Linked

Conquer LinkedIn.
Land your dream job.
Own your future.

OMAR GARRIOTT and
JEREMY SCHIFELING

D1125123

Workman Publishing
NEW YORK

Real Results from Our Clients

The insight Omar and Jeremy bring to the job search is unparalleled. Their down-to-earth approach makes even the hardest of steps seem easy. And in a world where recruiters primarily only use LinkedIn to connect to candidates, there's never been a better time for this book.

—JENNIFER BRIDGE,
Senior Director of Employer Relations
and MBA Program, UC Berkeley Haas

I loved working with Omar and Jeremy because they're not only extremely knowledgeable, but also genuinely passionate about helping people get on the path toward their dream career. Based on the course and their guidance, I've had twice the amount of networking calls than before and feel much more confident.

—SPENCER BOZSIK, Student

Our students and alumni around the globe overwhelmingly vote The Job InSiders' trainings #1! Their knowledge of how to expand professional networks and turn your profile into a powerful tool for the individualized job search tool is unmatched.

—MARK BROSTOFF, Director of
Graduate Career Services,
USC Marshall School of Business

The networking recommendations are gold! I successfully used several approaches to reach out to folks working in tech. After connecting with some nice people, I was able to get referred for a job at Google. I'm now a Google Data Engineer . . . and my referrer got a nice bonus. A win-win.

—DIEGO VARGAS SECAIRA,
Data Engineer

Whether you're in college or mid-career, these former LinkedIn insiders share expert advice to help you stand out among the "In" crowd and harness the power of the world's largest professional network for your own unique and evolving career goals!

—EVA KUBU, Associate Dean for
Professional Development & Director of
GradFUTURES, Princeton University

These lessons provided the professional touch I needed during outreach, increasing my accepted connections by 25 percent. Jeremy and Omar's personal feedback on my profile has resulted in recruiters contacting me directly thanks to what they taught me about the algorithm. This never happened before!

—BRENDAN SMITH, Student

Before adhering to your advice, I'd been receiving one message every month from recruiters asking if I'd be interested in their openings. Now I get at least three every week! I'll never fully understand how these algorithms work, but I'll take these results any day.

—ARI SALUD, Senior Analyst

LinkedIn, uniquely, is how Education Leaders of Color build our professional footprints. The strategies here show us how.

—SHARHONDA BOSSIER, CEO,
Education Leaders of Color

As a mid-career changer, Omar and Jeremy's insights are crucial. I needed to know the latest requirements for successful job hunting—an up-to-date profile, a good headshot, a ton of practice interviewing, and lots and lots of networking.

—DR. SARA LASKEY,
Product Strategist

I recommend Jeremy and Omar's content to all of my clients. Their advice is simple, easy-to-follow, and captures years of collective experience as actual hirers and coaches. If you're seeking sage wisdom as you launch your search, look no further.

—LISA MORGAN,
Career Coach, University of Michigan
Ross School of Business

LinkedIn is the dominant tool many companies use to find job candidates, but few job seekers understand how it works. This is a practical and insightful guide to using LinkedIn to get the job you want.

—DR. STEVEN T. HUNT,
Chief Expert for Technology & Work
and Author

Trust is a key component in the job search, which also extends to the people giving you advice on how to navigate it. Omar and Jeremy are both former colleagues at LinkedIn and highly dependable guides through the employment process.

—JOHN HILL,
VP of Network, Techstars

Omar and Jeremy cut through the mystery behind understanding what it takes to be an ideal candidate for your dream job. Their program guides you with simple and actionable tasks that help you put your authentic self forward in a way that gets results. Well done, guys!

—JAQUES OSTROWSKI,
Strategy Manager

I thought I knew LinkedIn, but you took it to another level! I love how you show users to effectively set themselves up as the best candidates. I have shared your course with everyone who wants to step up their game to job search and to network.

—LISA ROBLES,
Instructional Designer

Omar and Jeremy always teach me something new with LinkedIn. Their expertise and positivity combine to provide an easy-to-follow presentation that inspires every professional to get the most out of the platform.

—MICHAEL STEELMAN,
Director of Alumni Career Management,
William & Mary

I have to thank Omar and Jeremy for revealing all the LinkedIn secrets, tips, and tricks that job seekers must know about. I passed on their wisdom to my clients, and it always helped them to gain valuable contacts and optimize their job seeking efforts.

—ISABELLA PINUCCI,
Executive Career Advisor and Author

At first, I wasn't really confident about finding opportunities using LinkedIn. But now I feel more than able to connect with people and take the right steps for effective job hunting.

—SAAD IFTIKHAR, Student

Omar and Jeremy have helped our undergraduate students take those crucial first steps in their job exploration. Their step-by-step approach takes an intimidating task—networking—and breaks it down, getting students started and connecting on their own with the right people before they even realize it.

—EVERETTE FORTNER,
Associate VP for Career and Professional
Development, University of Virginia

Library of Congress Cataloging-in-Publication Data

Names: Garriott, Omar, author. | Schifeling, Jeremy, author.
Title: Linked: conquer LinkedIn. land your dream job. own your future. /
  Omar Garriott and Jeremy Schifeling.
Identifiers: LCCN 2021045304 | ISBN 9781523514168 (paperback) |
  ISBN 9781523514168 (ebook)
Subjects: LCSH: LinkedIn (Electronic resource) | Job hunting. |
  Employees—Recruiting.
Classification: LCC HF5382.7 .G378 2022 | DDC 650.14—dc23
LC record available at https://lccn.loc.gov/2021045304

ISBN 978-1-5235-1416-8

Design and cover by Sarah Smith

Photo Credits: **Getty Images:** Drew Angerer/Getty Images News p. 116 (top); fizkes/ iStock p. 116 (bottom); Hispanolistic/E+ p. 127; Rich Legg/E+ p. 121 (construction site). **Shutterstock:** emperorcosar p. 121 (Seattle); fizkes pp. 29, 77, 95, 105, 134, 222, 227, 274; HAKINMHAN p. 119 (graph); insta_photos pp. 118, 119, 121; Berk Ozel p. 119 (board).

Workman books are available at special discounts when purchased in bulk for premiums and sales promotions as well as for fundraising or educational use. Special editions or book excerpts can also be created to specification. For details, contact the Special Sales Director at specialmarkets@workman.com.

Workman Publishing Co., Inc.
225 Varick Street
New York, NY 10014-4381
workman.com

WORKMAN is a registered trademark of Workman Publishing Co., Inc.

Printed in the United States of America
First printing March 2022

10 9 8 7 6 5 4 3 2 1

For anyone who believes in the possibility of a better life.
And who wants to go create it.

Contents

Why Job Seekers Need Hedgehogs

Job hunting is hard.

I've been researching, writing, and speaking about career development for almost twenty years, and I've never heard anyone say, "I just *love* the job search process!"

I get it.

It's hard to distill your work experience into a few pithy bullet points. It's hard to ask people to spend their time helping you make connections. It's hard to sell yourself and your skills in a formal job interview. Now, do all of this in the wake of a global pandemic and the difficulty level rises exponentially.

But here's the good news about job hunting today: You don't have to figure it out alone. There are countless books, websites, and experts available to help you [*cough, cough . . . raises hand*]. And here's even better news: You've found *the* book, about *the* website, written by *the* leading experts on job hunting through LinkedIn in this unique moment in time.

Whether you're a recent grad, mid-career professional, career changer, or any other category of job seeker, you'll soon learn how to navigate the most important tool in the modern job search: LinkedIn. Omar Garriott and Jeremy Schifeling, known as The Job InSiders (I'm long used to their "In" jokes—when I had my daughter ten years ago, these guys gifted her a onesie that said "InFant"), will teach you absolutely everything you need to know.

I first met Omar and Jeremy when they led the education team at LinkedIn and I was a consultant to the company, running public webinars on how to maximize the platform for career success. While I spent a lot of time learning the nitty-gritty details of LinkedIn so I could teach about it effectively, Omar and Jeremy were always one step ahead. In the many years since, they remain my go-to resource for any and all LinkedIn questions, and their advice is featured all over my blog, podcast, and books.

This is why our work has been so complementary for so long. Maybe you've heard the theory of the fox and the hedgehog. Originally traced to the Greek poet Archilochus's line, "The fox knows many things and the hedgehog knows one big thing," the fox vs. hedgehog dichotomy is often applied to professionals in the workplace. A fox is characterized as a worker who has a breadth of knowledge across a wide range of topics—a generalist. A hedgehog is a worker who has a depth of knowledge in a specific discipline—a specialist.

In this scenario, I'm definitely a fox. I like to look at big workplace trends, pull together lots of different ideas on success, and take the 30,000-foot view of career development. Omar and Jeremy are the hedgehogs. Their depth of specific knowledge about how to use LinkedIn in a job search is truly unparalleled. And to get ahead in the new digital job search, you need hedgehogs for LinkedIn—the topic that matters most.

As you'll discover in the pages to come, Omar and Jeremy have made it their mission to stay current with every—and I mean *every*—feature, update, tool, and strategy that LinkedIn affords, and they share their knowledge with clear, actionable, and highly detailed advice. Their enthusiasm for what many career starters still think of (to their own detriment!) as "social media for old people" is encyclopedic and contagious, I promise.

Linked's five-step framework will provide everything you need to conduct a proactive and productive job search that results in a position that meets your unique goals. Omar and Jeremy's many happily employed clients—and their own successful careers as tech execs—attest to the value of the information you're about to receive.

After you read through this book, I have no doubt you'll succeed in your current job search and build a strategy to ensure that future career opportunities start coming to you. Yes, job hunting is hard, but if you follow Omar and Jeremy's advice, the results can be life changing.

—Lindsey Pollak
Spring 2022

INTRODUCTION

Get Ready to Launch

The privilege of a lifetime is being who you are.
—JOSEPH CAMPBELL

The Journey Begins

Congratulations! You've just taken a huge step forward in your career. Believe it or not, by opening this book, you've invested in yourself. Why? Because this isn't your typical self-help book about finding yourself. Instead, it's about *manifesting* yourself.

Becoming who you are is both the privilege and the adventure of a lifetime. And adventures are to be embarked upon—so we favor action. Our goal is to help you turn your dreams into reality; to bring you down gently from the clouds and find your earthly footing.

Plainly and practically, we'll walk you through how to take advantage of the seismic changes to the job search. We'll hold your hand through this new terrain, post-earthquake-and-aftershocks.

The promise of this book: finding, getting found for, and ultimately landing your dream job. The premise: believing *both* that your dream job awaits, and that there are concrete, actionable steps to attain it. Because putting yourself out there in the ways we outline will get you results. Your bravery will be rewarded.

The way you find and land your dream job—and then vet it—is by adopting a posture of positive proactivity. This runs counter to the purely reactive approach that the vast majority of job seekers take. They merely browse job boards and company websites and apply cold to as many positions as possible. They cross their fingers and lose track of the best-fit opportunities as crickets chirp. They focus on volume and convenience instead of diligently assessing roles, strengthening their candidacy for the most exciting opportunities, and networking their way in.

Maybe this reactive strategy has been your tactic thus far. If so, it won't be for much longer. You hold in your hands the guidebook to a proactive and productive job search, one that focuses your limited time on the information and techniques that truly matter and will bear fruit. We've seen it happen over and over.

Throughout this new job search process, remember that *you* make your future. You don't just stumble into it; you create it. And if the notion of a dream job seems like, well, a pipe dream, we'll help you bring it into focus. Or maybe your bar is a bit lower: You're seeking escape from unemployment or are flexible and looking for learning opportunities. Either way, we encourage you to see the baby step of a good-enough job and the quantum leap of a dream job as non–mutually exclusive. The open jobs out there now, including those that only superficially seem like a good fit for you, are not an impediment to landing your dream job; you just need to learn to spin multiple plates at the same time. The job search is continual. Just like you, it's always a work in progress.

Here's an analogy from the tech world. Beta is the phase of product development that is full of testing and iterating. Because the product is not yet finished, Beta is all about experimentation, trial and error, revisiting assumptions, considering new information, and adjusting in real time. It requires an open mind and a growth mindset. As Reid Hoffman, who started LinkedIn in 2002 in his living room, writes in his book *The Start-up of You* (and told us often when we were on staff), you want to be in "Permanent

Beta" when it comes to your career. You are never a finished product, and you learn by doing and trying.

When you think this way, you quickly realize that a better job is *always* around the corner—even if it's not posted at this very moment or if it takes some intermediate steps to arrive at. You are simply accumulating experiences, stories, perspectives, and connections to position yourself for the next thing, then the next thing, then the next thing after that. At some point, probably without even realizing it, it will not just be a *better* job; it will be your *dream* job.

This is paramount: Think of your dream job not as a destination, but as a *process*. In this book, we help you navigate through that multistep process.

The New Reality: LinkedIn

The simple fact is that the employment landscape is wildly different than it was thirty, twenty, and even ten years ago. Whereas taking certain well-codified steps—getting a good education, writing a stellar resume, collecting impeccable references—used to all but guarantee you a job, we now find ourselves in uncharted waters. And to make things even trickier, there's now more competition

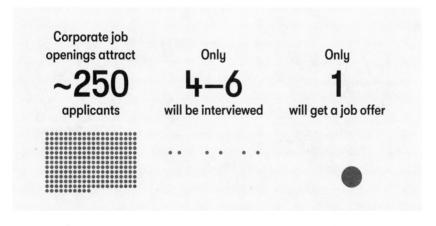

Corporate job openings attract	Only	Only
~250	**4–6**	**1**
applicants	will be interviewed	will get a job offer

Getting hired is about getting noticed and getting in. Not fitting in.

than ever. Many online job postings get hundreds of applicants, and the most sought-after roles at the most sought-after employers routinely attract more than a thousand candidates.

The good news is that, like many things in life, the process of landing your dream job is a game. And when you understand how the game is played and learn to play it well, you'll no longer be intimidated by it. What's more, you can leverage this know-how to get a leg up on the intensifying competition—and put your dream job in the crosshairs. We're here to help you do just that.

The key is knowing how to cut through the clutter and build your personal brand to get noticed, then to stand out from everyone else to get an interview and score a job offer. And the best tool for doing all of that? LinkedIn.

LinkedIn is where most every recruiter lives all day long. Their employers pay a hefty sum for the powerful access to candidates it gives them. This is true in every economic sector and every corner of the world, no matter the seniority of the open role.

Here's why: LinkedIn changed the game for every organization that needs to hire (which is . . . wait for it . . . *every* organization). Now nearly the entire world of work relies on LinkedIn and plays by its rules. So too, then, must the job seekers.

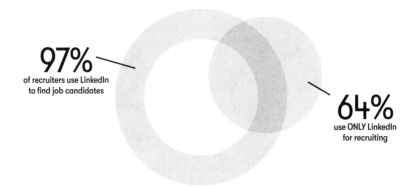

97%
of recruiters use LinkedIn
to find job candidates

64%
use ONLY LinkedIn
for recruiting

You'd be hard-pressed to find a recruiter who doesn't use LinkedIn.
Nearly two-thirds of them use it alone to source candidates!

In fact, recruiters and hiring managers are so obsessed with LinkedIn that they will *always* look at your profile, no matter where or how you apply to the job. Why? Because your profile can and should be leaps and bounds richer than a resume. (Do it right and it can even replace a cover letter.) We've collectively hired for dozens of roles and never once asked for a traditional resume. Sure, we may be LinkedIn fanboys, but we're no outliers!

For hirers and job seekers alike, LinkedIn simply has no true competitor. With more than 770 million global members and more than 180 million in the United States alone, LinkedIn is *the most efficient and effective place* for you to focus your energy—whether you're actively looking for a job or keeping one eye half open for new opportunities. It has by far the highest return on your effort investment.

No more wasting time on the futile routine of applying cold on job sites. Instead, in these pages you'll learn how to build a purposeful network and get recruiters to come to you. Because, on average, candidates who only apply cold have *less than* a 1 percent chance of

Everything That Matters—and Nothing That Doesn't

As product marketers at LinkedIn, our job was to convince you that every part of the platform is essential to your success. But now, as career coaches, hiring managers, and, of course, your trusty authors, we know that's not quite true.

LinkedIn is packed with tools and features, and the site can get a little overwhelming—especially for newer or less experienced users. So we've made a conscious decision to include only the most important parts of LinkedIn in this book because your time is too valuable to waste on stuff that doesn't matter. We want you to be confident that every step you take with us is a step toward your success!

being hired—while candidates who get referred have a 10x advantage. Said another way, when sourcing from job boards alone, large companies must sift through 129 applicants on average to find a single great candidate—but only eight applicants when sourcing from referrals or recruiter outreach.

If you were a hiring company, where would *you* focus? It's not a rhetorical question. It's vital. Because finding a great job requires shifting your orientation toward that of the hirer—to understand how they spend their time and what their process looks like. As you'll soon see, getting in the mindset of recruiters and hiring managers is an animating thrust of this book.

Here's just one example of why this matters for the successful modern job search: Hirers know that employee referrals and targeted online searches are the most efficient ways to find the best talent. But most job seekers haven't caught up; they don't know how to capitalize on these new realities. That's exactly what we'll show you how to do.

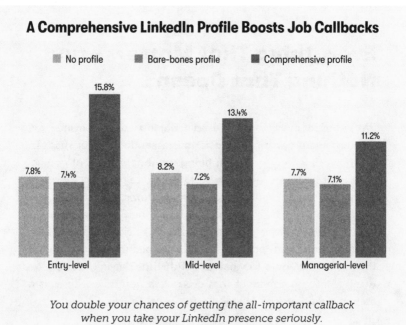

A Comprehensive LinkedIn Profile Boosts Job Callbacks

No profile   Bare-bones profile   Comprehensive profile

Entry-level: 7.8%, 7.4%, 15.8%
Mid-level: 8.2%, 7.2%, 13.4%
Managerial-level: 7.7%, 7.1%, 11.2%

You double your chances of getting the all-important callback when you take your LinkedIn presence seriously.

Defining Hirers

Careful readers will notice that we've started to lump in the term "recruiters" with "hiring managers." We'll do this throughout the book. And when we use those terms, here's what we really mean: those who use the (pricey) LinkedIn Recruiter product to find candidates.

We will also often use the word "recruiters" alone as shorthand; they are the hired guns who tap the power of LinkedIn Recruiter, and LinkedIn's algorithm for matching, to fill their funnel with possible fits for specific roles. Their main goal is to figure out whom to pass on to the hiring managers; they exist on a continuum from initial vetters and phone screeners to strategic and valued thought partners.

When we use "hiring managers" alone, by contrast, it is an intentional reference to leaders within organizations who have advocated for a job to be opened up and have the most acute need to fill it. They are either the final decision-makers on whether a candidate gets hired or championing their preferred candidate to the final decision-maker or hiring committee.

Your Job Search Guides

So who the heck are we, anyway? Here's a bit to know about your authors, Omar and Jeremy, aka The Job InSiders.

Having been on both sides of the market for talent, we've had an up-close view of this yawning chasm between old and new job-search methods. Both of us are hiring managers who also previously worked inside university career services offices as career counselors. Together, we started and led the College and New Grad product marketing team at LinkedIn for several years. We launched new features on the site and made students LinkedIn's fastest-growing demographic. (It was no small feat given that when we started out, they'd tell us in focus groups, "Yeah, I know LinkedIn. It's like . . . Facebook for old people!") Don't worry: We won't hate you for thinking the exact same thing. But we *will* change your minds. And in the time since:

- It's actually Facebook (ahem, Meta) that has become . . . Facebook for old people! Meanwhile, LinkedIn has proven its unique value as a career management tool. It's the present *and* the future of truly useful social media. For multiple years running, a Business Insider survey has shown that LinkedIn is the most trusted social platform (Facebook is last).

- We've helped tens of thousands of job seekers—from high school dropouts and undergrads to MBAs and alumni of all ages—take their job search game to the next level.

- We've consulted and run trainings for nearly every top business school in the world; been one-on-one career coaches; keynoted conferences; and created a wildly popular and five-star-rated online course on modern job search techniques.

In the process, we've learned a ton, and we've distilled it all down in these pages to give you the tools you'll need to stand out in the ever-shifting and hypercompetitive world of hiring. Far too many self-proclaimed job search "experts" dish out a regular platter of ineffective or obsolete suggestions. But we've been in the belly of the beast and earned our stripes; our track record is our proof.

Sure, we work in tech. But job seekers love us because we aren't in a Silicon Valley bubble. We've intentionally popped that bubble by working with real people in the real world, with legitimate and widely shared concerns and questions, every day.

Okay, okay. But what makes our particular insights so . . . insightful? It's because we separate the job-seeking gold from the pyrite so the clients we work with can remain laser-focused on what really matters in the job search. We cut through all the noise and "should-dos," much of it coming from those supposed experts and LinkedIn itself (which wants the site to be "sticky," i.e., reasons for you to visit, stay, and come back). The methods we lay out *actually work*. They have led to countless job offers, new connections that turn into referrals, and exponentially increased interest from recruiters. We are certain they will do the same for you.

Angelina, an international MBA student, wrote to us:

"These strategies are very insightful and can be life-changing for many people. So I really want to show gratitude. A heartfelt thanks!"

We're also true believers ourselves. Not only have we seen first-hand how our approach can change the entire course of someone's professional life, *it's changed our own*. Despite many job changes, neither of us has applied for a job in more than a decade. Why? We know the secret sauce to having recruiters and hiring managers seek *us* out on LinkedIn—a recipe we will share with you.

No matter where you are in your career—whether you're actively or passively searching for a new gig, just getting your start or have been out of the job market for years—you will absolutely benefit from these methods. What makes us so sure? Of the tens of thousands of job seekers who've taken our courses, *a grand total of one person* has taken us up on our money-back guarantee. Not too shabby.

Your Life's Work

We know. Looking for a job is daunting. You've got to put yourself out there, hone how you talk about yourself, and take risks. You have to update your resume and LinkedIn profile, figure out what you *really* want to go after, network (ugh), and face near-certain rejection. It's no wonder that many job seekers have inertia—often with a big helping of complacency and confusion mixed in.

We hope this book can be a catalyst to reimagine what's possible for you. It's time to tell your own story, build your own brand, and create your own network. Boldly and strategically. The payoff? Landing your dream job and owning your future.

Why? Well, because life's too damn short not to. We spend more of our waking hours at work than doing any other activity. Our jobs have an outsize impact on our happiness and sense of purpose in the world. At its best, work imbues our lives with meaning; at its worst, it can be soul-sucking.

Poet Mary Oliver reminds us we have "one wild and precious life." Making the most of it—and reenergizing yourself along the way—first requires a strong desire to be in constant motion toward something better. That's *why* we wrote this book. But you also need a path for that forward motion. That's what's in this book.

We know there's a massive hunger for this. And *you* must know you're not alone. Far from it. For too many people (in fact, for a majority of the workforce, as we'll see in the first chapter), a negative work situation feels paralyzing. You'll never be able to really launch your career if you're stuck doing something you don't love. And it's the "not-quite-ideal-but-kinda-sorta-good-enough" job situations that can make you feel the most trapped.

But here's the good news: Career transformation no longer solely relies upon "old boys' networks" or having an elite alma mater. It's universally attainable. Because something pretty radical has happened in recent years: Anyone online now has access to the people and information that determine opportunity. Anyone! It's that potential to drive sweeping equity that most fires us up about LinkedIn.

Whether you feel stuck at the beginning or the middle of your career, you're not trapped on the sidelines—the tools of

Gauging Fit:
What Makes a Great Job Great

People leave jobs with more frequency now than just a generation ago. Millennials, who now make up most of the workforce, have been called the "job-hopping generation." According to Gallup, 21 percent of millennials change jobs each year, which is three times higher than non-millennial age groups. And only 60 percent plan to stay with their current employer for the next year.

Many factors drive these trends, such as rapidly evolving technology, economic instability, massive student debt, and wage stagnation. In addition, there's an increasing desire to do impactful work that improves society, which might outweigh factors like salary or job security. But this much is time-tested: Relationships matter (quite often people don't leave jobs; they leave managers). So does our hunger to grow, both as people and as professionals, and our need to make a difference.

The foundation of our approach is that you can and deserve to find not just a good, but *great* job. So what makes a great job, anyway? The writer Christopher Morley once famously quipped, "A happy life is spent learning, earning, and yearning." We'd amend that slightly. At base, a great job sits at the intersection of three things:

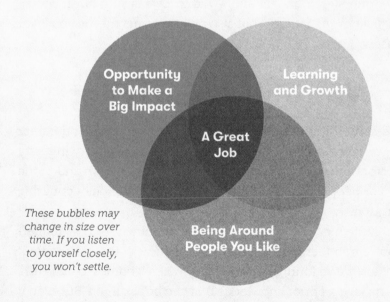

Opportunity to Make a Big Impact

Learning and Growth

A Great Job

Being Around People You Like

These bubbles may change in size over time. If you listen to yourself closely, you won't settle.

continued . . .

This is your starting point. You will have to define and redefine for your-self what this looks like throughout your career—and your job search. At different points, a given criterion (like not working with jerks!) may be more important to you than others. Or you may find that stretching your skill set is less attractive than doing what you're really good at or enjoy.

Your conception of "impact" may change over time, as well. For Omar, this had been all about "doing good": making professional choices based mainly on helping to solve important and intractable problems. But when he got cancer at thirty-five, that definition morphed into making a more regular impact on his coworkers (and anyone, really) in little interactions and in life's easier-to-miss moments. Grandeur gave way to presence.

Keep these three criteria top of mind as a basic rubric as you seek new opportunities. You may have to compromise on one or more of them in the short-term and take a "good-enough" job. But eventually, if you keep your antennae up, you won't! A great job—dare we say, a dream one—beckons.

empowerment are right at hand. What follows is your crash course on not just how to get a job, but also on how to get the life you want and deserve.

Who This Book Is For

There's something here for everyone. For every age and career stage. For every level of educational attainment. For every industry and sector of the economy. For citizens of every nation and of the world. For people of every ethnicity, gender, and socioeconomic background.

And, yes, this book is for all levels of fluency in today's digital-first job search techniques. Having worked with the full range of job seekers, we've found that, especially when it comes to LinkedIn, there's no level of prior knowledge that can be assumed. But even if you feel like you have a sturdy handle on this stuff, rest assured that we'll still help you take a giant leap ahead.

Frankly, if you're in the job market—whether actively searching or passively dipping in one toe—you will learn at least a few key lessons. That's our pledge to you. But here's who will get the *most* out of this book (and for whom it's specifically written):

1. Career Starters and New Grads: Whether you're currently a student (high school diploma/GED, associate's, undergrad, MBA, or any other program) hitting the job/internship market for the first time or re-hitting it while you pause to complete your studies, LinkedIn is essential. This is where the entire world of work you want to enter lives and breathes. (It's not *just* social media for old people, it's like TikTok for responsible grown-ups!)

Remember, at LinkedIn, we built the team and the products focused on college students. Since then, the platform has only grown in importance to career starters—so much so that we can't keep up with the demand from university career centers for our trainings. Even those schools with amazing employer relationships and an eager-to-give-back alumni base know that investing in LinkedIn will reap rewards for their grads. We want you to kick-start your careers, to build your professional brand in a purposeful way, and to set yourself up for a lifetime of success—however you define that. As former teachers, students are our passion.

Think of this book as the companion graduation gift to Dr. Seuss's *Oh, the Places You'll Go!*—the practical peer to Dr. Seuss's whimsical inspiration.

Here's a revelation from a new grad, Abhay, we coached:

"I didn't realize that recruiters were searching for people. I thought candidates had to do all the work, but being GIVEN interviews based off my LinkedIn presence was an amazing change of perspective."

2. Mid-Career Searchers: Been out of the online job-seeking game for a while and feel like the whole thing has passed you by? Looking to make a career change or a half-pivot? Suddenly finding yourself out of work and wondering how relevant your experience and skills are? Some of our most engaged trainings are with people just like you. They're grateful because they know things have changed, but they don't quite know what to do about it.

> Amy, a mid-career changer, advises:
>
> **"For older job seekers who might be hesitant about using social media or similar platforms, it's worth the investment to learn how to use this platform. And it's easier than you think."**

We work with a number of alumni and professional associations, veterans' organizations, and placement firms focused on career switchers. You're in good company. If you already know the color of your parachute, we'll show you how to get out of free fall and land right on your target.

3. Underrepresented Candidates: Let's face a hard truth: Job seekers who are people of color, women, disabled, LGBTQ+, non-college-educated, or otherwise don't fit the mold of the current power structure (or specific company/industry norms) are often at a distinct disadvantage.

Our beloved tech sector, for example, has shamefully abysmal numbers of women and minority employees. It's a reality that permeates our entire economy. In fall 2020, on the heels of Black Lives Matter protests around the country, Wells Fargo CEO Charlie Scharf scapegoated his bank's lack of diversity on "a very limited pool of Black talent to recruit from." That's not exactly our idea of enlightened leadership. Real leaders take pains to be part of the solution, not just make excuses. And solutions are needed: Studies show that Black and Asian applicants who "whiten" their names on a resume are up to twice as likely to get called back for an interview.

There are efforts by employers to respond to these disparities en masse. We feel encouraged by the growing adoption of innovations in the use of technology for hiring, such as blind interviews to reduce human bias. But they need to be much more broadly implemented throughout the entire candidate funnel. One seemingly simple must-do on a LinkedIn profile, for instance, is to have a closely cropped profile photo; many candidates of color, however, hesitate for fear of subjecting themselves to bias. And in the same vein, the platform's algorithm favors job seekers who have, by virtue of their proximity to influential and connected people, *already punctured* the "inner circle." That, of course, creates some not-exactly-meritocratic ripple effects for who does and doesn't get into the recruitment and consideration process.

Indeed, LinkedIn itself has work to do. "Black LinkedIn" has become a thriving digital space for authentic tale-sharing of needed workplace reforms, but real talk doesn't always feel welcomed on what some perceive to be a sanitized, put-your-best-foot-forward platform. There is also the common implicit bias afflicting many a tech company: They build and design mostly for people who are just like them (that is, disproportionately white and male). We saw that happen at times at LinkedIn.

In this book we'll discuss why LinkedIn nonetheless is the most important place to tell your story and amplify your voice, and why it's the "Great Opportunity Democratizer," no matter who you are or where you come from. We'll show you how to level the playing field and showcase your abilities with real-world examples and how-tos from across the job-seeking spectrum.

4. The Scrappy—and Savvy—Among Us: LinkedIn is well-established as the place where business gets done. Job seekers— from young up-and-comers to entrepreneurs, side hustlers, and small business owners—use it to take matters into their own hands.

Economic fluctuations often disproportionately impact younger job seekers and part-time workers. But you don't have to sit idly by. Those in the gig economy—as well as Gen Zers and FIRE movement-ers—know how to scrap. They've *had* to. They've come of age surrounded by uncertainty. And they can unleash LinkedIn to put professional pieces together: to build their brands, to market their services, to find project- and contract-based work, and identify mentors and investors. Even if you're not in a nine-to-five, LinkedIn is worth the full-throated investment.

How to Use This Book

Here's a quick overview of everthing you can expect in the pages to come. In Chapter 1, we'll explain how the modern job search works—how the game is now played. Then, in Chapter 2, you'll learn about the hidden (aka the *real*) job market, the powerful concept of network effect, and how to motivate yourself to create healthy job-seeking habits. And most importantly, we'll introduce you to an easy-to-follow, five-step framework to help you win that game. It goes like this: **Explore, Position, Search, Network, Research.**

Chapters 3 through 7 will walk you through each of those five steps in detail. Every step has a concrete set of actions you can take (mostly on LinkedIn but occasionally dipping into other parts of the web, too). We err on the side of the pragmatic, but add context when it's important for you to understand the concepts (the *why*) behind the tactics (the *what*). Each of these chapters ends with a checklist recapping the must-do actions.

Finally, Chapter 8 contains next-level tips and tricks for advanced job seekers, and we conclude with a helpful recap, with some job market prognostication for good measure. This structure is intentional; we don't want you to get overwhelmed, focus on the wrong things first, or bite off more than you can chew in one sitting.

Time-Tested Strategies

As you put the concepts in this book into practice IRL, you may periodically come across some screenshots of LinkedIn that don't map exactly to what you see on the site at a given moment. Don't fret: The site's core functionality rarely changes. LinkedIn does sometimes tweak the look-and-feel ("User Experience," in tech parlance), alter how you navigate to a certain area, or, even rarer, add a new paywall or discontinue a feature. But the methods to perform each step of the job search process basically remain the same. If it ain't broke, don't fix it!

One note: Although the book is meant to be read sequentially, the job search itself doesn't quite work that way. You should feel free to circle back to specific strategies over and over again as you put them into practice. If you find yourself doing this, you're using this book the *right* way!

Mark up and dog-ear pages as you go through; take notes in the margins. Make your *own* list of where you need to dedicate the most time, and use additional tools we've created—to which you now get access—to make meaningful progress (see the Online Resources section on page 293 for your special code to our on-demand course).

Just like your newfound approach to the job search, the book itself is meant to be engaged with actively, not passively. Get out a pen, pull up LinkedIn, and get going!

CHAPTER 1

The Old Game— and the New

Understand the shifts to play the right game the right way

Don't ask yourself what the world needs; ask yourself
what makes you come alive. And then go and do that.
Because what the world needs is people who have come alive.
—HOWARD THURMAN

The Job-Seeking Majority

The first and most important thing to know is this: Though seeking a new job can feel frustratingly isolating, you're not alone. Not by a long shot.

In fact, *most* people are in your seat. Studies show that more than seven in ten employees in the United States want a new job. Four in ten want to quit their current position. Job dissatisfaction is arguably at national-crisis levels—63 percent say their jobs significantly impact their mental health and have induced unhealthy behaviors, such as drinking or crying regularly.

It's even worse for the largest part of the workforce, millennials (often defined as people born between 1981 and 1996): Nearly three-fourths are disengaged at work. These workers, along with those of Gen Z coming up behind them, are more willing than previous generations to change jobs in pursuit of personal meaning and other nonmonetary factors. Estimates show that they will have *at least twenty and as many as forty jobs*, each with their own searches and transitions, in their lifetime. This is the new normal.

There are many factors at play here, including globalization, automation, wage stagnation, and underemployment. Then there are shifting attitudes about what workers want out of their jobs and how they derive a sense of purpose and identity from what they do. (Millennials and Gen Zers, for instance, are society's most passionate advocates for change—and they don't want to separate what they do from what they believe in.)

A huge slice of society wants something very different out of work.

And, of course, the COVID-19 pandemic sent a fundamental shock throughout the global economic system, changing both where and how we work in dramatic ways. But the end result is that a great many of us want something very different out of the thing that occupies more than a third of our waking lives.

So do us a favor, right now. Put down this book for ten seconds and take a deep belly breath. Exhale for as long as you're able. Ground yourself in the knowledge that you're not the only one struggling to make the most of your one wild and precious life. Try to visualize this huge community of fellow seekers. Breathe in the thought of being surrounded by immense possibility, and breathe out feelings of loneliness and unworthiness. You might think this is totally corny, but it's so worth it.

(*Rest of page left blank intentionally to ensure deep breathing and positive visualization. Do it!!!)

How Hiring Has Changed

Okay, now that you've (hopefully) reached a wiser place, you're ready to launch forward into unknowns with greater calm, confidence, and clarity. We'll soon explore how to stand out given the new rules of the job search. But first, let's immerse ourselves in the four main ways in which hiring dynamics have shifted since the Great Recession of the late 2000s and the global pandemic, both of which have only accelerated paradigm shifts that were already in progress. Perhaps some of these new realities are all too familiar to you.

New Reality #1: Technology and persistent economic trends give employers more power.

Digital tools (ahem, LinkedIn) allow recruiters to be more proactive. Companies have cut out many of the traditional hiring processes and can search for exactly who they need. Most inefficiencies have been erased.

The most in-demand employers—the places you really want to work—no longer waste time tabling at job fairs or sifting through uninvited resume piles. And, on average, you only get a six-second scan even when your resume *does* get a look.

Another cause of heightened employer power is underemployment, a nasty relic of an economy hit by the one-two punch of the 2008 financial crisis and the COVID-19 pandemic just twelve years later. Underemployment typically afflicts college grads who find themselves in jobs that don't require a bachelor's degree. More than forty percent of new grads fit that bill, and the trend line isn't encouraging: About three-fourths of those new grads remain underemployed a decade later.

Wages in the United States have been mostly stagnant for decades and are now only increasing in the hospitality and retail sectors, specifically due to a dearth of workers. (Indeed, in recent years, the so-called "Great Resignation" has given workers a little extra breathing room in industries historically rampant with under-employment.) This all, in turn, drives the high levels of disengage-ment and dissatisfaction we mentioned earlier.

You (probably): *"Umm, major buzzkill, guys! I know, it's rough out there. So what does all this mean and what can I do about it?"*

Well, for starters, you need to accept that there are no silver platters in the job search, regardless of your career stage—whether you're in a top MBA program, super experienced, or just starting out. You may be thinking, "Yeah, that goes without saying." But it's actually a massive change over only the past fifteen or so years, so . . . it's worth *saying* it. The strategies we lay out in this book are centered on effectively responding to these changes. You may be highly educated and/or highly qualified on paper, but, sadly, the modern world of work is anything but a pure meritocracy.

So let's take the power back!

New Reality #2: In this brave new world, a personal brand isn't a mere nice-to-have, or something just for "influencers." It's a necessity. For everyone.

According to CareerBuilder and the Harris Poll, 20 percent of employ-ers expect job candidates to have an online presence. While this number is steadily ticking up, the more significant statistic is this: Nearly half of employers (47 percent) report that they are less likely to bring in a candidate for interviews if they "can't find" the candidate online. They're simply seeking more information before making the interview decision, and two-thirds use search engines to do so.

And what are they looking for when researching potential inter-viewees? Half say, "A professional online persona," which includes confirmatory (or detractive) information about a candidate's fit for the job, as well as recommendations from clients and colleagues. Employers prefer a clear and coherent narrative for your academic and career pursuits, primarily on LinkedIn and then reinforced by other web hits (like on-brand things you've written elsewhere).

They of course also want to ensure that you don't have any red flags online (so you might want to make that Instagram feed private, and shut down or rename that flamethrowing Twitter account). A Jobvite survey of 1,600 recruiters found that 93 percent of them look at a candidate's social profile.

Remember, recruiters and hiring managers often do plain old Google searches of applicants *before* the serious consideration process even starts. And what's the ideal first search result when they do so? You guessed it: your LinkedIn profile. (*Not* those random tweets, party pics, or blog posts about the best burrito in town.)

How do you build or enhance your brand to ensure that your professional profile rises to the top? And how do you search-engine-optimize yourself? In a nutshell, it entails:

- Weaving a good story

- Carving out your own niche

- Creating a custom LinkedIn URL

Says DeAnn Sims, a social media consultant:

"**Whether it's intentional or not, not having a [strong] profile always feels like you have something to hide. Either you've specifically taken steps to make sure you can't be found, or you're using a childish byname—neither of which feels very professional.**"

- Reaching profile completeness (but disavow yourself of the idea that there's such a thing as the "perfect profile," or even "All-Star," to use LinkedIn's terminology; there's only a perfect profile *for a specific job*)

- Utilizing strong keywords

- Showing not just telling (i.e., the original content that Google loves)

Let's hit pause right here to highlight the criticality of the first item: storytelling in the digital world.

Your task is to capture the limited attention of recruiters; you'll soon be learning and using sophisticated tactics to land at the top of their algorithm-dictated searches. But the very first thing to realize about recruiters is that they are humans. And like all humans, they're built to love stories. Our brains, since those cave-dwelling days around the fire, are wired to respond to compelling narratives. (In fact, stories trigger the release of the neurotransmitter oxytocin, which is the foundation of human trust and empathy—and ultimately connection.)

Simply put, your story is your professional brand. So it's worth spending the time to make sure it's uniquely you. Of course, we're all works in progress. But recruiters and hiring managers are perpetually overwhelmed, so they need an easily discernible narrative onto which they can latch. A surefire way to *not* stand out is to expect the recruiter to connect the dots of your career.

The best narrative is one that checks their boxes while helping you stand out. This takes massaging, testing, and refinement, but when it comes to your unique professional brand—expressed mainly in places like LinkedIn and on your resume—it's all about condensing. Because a key tenet of job searching in a super-noisy world is this: Less is more. You cut through the noise only by being found, and someday even *known*, for a specific thing. Even if you think of yourself as a generalist (say, a Project Manager), perceived specialists are the ones who get traction in the job market. Perception is reality.

Your story is your professional brand.

So ask yourself: What do you want to be known for, to be found for? What are you awesome at doing, now or perhaps sometime down the line? In other words, don't worry about trying to be great at everything (a pretty unrealistic goal to begin with—after all, there's only one LeBron James!). Instead, you want to pick a lane (like Steph Curry's three-point shooting prowess) and be great at that one thing. Or, more commonly, show up *appearing* to be great at it, and then just figure it out as you go!

And so, it's all narrative. There are excellent methods to create a stellar self-brand, but at the end of the day, nothing beats the power of a great story—one that makes sense, connects threads, feels focused, and plucks specific professional examples that bring that compelling narrative to life (and leaves out the stuff that doesn't).

Here's the hopeful part: No matter who you are—whether you're a dropout, a new grad, an MBA, a veteran transitioning into civilian life, or in your professional twilight with employment gaps—you have a story to share!

New Reality #3: Networking—and ultimately getting a referral—is your ticket to the most sought-after jobs in the world.

We've all heard it a million times: "It's not what you know, it's who you know."

Clarification: It's not who you know, it's who *they* know.

This is also known as network effect. Think about it. If you build a network of 500 LinkedIn connections, and each of those connections has 500 (or more) connections, you're now only one degree removed from millions of people. You can be the node of a network that spans geographies, industries, and companies. (500 connections, by the way, is the threshold at which LinkedIn's ridiculously smart data scientists have found that you're harnessing the power of network effect. It's why LinkedIn just shows your network as "500+" when you cross that specific milestone.) Owing to that sheer volume, these seriously useful "weak ties"—connections of connections—are how an estimated 80 percent of jobs are found.

This element of the modern job search is what's so exciting about LinkedIn. Never before in human history could one build an easily visible, quantifiable, highly searchable professional circle. We like to say that this makes LinkedIn The Great Opportunity Democratizer: It gives a leg up to anyone who's willing to put in the effort to build a network, using shared affiliations, interests, or connections as a wedge to get in the door. It matters less which school you went to, or if you were born with a silver spoon in your mouth. It *does* matter what you can do, and that you value relationships. That old, narrow path is giving way to greater access to opportunity, driven by the hunger of hirers to find the best people and of job seekers to break down barriers.

Gap's Global Head of Talent Acquisition, Meghan Kelly, wants to democratize opportunity:

"We're always looking for more inclusive pathways for qualified talent."

Still, we work with many job seekers who have negative connotations—or at least hesitations—about networking. They think it's some combination of unnecessary, slimy, confusing, and/or complicated. If you harbor such sentiments, please, please, *please* let go of them by the time you . . . finish . . . reading . . . this . . . sentence. All better?

Not only is networking the real way most jobs are found and filled, but it's also a strategy that's available to everyone. And if you're not making the absolute most of it, you can be certain that someone else who wants the same job is. Someone who *really* knows the value of developing relationships—and knows that LinkedIn is the new business card.

Part of why the focus-on-your-resume-alone game isn't paying off the way it used to is that *every* job search is now network-based. It's what college career centers sometimes still call "off-campus." By that they simply mean you've got to navigate your own way by building your personal brand and connections. If you're still in school, that's even true for the rapidly disappearing "on-campus" opportunities where jobs arrive directly at a student's feet. Someone must get you in the door and validate you.

Old vs. New Processes

Have you been out of the job search game for a while? Well, there have been seismic shifts and the rules of the game have changed forever. And even if you're a career starter, it's helpful to know how these changes have cohered into a new reality for every job seeker.

Here are the top ten ways the reality of the job search has shifted over the past decade or so:

OLD	NEW
1 Submitting a resume	Getting found online
2 Trusting in a meritocracy	Trusting in the power of weak ties
3 Attending job fairs and info sessions	Being the needle in the (smaller) haystack
4 Submitting an application when it's super polished	Getting a warm lead and getting in right away
5 Tedious, inefficient networking (exchanging business cards after a forced conversation)	Purposeful, efficient connecting (saying "I'll find you on LinkedIn" and then paying for coffee)
6 Writing a thoughtful, custom cover letter	Writing a thoughtful, keyword-laden About section on LinkedIn
7 Expecting employers to pick out what's relevant	Purposefully connecting your professional dots
8 Shotgunning: quantity over quality	Focusing: quality over quantity
9 Learning the hard way what a job is really like	Identifying insiders in order to vet a job *before* you take it
10 Finger-crossing and wishful thinking	Constantly improving and having a growth mindset

And this people-first approach is most definitely true for each of the dozens of jobs you'll have throughout your career. So here's an essential, lifelong career mindset: Think of the job search as a process that hinges on your network, and figure out how to use that fact to your advantage at every professional transition point.

We, your trusty authors, came to this realization quite suddenly. As we both graduated from top-ten MBA programs about a decade ago, on-campus recruiting was robust and most of our classmates—roughly 80 percent—found internships and jobs using that old-school route. Heck, we did, too. We all thought, "Yeah, that's what we paid for!" But only a few years later, business schools started calling us up, knowing we had led the student and university team at LinkedIn, and explained that things were changing rapidly.

Here was their new reality as of the mid-2010s and continuing to this day: Even at top-tier programs, the ratio had been flipped upside down. As many as 80 percent of students were now finding jobs off-campus via networking (often within their alumni base), whereas only 20 percent were doing so through traditional on-campus recruiting. (We've verified this with our clients and in multiple presentations at the global conference for MBA career centers.) LinkedIn had become such a powerful sourcing and networking tool that even the world's best business students (at least, those without an optimized online presence and network) couldn't expect results in the traditional on-campus job search. So our business, The Job InSiders, was born, and helping job seekers get noticed and find leads that could turn into referrals was our goal.

Think of the job search as a process that hinges on your network.

Ah, the almighty referral. Referrals usually ensure your resume gets a look—even if it's only for an average of six seconds. They are the single biggest predictor of whether you get an interview. And shared connections that might ultimately lead to referrals help you

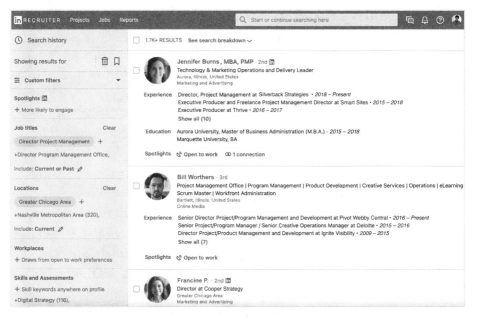

A screenshot of candidate search results in the LinkedIn Recruiter product. How are you going to stand out?

both sit atop search results and pass through the filters on LinkedIn Recruiter that most every recruiter uses all day long.

Here's the rub: Although at least 70 percent of people get hired at companies where they have a personal connection, a whopping 51 percent of millennials (remember, the largest part of the workforce) are uncomfortable reaching out to connections for a referral. Tragically, 40 percent avoid this step altogether during their job search. To which we say: What's the point of having connections if you're unwilling to use—ahem, *ask*—them to help you?

Though referred candidates make up only 7 percent of total applicants, 40 percent of new hires are referrals. That's an amazing return on your relationship-building investment! (And it's also why companies throw lots of money at current employees to make referrals; they all know that referrals are the best source of talent.)

New Reality #4: Surprise, surprise—LinkedIn is the default tool for job hirers and job seekers.

With nearly a *billion* members (just under half of whom access it on a daily basis), 50 million corporate clients, tens of millions of jobs, and heavy engagement from nearly every recruiter in the world, LinkedIn has cornered the job-seeking-and-finding market, matching supply to demand at massive scale. It's why Microsoft and Salesforce got into a bonkers bidding war over the company (Microsoft won, at the hefty price tag of $26 billion).

Recruiters are all-in on LinkedIn. They pay a lot to be able to slice and dice information about passive and active job seekers in myriad ways. They're deeply invested in the site's Recruiter tool—to the tune of tens of thousands of dollars a year *per user*. In fact, LinkedIn takes in the lion's share of its revenue from this subscription-based product that recruiters spend their entire work-days using. So the company is constantly endeavoring to make the platform ever more valuable to this very specific audience: those looking to fill open roles.

The whole idea is quite ingenious, really. Give job seekers (and let's face it, we're all job seekers on some level) a place to network and post their professional details; then charge recruiters and hiring managers an arm and a leg to find and reach them.

Even so, the value outweighs the cost. Year after year, nearly every recruiter, at nearly every firm on the planet, utilizes LinkedIn as their primary tool. They know it works. So LinkedIn's business model works. (But we won't tell you about the company's gourmet food or pricey parties!)

You, again (probably): *"Okay, but what does that mean for me?"*

It means there's only one place that matters for the modern-day job seeker. Only one set of tools to learn. Only one site to build a net-work, to search for (and be alerted to) jobs, to explore career paths, and to build your brand.

It's more than just an online resume. It's a job board, a Rolodex (Google that word if you must!), a repository of professional content, and an advertisement for yourself, all rolled into one. And, just like for the recruiters, it works beautifully for the job seekers. Think of other competing sites like Indeed, ZipRecruiter, or Glassdoor as one-trick ponies: They might have lots of job listings but very few ways to help you win those jobs. Or they might be social networks that try and fail to move beyond purely social networks, or only focus on niche industries or types of talent.

Think of LinkedIn the way recruiters do: as your "resume-PLUS." It's your resume PLUS a human narrative that ties together your experiences, skills, and passions. Your resume PLUS additional details such as your professional blog, the causes you care about, your job experience (reflecting back), and your aspirations (looking forward).

So amidst the chaos of the new job search, there's this bit of good news: We at least know the single place where recruiters and hiring managers congregate. Getting to them would be infinitely harder if they were dispersed all over the internet, and fortunately this is not the case. Armed with that knowledge, you're going to learn how to take some of the power back to get into the job that you want, both now and as your career progresses. So how do we do that? By gaming both the recruiter *and* the algorithm on which they rely: the human and the machine.

Playing the New Game

Some employers' haystacks are more like hay *mountains*. Hay Himalayas, even. Google, for example, gets 3 million applications each year for just 7,000 openings. It's expensive and inefficient to hire an army of recruiters to read every single resume. So, just as companies have been doing since the Industrial Revolution, they bring in machines to help out. In fact, the CEO of ZipRecruiter, Ian

The Best Coaches Rely on LinkedIn

Liz Cohen, Founder and Head Coach at Next Step Careers, is one of our favorite career coaches—sharp, savvy, seasoned, and sensitive. Here's why she finds LinkedIn so central to the success of the job seekers with whom she works. In Liz's words:

As a career coach, LinkedIn is a key tool that I help my clients leverage to advance their careers. Clearly, it offers an unparalleled number of job opportunities and features for exploring career paths, companies, and individuals. But most importantly, LinkedIn gives my clients the opportunity to turn strangers into friends—making job searching more human and effective.

I hear it every day: "Liz, job searching is about who you know, and I don't know anyone." For even the most accomplished job seeker, and especially for individuals struggling with impostor syndrome or the possibility of workplace discrimination, the barriers to entry can feel overwhelming and insurmountable. But LinkedIn allows my clients to strategically identify and reach out to people who work at the organizations they most want to join. It allows them to start a conversation based on shared experience, identity, or interest, instead of an already-established relationship. A message begets a phone call, which begets a referral, which turns into an interview, a job offer, and oftentimes a new, lifelong connection.

One client of mine, Janie, wanted to work at one of the most competitive, hard-to-break-into tech companies. She was inspired by their mission but feared that as a woman of color having spent her career in higher education, she wouldn't be given the time of day. With LinkedIn, she identified a fellow woman working on the team she wanted to join. Janie reached out to connect and share her story, and five weeks later she received an offer to join the company.

So even if job searching is about who you know, with LinkedIn, you can get to know just about anyone. Which means the possibilities are endless—if only you're willing to muster up the courage to try, and to say "Hello."

Liz Cohen · 1st
Career Clarity & Job Search Coach | Founder of Next Step Careers (ns-careers.com)

Siegel, estimates that more than 70 percent of resumes are now reviewed by robots before they reach a human reader. Artificial intelligence, or AI, is now built into the "Applicant Tracking Systems" used by 95 percent of the Fortune 500. It's designed to ease the process burden for recruiters and hiring managers, screening out any applicant who doesn't seem like a great fit to its cold, robotic eyes. Brutal.

But we're happy to report that your AI "opponent," the bot you've got to beat, is not some superintelligent supercomputer hell-bent on humankind's destruction—as much as those automated rejection letters might make you think otherwise. Instead, it's much more like a basic pocket calculator, or that preschool plaything Mr. Spell from *Toy Story*.

We're only exaggerating slightly. Before a real, bona fide person even reads your resume and LinkedIn profile, it will be screened by a relatively simple text search. Applicant Tracking Systems and intelligent job boards use quick filters to do the heavy lifting of candidate screening. These AI tools have proliferated as employers focus precious human time on the most qualified—and connected—candidates. So what are these computer algorithms looking for? Basically, they scan for keywords that indicate you're worthy of consideration by their human overseers.

Applicant Tracking System (ATS): software that recruiters use to scan the resumes of people who have already applied

LinkedIn Recruiter: subscription-based product that recruiters use to scan profiles for people they'd encourage to apply

(These are two different pieces of tech, but wired quite similarly— e.g., highly focused on keyword matching thresholds.)

Once you've passed through these algorithmic gates, the much tougher challenge any job seeker confronts is the flesh-and-blood human reading your resume or profile. Why? Because unlike the computer, whose cold, hard logic can be reverse engineered easily enough, our species' fuzzy decision-making is much more difficult to nail down.

For example, even some of the best recruiters we know have a hard time explaining what made them choose one resume over another. "I just know a great candidate when I see one" is a common refrain. And of course, that willy-nilly qualitative approach can be fertile soil for process inefficiencies and harmful biases (both implicit and otherwise—e.g., preferring applicants who look like others at the firm or even the recruiter themselves). It's another reason why networks matter: as source validation in a noisy world.

Everyone is busy. So we take heuristic shortcuts, for better or worse.

Hacking, Hiring, and Believing in Yourself

LinkedIn is your job-seeking Swiss Army knife. Knowing how to use this nifty new multi-tool begins with understanding the hiring process. Why? So you can reverse engineer that process and rise to the top for both human and machine. In the next chapter, we'll explain the real way that hiring works, and the tactics to hack each part of the process. We'll lay out a five-step approach for the new job search, which each subsequent chapter will detail. By the time you've finished this book, you'll be an **expert-level Job Search Hacker**.

We want you to confidently embrace that moniker, and really believe your dream job is within reach. Once you're equipped with these strategies, we know for a fact that you'll stand out from all

How We Humans Hire

Here's our own approach as hiring managers at several companies over the course of our careers. (Note: Keep in mind we have nowhere near as many positions to fill as a typical recruiter, who is spending most of their day screening—and mostly saying no.)

- In the midst of a busy day, we *might* carve out thirty minutes to peruse fifty or so resumes. Allowing time to evaluate them, this equates to about fifteen seconds per resume. This is generous because they've already passed through a first filter (i.e., a recruiter has already selected these). Remember: Recruiters spend an average of *only six seconds* per resume. That's right. TL;DR is the new norm, even with hirers who are heavily invested in filling key roles.

- With so little time, we quickly scan each resume for solid, attention-capturing phrases that indicate things like specific skills ("email marketing"), big numbers ("increased CTR 30 percent, driving 25,000 new visitors to the site"), signifiers of quality ("authored two viral posts on digital marketing"), or interesting stories that demonstrate scrappiness ("created a social media strategy pro bono for a local nonprofit"). If these descriptors seem like a foreign language to you, no worries; we're just using marketing examples.

- Time's up! An applicant makes the interview list if we answer "Yes" to two questions:

  1. *Could this person do the job?* This assessment is based on prior experience, skills, and ability to learn quickly.

  2. *Am I excited about this person?* This assessment is based on whether or not they come across as a star or rising star who has consistently gone the extra mile and taken initiative, versus merely completing responsibilities. We want to know what they've accomplished, not just what their job(s) were.

When hirers are going to spend more waking hours with this candidate than possibly any other one person in their lives, they want to make absolutely sure that time will be well spent. Can you blame them? Life is just too short to work with mediocre, dull teammates!

those other green- and purple-belt job seekers. We've seen it happen time and time again.

But before we dive into the tools and tactics to land your dream job, we want to provide a note of encouragement and perspective. Having now examined the four new realities of the modern job search, here's how to approach LinkedIn: Don't try to *be* the best candidate for a job (yet). Rather, try to make a connection that can help you find and then evaluate your next best opportunity—one that matches your skills and experience—and then *present* yourself as the best candidate for it.

If the hirer doesn't agree, well, they won't hire you. And if you get the job and it turns out to not be right for you, or you're not set up to be successful in it, well, you can leave. But don't let fear of the unknown or not checking every single box on a job description stop you from trying.

Do you know the most common problem afflicting workers? And for anyone who dreams big or wants to grow and develop?

Expanding your set of job possibilities is fundamental.

It's "impostor syndrome." From career starters to corporate executives, we humans have a negativity bias that makes us rather adept at knowing what we're *not* good at, quite often at the expense of seeing and really appreciating what we are *great* at.

Here's the simple antidote to impostor syndrome heard 'round many an office watercooler and in mentoring meetings: "Fake it 'til you make it." We'd amend that nugget of wisdom slightly: "Confidently put your best foot forward and convince an employer that they need what you alone bring. Then, have a growth mindset and learn on the job!" (Okay, not quite as snappy, but oh, so true.)

A huge hindrance to finding a rewarding job is not thinking broadly enough about possible opportunities and limiting yourself only to those that feel like the perfect fit. Expanding this set of possibilities—and believing you can be both competitive and ulti-mately successful—is fundamental to the new, digital job search. Because you can't tell a compelling story about yourself that's tai-lored to a job—much less get found and chosen for it—when you don't really believe you can do that position in the first place. Self-reflection, self-awareness, and self-compassion are the building blocks of deeper self-belief.

Sufficiently motivated? Super-skeptical? Somewhere in between? However you feel, we get it. Putting yourself out there for a new or different kind of job requires vulnerability. Embrace the questions that come from sitting in that vulnerable place. And recognize that building confidence in the job search doesn't happen overnight. It's an iterative process. A huge chunk of that confidence comes from knowing that you're employing the right strategies.

Now, as for those strategies: Let's dive in, shall we?

Don't (Just) Take Our Word For It: From Recruiters' Mouths

Linkedln hasn't just helped level the playing field for job seekers. It's also done so for job *hirers*. Across every industry, it's indispensable to top recruiters and human resource leaders. Here's what some of them say:

> LinkedIn has become the dominant platform for sourcing talent in our industry, including creative talent. Candidates who have well-developed profiles stand out. The more we can learn about the unique experiences and capabilities of talent through profiles, the better able we are to assess fit with our particular studios and teams.
>
> **—MALA SINGH,** Chief People Officer, Electronic Arts (EA)

> With every investor dollar for my high-growth startup comes new demands to hire great people. I rely on LinkedIn day in and out to find the high-quality candidates needed to keep my company growing.
>
> **—NAVEEN SIKKA**, CEO, TerViva

> If you're truly an exceptional educational professional, you're probably on LinkedIn. So it's become a really great source for us.
>
> **—DON GLADISH,** Director of Leader Recruitment,
> IDEA Public Schools

> LinkedIn has become the running water of recruiting and job seeking. If a business professional tells me today that they don't have a LinkedIn account, I'm as shocked as I would have been if the same person told me, 10 years ago, that they didn't have the internet.
>
> **—WILL CHAMPAGNE,** Founder and Managing Partner,
> SCGC Search (VC and Startup search firm)

LinkedIn plays a critical part in my role as a talent advisor. It's the single most used platform I use to find candidates, pull talent insights reports, research companies, and view updates from my network. I can easily message potential candidates and keep in touch with former colleagues. It would be truly challenging to successfully do my job without LinkedIn.

—**GINA PAK**, Recruiter, Benchling (formerly a recruiter for Goldman Sachs, Google, Salesforce, and Slack)

It was like Christmas morning when my team finally had access to LinkedIn's products. We were finally able to proactively source people and make informed, data-driven decisions.

—**BRENT MORRELL**, Director of Talent Acquisition, State of Indiana

In the vast, emerging markets of Asia and beyond, LinkedIn has set a new standard for trust, value, and community on the internet. . . . Not a day goes by where I don't search for or strengthen a relationship via LinkedIn in the markets that matter to my mission; indeed, it's now where culture happens.

—**RISHI JAITLY**, Founding CEO, Times Bridge (a *Times of India* company)

Recruitment IS marketing. If you're a recruiter nowadays and you don't see yourself as a marketer, you're in the wrong profession.

—**MATTHEW JEFFERY**, Global Head of Sourcing and Employment Brand, SAP

LinkedIn has played a critical role in getting CHRISTUS Health's brand out there and helping us recruit the healthcare professionals we need—especially nurses!

—**RON CROY**, VP of Talent Acquisition, CHRISTUS Health

CHAPTER 2

A Five-Step Framework for the Modern Job Search

Know how hiring works so you can game each step

> Destiny is no matter of chance. It is a matter of choice.
> It is not a thing to be waited for, it is a thing to be achieved.
> **—WILLIAM JENNINGS BRYAN**

Process Makes Perfect

It's time to train you to become an expert-level Job Search Hacker. In the rest of the book, we'll guide you through everything that *actually* matters when it comes to both finding a great job and getting found for one. You'll learn to cut through the clutter of LinkedIn, and pay no mind to all the misleading laundry lists out there from purported experts.

Our starting point is an overview of two key processes. These are the tip-offs to the new job-seeking game, the one you're eventually going to tilt in your favor. These processes are:

- **The Hiring Process**—how employers zero in on new hires

- **The Five-Step Job Search Process**—how candidates ensure they stand out

Not only will you be more successful when you dig deeper into these processes, but you'll also feel more in charge of your own

Adopting a Mindset of Resiliency— and Infinite Possibility

I ndulge us while we channel our inner Tony Robbins. Because your belief system about what's possible for yourself is going to get you farther than any one tactic in this book.

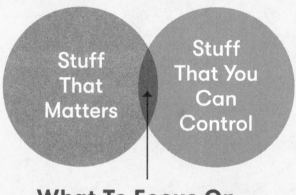

What To Focus On

You spend one-third of your waking life at work.
It matters. But it's not all controllable.

In our experience, the people who are most effective at going from job seeker to job getter are those who have an internal locus of control. They know that they can shape their own professional brand, build their network before they need it, keep close tabs on opportunities so they can jump on them, and put their best foot forward for hirers.

career destiny—even if the odds feel stacked against you. That knowledge will give you a greater peace of mind and a sense of control. Even though you can't do much about larger economic realities (apologies to the Fed Chair, if you're reading this), there's a lot you still *can* do to take the power back and create your future.

Let's look at how.

You have significant agency in how your career unfolds. Adopting this mindset is anything but trivial for many people, especially if you have professional battle wounds or are a rookie to the game.

But it is crucial—fundamental, really—that you approach the job search with a deep and abiding sense that a) you shape your fate; b) something better is always on the other side—of a failed networking attempt, of an interview that flopped, or of the work you're doing to put yourself out there; and c) no matter what, you'll be okay.

This sense of agency isn't just some silly mind game. It's real. No one—no company, no hiring manager, no recruiter—has as much control as you do in landing your dream job. You create (and can recreate) your professional brand, your story, your work and volunteer experience, and your network. If you believe this, you will manifest opportunities.

Bet on yourself. We're pushing our chips up behind yours. Because you're holding in your hands an ace card to taking greater control of your future.

Positivity. Proactivity. (Infinite) **Possibility.**

These three Ps will be the hallmarks of your new mindset for the new job search. Because if you don't tell yourself (repeatedly) that you are in control—well, then, you won't *feel* in control. And that feeling is a crucial part of not only playing the right game, but playing it to win.

We know, that work is hard and ongoing. So here's how you can gauge your progress: As you encounter the inevitable obstacles, you will find yourself increasingly feeling like Teflon. "It's okay, this is all part of the process," you'll start telling yourself. "All of this is a work in progress, and something better always awaits."

Speed bumps. Not roadblocks.

The Hiring Process, Explained

As you might have learned back in economics class, markets are all about supply and demand. The Invisible Hand that Adam Smith described makes them efficient. The job market is no different, right? Employers (the demand) will match, at enormous scale and with optimal efficiency, to the best-fit employees (the supply).

Wrong.

The reality is that hiring is messy. *Quite* messy. It's rife with inefficiencies. That's because in the real world, the hiring process is highly dependent on relationships, timing, and location.

The ways in which talented job seekers (whether "active," "passive," or "tiptoers") connect to the perfect job at the right employer (and vice versa) are quite often serendipitous: Who happens to be top-of-mind for the recruiter or hiring manager precisely when a job comes open; who happens to rise up to the top of a basic LinkedIn search as they outsource the work of finding candidates to its algorithm; with whom the manager already has a relationship. Good timing matters a lot. And so does a healthy dose of luck.

According to *Forbes*, about 70 to 80 percent of jobs are never even publicly listed. And many of those that are seem to be nothing more than mirages—they already have internal candidates who are all but shoo-ins. (In some cases, the job descriptions are even written *for* the specific person the manager has in mind.) Other jobs

Active job seekers: Those eagerly searching and solidly on the job market, usually due to unemployment, underemployment, career starting, burnout, and/or a toxic work environment.

Passive job seekers: Those not seeking a new job who will respond only to recruiter or manager outreach—and only if the timing and role are right.

Tiptoers: Those somewhere in between the first two categories, on a spectrum from modestly networking, to starting to lay seeds, to proactively monitoring jobs that come open but not usually applying to them.

are posted to satisfy legal or company policy requirements and are usually listed for a ten-day minimum.

This all may seem unmeritocratic and, frankly speaking, unfair. But having worked with lots of recruiters and speaking as hiring managers ourselves, we know firsthand why there's a thriving "hidden job market." As we mentioned in Chapter 1, recruiters spend all day trying to fill the candidate funnel, and managers get job openings approved because they have acute hiring needs. Except for the most senior positions (for which entire search and approval committees exist), neither recruiters nor hiring managers want to waste extra cycles digging deeply for the perfect candidate. Especially so when a "good-enough" one is available, either through their networks or the early applicant pool (i.e., via a referral).

Your goal is to perch atop this list of low-hanging fruit, both for the jobs that are posted and those that aren't (or aren't *really*).

How? That starts with knowing how hiring happens. This is how it all unfolds:

1. Recruiters seek focused candidates.

What this means in practice: The lowest-risk, lowest-hanging candidates are those who look, swim, and quack precisely like the duck that recruiters are trying to find. No recruiter in history has ever been fired for screening a Brand Marketing Manager for . . . a Brand Marketing Manager role.

2. They then look for serious candidates.

What this means in practice: Candidates who appear to be unserious get filtered out. This can take a variety of forms—like not knowing about the company or not raising your hand on LinkedIn that you're open to opportunities (see page 100). And it goes well beyond the most basic and all-too-common problem of a sparse or outdated profile—or one without a photo.

3. Hirers rely on internal referrals as *the* crucial source to generate high-quality candidate leads.

What this means in practice: Throughout the entire hiring process, employers give special consideration to applicants who've been referred. As hiring managers, we've been in situations in which we narrowed down a short list of very strong candidates—only to have an internal referral come in at the eleventh hour and reorder the carefully stacked ranking. "I only hire referrals" is not an uncommon hiring-manager refrain.

4. Candidates get chosen for interviews based on both their connections to the employer and their knowledge of the organization.

What this means in practice: The easiest, lowest-risk hires are internal transfers—the ultimate connection. They're known quantities, and it costs less to retain an employee than it does to find and onboard a new one (it takes, on average, between one to two years for a new hire to produce a positive return). But the transfer dance can be disruptive on a large scale, and companies eventually need to grow their ranks. Job seekers looking to break in need to puncture the inner circle and make themselves appear as low-risk as possible.

5. Hirers, we all know, do background checks on candidates before they extend a job offer.

What this means in practice: Think of the term "background check" broadly. It's not just a verification of criminal, credit, and/or job history *after* an offer is extended. It's also a continual and less formal undertaking throughout the process—what's sometimes referred to as "backchanneling." This is when a recruiter—or more often the hiring manager—reaches out to a shared connection to get intel on a candidate while they're in the consideration process. In fact, background checks and backchannels can even inform which candidates get interviews and which are ruled out in the first place.

Recruiters also check your digital footprint. According to a Jobvite survey, 93 percent of recruiters are likely to look at a serious candidate's social media profiles (primarily but not only LinkedIn). And CareerBuilder found that of those who do, 57 percent have found content that caused them *not* to hire a candidate.

Hacking the Hiring Process

That was the hiring process in a nutshell. Now here's how to crack it and play the game the *right* way.

1. If hirers are hunting for focused candidates, you need to **build a LinkedIn profile that's laser-focused** on exactly what hirers are looking for.

What this means in practice: Since recruiters are risk-averse, you must look like a safe choice. They want you to have the right background, titles, experience, connections, and more *for the specific job* they're seeking to fill. Utilizing strong keywords on your profile is a big part of this strategy, as we'll soon see. But always remember: When developing your professional brand, less is more. That all-purpose advice applies to both short- and long-term career goals, from the baby step of landing your next gig to the quantum leap of your ultimate dream job. Focus, focus, focus.

Erin Cardenas · 1st
Senior Project Manager
San Mateo, California, United States · Contact info

William Lewis
New Business Development | GTM Strategy | Program and Product Manager | Entrepreneurship | Personal Finance Guru
San Francisco, California · Contact info

In a world of unfocused Williams, be an Erin.

There's usually hard work required to figure out *how* you want to focus yourself to win the next job. It's a mix of deep, personal self-examination and a whole lot of exploration of what (and who) is out there. Chapter 3 will walk you through some tips to do this, such as finding and learning from people who've blazed trails. Trade-offs abound because, hey, we're all far more complex, curious, and capable people than a resume or LinkedIn profile can adequately convey, right? But you will get much more bang for your digital job-seeking buck by putting a simple stake in the ground that says, "this is who I am"—or at least, "this is what I want to be found for." Less. Is. More.

Perhaps you can draw inspiration from legendary jazz bassist Charles Mingus, who said:

"Making the simple complicated is commonplace; making the complicated simple, awesomely simple— that's creativity."

2. If hirers are looking for serious candidates, you must **demonstrate engagement**—with the firm, with connections who are "network nodes," and with the job market generally.

What this means in practice: A seemingly disengaged candidate fails to send the right signals on these three dimensions of the employer, the people, and the market. Shining these signals on LinkedIn, though, might include your openness to new opportunities, your connectedness to your desired employers, and your explicit interest in them.

LinkedIn continues to do a lot to make it easier for recruiters to find candidates who give off that vibe—and to filter out those who don't. Remember, helping recruiters and hiring managers pinpoint the exact candidates they need is, and will always be, LinkedIn's core business. And as the company continually strengthens its value to hirers, it becomes increasingly important for you to show up the right way on the platform.

The Job-Seeking Gap

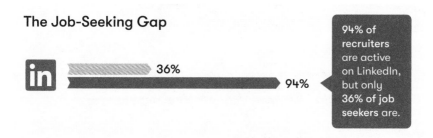

94% of recruiters are active on LinkedIn, but only 36% of job seekers are.

Wanna get hired? Be where the hirers are.

3. If hirers constantly solicit referrals, your task is to **find and culti-vate a warm lead**—at every one of your target employers.

What this means in practice: You might've heard wild stories about all-night ragers in Silicon Valley start-ups or Wall Street brokerages, but organizations aren't generally in the business of throwing away money. So why do almost all of them—for-profit, nonprofit, and public sector—have referral programs, with bonuses that can reach tens of thousands of dollars? Because those organizations—and their recruiters and hiring managers—know that employee referrals are the best source of talent with the highest return on investment. Referrals are validation-providing and confidence-boosting. They offer comfort to hirers in a chaotic world.

A savvy job searcher never *only* applies to a job and hopes for the best. Starting now, you will find organizational insiders to refer or vouch for you. Don't fret about getting the perfect, most senior person for a referral—or even someone directly connected to the hiring manager or recruiter (who is sometimes listed on the job posting itself). Level doesn't matter as much as speed. Most first-round decisions about who gets in for the first batch of interviews are made *within the first 72 to 96 hours* that a job posting is live.

Ideally, you will build at least one solid relationship with a contact at your target company who can refer you right away via their internal process *before* your perfect role is posted. But if you haven't, it's more important that you get your application in within

---

> **Referral Request**
>
> Hi Nikita,
>
> Hope you're well! I just saw that your team at Nike is hiring a new
> designer for the Jordan brand. Given my background in cutting-
> edge apparel design and branding, would you be open to referring
> me for the role?
>
> If so, I've attached my resume here.
>
> Thanks for considering!
> -Cyndi

*Here's a typical referral request. Company insiders are incentivized
to make referrals—you're just giving them that opportunity!*

---

the first four days and work simultaneously to have a current
employee flag your materials and candidacy in the meantime—or,
worst case, in week two. Remember, they often have a vested interest to do so. It shouldn't be too difficult (or scary) of an ask, even for
a contact whom you don't know well.

4. If hirers select candidates based on their connections and knowledge, you must **build both your network and your understanding
of the company, industry, and people**.

What this means in practice: Employers trust people they know. To
break into a new company, job seekers must puncture the inner circle. But how? Being 1st-degree-connected to recruiters and hiring
managers—or at least to those who *they* are connected to—ranks
you higher in the search results. And just like with any Google
search, if you're not in the first page or two of results, you might
as well not exist. This may seem frustrating, but you can turn up
higher in searches by building a relationship with almost anyone
on LinkedIn.

Broader, more diverse networks are stronger networks.
"Network effect" is a crucial concept to understand and work to

1st-degree connection: Someone you know already on LinkedIn

2nd-degree connection: Someone who knows someone you're 1st-degree-connected to

3rd-degree connection or above: Someone who's more distantly connected to you

Network effect: The very real phenomenon of everyone benefiting from something the more it's used. Way back when there were rotary phones and fax machines, the more people who used them, the more valuable they became. These days, the concept typically applies to technology platforms that grease the wheels of connection and help close market gaps. LinkedIn was built on this premise—and has no true competitor because of it.

your advantage. Why? Because three-fourths of jobs are never even posted—uncoincidentally, the same percentage of jobs that are found via connections—and most of *those* jobs are found not by whom we know directly, but rather, whom *they* know. It's these weak ties—the 2nd- and 3rd-degree connections—that give us the volume we need to peer into millions of people's networks and find lots of ways to get those precious referrals.

So how do you tap into network effect and put the incredible power of it to work for you? Connect broadly. Not quite indiscriminately, but very liberally.

At the same time, network intentionally, not just randomly. You need to build a purposeful network—with the *right* people. Specifically, these are the insiders at the organizations where you want to work. And by networking with them, you'll be able to build your knowledge about their companies, their industries, and the movers and shakers that drive them. Which, in turn, will give you the information you need to land a job you love.

5. If hirers do background checks (remember: broadly defined, and at any time during the process), you must **do your own check**—also throughout the process, but most crucially at the offer stage.

What this means in practice: Why should employers be the only ones who get to snoop around? Good news: You can do a background check on *them*, too.

If you've been rigorous enough to hack each of the first four parts of the hiring process, and it's resulted in some serious potential inroads with an employer—or even an offer—it's not quite time to sit back with a margarita. Keep being proactive and on the hunt for data that can help you get the job and decide whether to take it. Namely, that means contacting *former* employees of the company, gleaning insights from shared connections to the manager or other team members on LinkedIn, knowing your worth for salary negotiations, and getting additional insider information from a review site like Glassdoor.

Why? Because when managers start to home in on a candidate, they shift from being the consumer (expecting candidates to sell *them* on why they should "purchase" their services) to the seller (trying to convince candidates that this is a great role, team, and organization). In this dance, you're never quite getting an inside look at what it's *really* like to work there. At this stage people tend to sugarcoat what the job is—and whom it requires you to work for. It's often all too true that people leave bosses, not jobs. So your background check is about arming yourself with the knowledge to make a decision—and to avoid an unpleasant situation before it potentially happens.

According to a Gallup poll,
75% of workers voluntarily left their
job for reasons related to the **manager.**

Your due diligence doesn't end with getting the offer.
Know what you'd be getting into.

Glassdoor: Half-Truths, Half-Useful

Glassdoor.com is a go-to destination for insider information on every-thing from company culture to salaries. For job seekers, it complements LinkedIn nicely. While Glassdoor can be helpful to read semi-candid insider takes—a step that absolutely needs to be part of your due diligence—it has two shortcomings:

1. OUTLIER BIAS: Crowdsourced reviews tend toward the extremes. Think about who would be most motivated to post company culture observations (and salaries) on a public website; it's those who have had either a great or an awful experience there. Most people, however, are probably some-where in between. If you throw in negativity bias (humanity's tendency to prioritize threats over rewards), the feedback can definitely skew toward the had-an-awful-experience extreme.

Companies are actively intervening to change this, and their HR depart-ments watch for negative feedback. A cynic, however, might say it's easier to intervene with the specific disgruntled employee (or ignore them if they've already left) than it is to institute systemic change to address widespread issues. And many companies now even run campaigns explicitly asking their employees to submit positive reviews.

2. GENERIC VS. SPECIFIC: In our experience, people often put way too much stock in the idea of "corporate culture." C-level leaders advance this half-truth because it helps their companies appear to be different from competitors that are also in the market for both customers *and* talent. In addition, stated values fall flat if they don't buy in at every turn. Glassdoor reviews typically pertain to general company-wide observations, which are only of minimal value to the discerning job seeker.

Why? Because the full truth is that no organization, of any size or sector, is a monolith. Sure, it's important to investigate at a general level how the company talks about itself, what its employees say, and whether the val-ues are real. But any organization is really just a bunch of individual teams. It's those teams, and their specific managers and the microcultures within them, that will affect your day-to-day work and your happiness more than any generic review (e.g., "visionary CEO & great coffee on the third floor"). While Glassdoor curates "Best Companies to Work For" lists, which are perhaps only marginally useful, what the job seeker *really* needs is a "Best Bosses/Teams" list. (We're now accepting funds for this genius start-up idea!)

The Five-Step Job Search Process

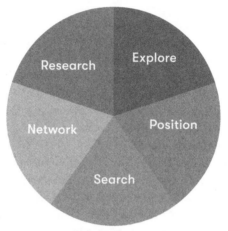

Our patented (well, not really) five-step process to landing your dream job.

Now that you understand the hiring process—and how to hack it—from top to bottom, let's turn to the job search process. It's what animates the rest of this book. The modern job search entails **five concrete sets of actions**. These are similar to the five strategies we just reviewed but take a far more positive and proactive approach, rather than one that's entirely based on reacting to recruiter behavior. The recruiter's process flows naturally into the job seeker's.

Here are your five steps to landing your dream job:

1. Exploring possible career paths so you can get focused.

In other words: figuring out the right role for you, and identifying at least five target companies that you really like, even if the right role doesn't (yet) exist there. Focusing your lists of both the roles and firms you want to go after will be informed by those who've forged professional paths before you. So you'll find five alumni at each of those five target companies to help you find that focus.

2. Positioning yourself for the job you most want next.

In other words: creating a clear personal brand in a cluttered digital world, and ensuring you stand out for that specific thing. One that goes beyond your resume and is your "resume-plus": resume-plus-narrative, resume-plus-aspiration, resume-plus-visual-elements, resume-plus-social-proof, resume-plus-showing-not-just-telling. Positioning yourself effectively is all about showing up and showing off your focus.

3. Searching for the *right* people, opportunities, and employers.

In other words: searching for and applying to jobs with the techniques that give you the best chance of landing an interview. Staying engaged. Keeping the forward momentum and driving interest, and leveraging digital tools to help. No matter where you are on the job-seeker spectrum—from desperately seeking anything to happily-but-not-ideally employed—you should *always* have at least one eye open on opportunities.

4. Networking in both broad and purposefully selective ways.

Job seeker Ari has seen a massive difference with a proactive and targeted approach (can you tell he's a financial analyst?):

"I refined my search, as opposed to the broad, shotgun approach (hit rate ~2 percent). When I contacted alumni, messaged recruiters, and sent tailored connection requests, I got much more traction (hit rate ~10 percent)."

In other words: standing out by getting in. Growing your connections, then mining them to build relationships at the places and with the people making the actual decisions *before* that perfect job is even posted. Then, when it is posted, not just applying cold, but tapping your connections to find and cultivate a warm lead who can refer you, so you're not just another minnow in an ocean of talent.

5. Researching to seal the deal. (And once you have, knowing what you'd be getting into before you accept the job offer.)

In other words: Doing due diligence on the employer you want to work for and the industry they're in; preparing for interviews with a nuanced understanding of the people you're talking to; performing your own background check—on the company, team, and potential manager—so you know it's a good landing spot once you get the offer; and using salary data to know your worth.

The Broad Buckets of the Modern Job Search

1. **Explore**
   Build your list of companies

Get Info

2. **Position**
   Become a recruiter magnet

3. **Search**
   Find the right jobs

Get Access

4. **Network**
   Get a referral

5. **Research**
   Ace the interview!

Get Hired

Want it even simpler? Here are the five steps placed into three straightforward buckets.

Success, Redefined: Repeating the Five-Step Framework

Up and to the right.

That's what we're all trained to believe successful businesses—and careers—look like on a simple line graph. Always growing, quickly or steadily. More money, more power, more influence—more, more, more. Anything different or less obvious means, well, you'd better get back on track.

But nothing could be further from the truth. Sometimes we need to go "off track," even seemingly backward, to later catapult forward. Sometimes global pandemics or painful economic realities like recessions or mass layoffs dictate it.

In applying our five-step framework, keep this top of mind: The fruitful job search—not to mention professional fulfillment—is never simply up and to the right. Our society doesn't celebrate failures as it should. Success rarely comes overnight, even if our cultural stories reinforce the silly notion that anyone can be rich and famous this very instant, if only their true talent can be seen. But life is not *America's Got Talent*.

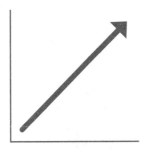

What people think
success looks like

What success
really looks like

Be compassionate with yourself as you seek new opportunities.

Go ask any ostensibly "successful" person: We bet they'll tell you their career path was anything but a straight line—rather, a series of mini-pivots. Professional success is much more likely to be the product of a lot of hard work, lucky (and unlucky) circumstance, ingenuity, scrappiness, and mess-ups. Job changes may be lateral or even pay less, but they can have other benefits—opportunities to learn, network, and build new skills. With the right attitude, we can learn much more from our misses or perceived slights than from our wins. (Trust us, we know this is easier said than done; one of us kept a list of "haters" in the first half of his career to prove wrong!)

Pablo Picasso encountered many difficulties on his path to greatness— poverty, dyslexia, depression. So perhaps you can take some believable inspiration from his observation and imploration that "Action is the foundational key to all success."

Before our careers at LinkedIn, we both worked at Apple. So we're obligated to mention our shared deity, Steve Jobs, and share a few words from his famous commencement speech at Stanford in 2005: "You can't connect the dots looking forward; you can only connect them looking backward. So you have to trust that the dots will somehow connect in your future."

There's a crucial implication—and caveat—for the framework at the heart of this book. Though we present the job search as sequential steps herein, it's really a fluid, nonlinear, and iterative process. That philosophy applies to your next job, as well as the twenty-plus more you might have throughout your life.

Keys to Staying Motivated

Let's face it, the job search can be exhausting and frustrating. Maddening, even. Far too many of us are unemployed or underemployed, and it feels like the economy—and what employers are looking for—is constantly shifting. We try to tell our stories into a void. The roles we really want always go to other people. Even when we do get interest from employers, it can be for jobs or companies that we have no interest in. We know. So it's vital to find ways to stay motivated in what can be a deflating—and lengthy—process.

Social science research has a lot to say about how we can make daily habits out of things that are good for us in the long run. The problem is that our brains' reward systems are biased toward the immediate. It's why questionable behaviors like gambling, eating junk food, or bingeing on Netflix feel so good.

What you need to do is make job-seeking a habit. It should be a regular part of your routine that doesn't require too much extra mental or psychic load. If it isn't, you'll do it half-assed (best case) or keep pushing it off (worst case). Every day, you can always do at least a little bit, making some progress here and there—touching up your profile, building your network, searching for and applying to jobs, or preparing to be vetted.

Here are the three keys to habituating yourself to being a voracious and proactive job seeker:

1. Get quick wins.

Ever heard this advice for starting a new job? Well, it also applies to starting a new job *search*. Don't think of it as needing to go whole-hog from the get-go; every bit of progress you make will have a benefit. For example, if you've given significant love to your resume, just update your LinkedIn profile with those exact same bullets. It's all to be refined and iterated upon as you figure out your focus.

You must also take special pains to acknowledge those quick wins, like the recruiter who accepted a connection request; the email offering time slots for a first interview; or the discovery of a brand-new target company that might just be a perfect fit. Remember negativity bias—we're so good at seeing what we're doing *wrong* that it obscures what's going well. If you let this happen to you in the job search, it will be much easier to beat yourself up and get discouraged than to keep going.

continued . . .

2. Set aside a time—ideally the same time—every day for the job search. And protect that time.

It may take several consecutive weeks or even a couple months, but eventually, making incremental (but regular) progress toward a new job will become second nature.

Many research studies have all found the same thing: People keep up behaviors, desirable or undesirable, not because they have more or less willpower and commitment than other people, but because they've done them over and over (to the exclusion of other behaviors). You can automate yourself!

Be aware of your behaviors, though. You might find yourself taking the "shotgun" approach: mindlessly applying cold to one job after another on job boards or LinkedIn's Easy Apply. If so, pause, check yourself, look or walk around outside, and then stop yourself from what will likely be more fruitless effort. When you're ready to get back at it, pivot to a more productive pursuit, like finding and connecting with actual humans at the places you most want to work.

3. Create short-term rewards for what is a long-term endeavor.

If what motivates us are short-term dopamine hits from activities like getting likes on Instagram, then you must aggressively seek out ways to get those hits routinely, in the short-term, for what will likely be a long-term process. Here are some examples:

- Start a daily gratitude practice (writing down five things you are grateful for)

- Publicly state your intentions (letting others know about your goals, and your incremental steps toward them, for greater accountability)

- Try "habit-stacking" (adding job search activities to well-trodden habits you already have)

- Treat yourself (taking a trip to your favorite restaurant after, say, making ten potentially valuable connections)

Get Ready, Get Set . . .

From finding the best companies to positioning yourself as irresistible to their recruiters; from keeping your finger on the pulse of potential dream-job postings to networking your way in and researching your way to interview success, *now* you're playing the new game. And you're playing it to win.

Ready to put these frameworks into action? Let's take a moonshot! So read on. Mark up these pages. Follow the checklists. Revisit the strategies as needed. Rinse and repeat. All the while, believe in yourself and exercise your internal locus of control.

And remember: Positivity. Proactivity. (Infinite) Possibility.

Let's go!!

CHAPTER 3

Get Focused: Exploring

*The journey begins with knowing
what's out there*

> But the eyes are blind. One must look with the heart.
> **—ANTOINE DE SAINT-EXUPÉRY**

Set Your Course Before You Set Off

It's time to take the plunge and land a job you love. No more settling. Pause for a moment and let yourself feel the excitement of new possibilities—now try to channel that excitement for what may lie ahead. You'll need it! Because the hardest part of any job search is, you guessed it: getting started. But fear not—we'll be with you each step of the way, from start to finish.

So just what is the first step in the modern job search?

Well, you could jump into action mode and do what we've all been trained to do: Work on your resume. Or you could fiddle around with your LinkedIn profile. Or perhaps the most mindless (and least impactful) activity: taking that stale, multipurpose resume and applying cold to every job you come across. With so many ways to browse and apply—with so many *things to do*—it's no wonder that lots of searches never leave the launchpad.

But here's the truth: All those actions won't yield results unless they're focused. While firing off your resume far and wide like a bazooka or clicking every "Easy Apply" button you see on LinkedIn may *feel* productive, it's not. It takes a laser-guided missile to hit your target (which might be new connections, emails from a recruiter, interview callbacks, and ultimately job offers). Your first task is to get to know thyself—then find what matches are out there and get discovered for them.

So here's a simple operating question to cut through all the analysis paralysis: *What kind of job would you actually love in the first place?*

If you don't yet know the answer to that question, that's okay. It takes time for lots of us. But until you start to develop a hypothesis about the kind of work that brings you fulfillment, every other step— building a resume, crafting a LinkedIn profile, even networking— could feel like a step through superglue. Without a clear North Star to guide you, every job search maneuver is just a shot in the dark. That's where the Exploring step comes in.

This is an absolutely critical, soul-baring, be-truly-real-with-yourself, no-shortcuts-allowed exercise. Because when it comes to your professional brand in the digital world, getting focused— on what you really want to do next, and then on how you position yourself accordingly—is the key.

Said another way: There's no such thing as a perfect LinkedIn profile. There is only a perfect LinkedIn profile *for a specific job.* What is that job for you, and for where you are right now in your career? Clarifying this will be your compass.

So to make sure you set off in the proper direction, let's take the first step together: finding the right path for you by exploring on LinkedIn. Let's do it in two parts: 1) understanding your options, and 2) testing your options.

Career coach Shelley Piedmont says:

"Take the first step of learning about other career options. That is the hardest one. All steps after that come much easier."

Part 1: Understand Your Options

To point your compass toward the right career path, you need to get a feel for what's out there. Once you do, chances are you won't have to blaze an entirely new trail. The galaxy of possibilities will be made more knowable and more manageable.

Here's a useful case study. Jeremy used to mentor a high school student in the South Bronx named Ian. Ian had impressive clarity about his future and was dead set on becoming a criminal forensic scientist. There was only one problem: Ian hated science. Kind of a job requirement. Oops.

Upon further investigation, it turned out that Ian didn't know any practitioners in the field. But he did watch a ton of *CSI*. Sure enough, he had trained his sights on the one profession that seemed cool—even though it was totally wrong for him!

Explore the trails that others have blazed before you.

Ian is no outlier. We have all done this, usually at earlier stages of our professional lives, but it's liable to happen at other key moments of our careers, like mulling over what comes next after a graduate program, or trying to break into a new industry mid-career. We get tunnel vision on a specific path that we've heard about—and then start to ignore all other possibilities. And we do so at our own peril, given that just seeing a role on TV or focusing on what our friends are passionate about may block out the other careers that are indeed a better fit for us.

To avoid this trap, you must get intimately acquainted with the set of real possibilities out there. The single best way to do that is to explore the trails that others have blazed before you. Especially those with whom you already have shared work credentials or a shared affiliation—like an alma mater—who are lower-hanging fruit to connect with.

When we worked at LinkedIn, our team built a handy product called the **Alumni Tool**. (Sure, we're biased, but we think it's the best-kept secret on LinkedIn.) And even though it's buried deep within the site, discovering it is like striking career gold: It shows the paths of *every alum at virtually every school*—colleges, universities, graduate programs, even many high schools—in the world.

So what makes these paths so valuable to you? And why the school-based approach to career exploration? The Alumni Tool gives you a sense of your most realistic, attainable options. After all, these alumni have been in your shoes, studied what you've studied, and gone on to land awesome opportunities across a variety of fields, locations, and employers. Not only that: Given your shared affiliation (Go Tigers/Aggies/Banana Slugs/Fill-In-Your-Goofy-Mascot-Here!), these contacts are also low-hanging potential referrals and informational interviewers. Their brains—and networks—are ripe for the picking.

Here's how to start mining that alma mater career path on LinkedIn:

1. Type in your school in the search box, and choose the "School" page option.

2. Click "Alumni" at the top of the college or university's page.

3. Welcome to the best-kept secret on LinkedIn! You now have access to all your school's alumni on the site (i.e., those who've listed the school in the Education section of their profiles—all easily filterable by location, company, job, major, and connection proximity):

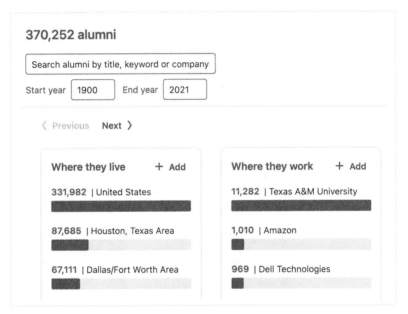

What to do next with this information depends on where you are in your career (e.g., a new or soon-to-be grad casting a wide net, or twenty years out with more focused requirements) and on what's most important to your search (e.g., living in a certain geographical area, or working for a dream employer).

Here are just a few examples of the myriad ways you can purposely slice and dice this alumni data to get precisely what—and whom—you need to help you focus your job search.

Geographic Filtering

Let's say you're a current college senior at Texas A&M University who wants to move to Austin after graduation. Select "Austin, Texas Area" from the *Where they live* column (if it doesn't appear in the first set of listings, click "Add," then search for your desired location). You have just cut down your list of 370,000+ alumni to one-tenth of that unruly number—only the 31,000+ in Austin:

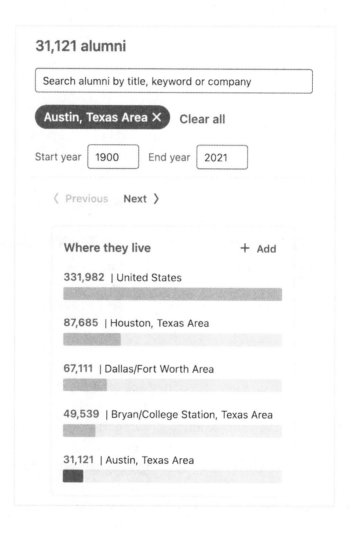

And best of all, everything else in the Alumni Tool dynamically updates based on any filters you apply. So in this example, you'll now see only the companies hiring alums in the Austin area in the *Where they work* column:

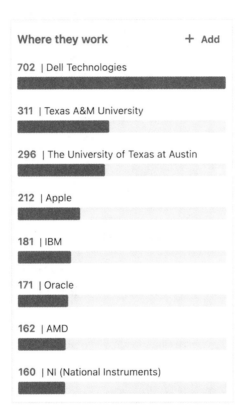

Okay, so what? Well, now you have a list of alumni in your desired city who are available to connect and from whom you can learn. (We'll get into that reaching out part later in this chapter.) Just as valuable, this is also your postgraduation employer lead list. Both factors can help you get focused. It's a custom-tailored directory of potential organizations to explore—ones in which your alumni base is *already working*.

Academic Filtering

Maybe you're a new grad who's not sure what to do with your psych degree. You're far from alone—it turns out that, according to LinkedIn, more than a thousand Texas A&M alumni *in Austin* walked in your shoes and navigated that very situation. Just click the "Next" button to toggle over to the *What they studied* column and choose your major:

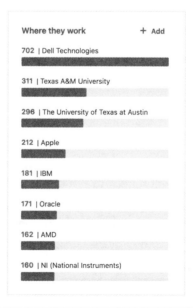

Now look at the *Where they work* column and behold all the most popular options at your disposal—from technology and business to academia:

Occupational Filtering

Let's say you graduated a decade ago and entered the health care sector but now want to switch into an information technology career. Choose your desired field (and perhaps also the function you want to be in) from the *What they do* column:

Again, notice that the other elements of this tool also update as you click into these filters. So toggle back and check out the various employers where others like you have landed jobs:

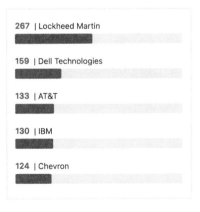

Other Best Practices

Here are a few more important notes to get the most value out of the Alumni Tool:

1. Be sure to conduct a similar search for *every school you attended*, in any capacity (including high schools, graduate programs, professional certificates, and even study abroad). Each new search expands your horizons even further.

2. No matter what kind of program you were in at a school, even if you didn't complete it—a certificate, an associate's, bachelor's, master's degree, or beyond—remember that the entire institution's alumni base is also part of your network.

If you got your MBA from Texas A&M, for example, you would of course want to peruse the Alumni Tool for the Mays Business School *as well as* the overall Texas A&M page. But don't skip other schools within the larger university, such as the School of Law or the School of Public Health. Whether you were part of the Texas A&M community for a semester or a seven-year PhD program, all these alumni are now at your fingertips.

> **An *entire* institution's alumni base is also part of your network.**

Why are they so accessible? Because graduates tend to feel an affinity for their larger institutions, not just their specific programs (just look at all the university logos plastered over bumper stickers, thirty years post-graduation). Omar, for example, went to UC Berkeley's Haas School of Business but always responds to requests he gets from anyone who's ever been affiliated with UC Berkeley. He loves Cal, not just Haas—and definitely not just MBAs.

3. You can custom-search far more than a location (e.g., "Austin, Texas Area" on page 68) with this tool. Don't see a specific company, skill, or area of study in the default list of the top fifteen results? Click the "Add" button atop any of these dimensions and use the search to find the right, LinkedIn-standardized match to narrow your list:

4. For any additional search criteria that don't fit within LinkedIn's standardized options, you can add them using the search box at the top of the Alumni Tool:

For instance, let's say you only want to see graduates who are in the field of Corporate Social Responsibility. Just do a search for that phrase (in quotes to capture all the words of the phrase together) and hit "Return." Now you can see all the alumni who have that specific field anywhere on their profiles, plus updated data on where they live, work, and more:

346 alumni

Search alumni by title, keyword or company

"Corporate Social Responsibility" ✕   Clear all

614 alumni

Search alumni by title, keyword or company

"Corporate Social Responsibility" OR "CSR" ✕   Clear all

Corporate Social Responsibility is also known as "CSR," so you can add an "OR" operator to catch more than one phrase and widen your search.

These focused methods of finding alumni are especially helpful at the outset of your job search. This way, no matter what's most important to you, you'll have a tailored list of pathways to explore. Instead of settling for just the jobs you know, you now have visibility into both a larger *and* more realistic set of potential jobs that you might actually, dare we say, enjoy! Just as important, you're laying the groundwork for a network of school-affiliated people who can help surface opportunities and eventually get you in the door.

Now let's get into how to tap the power of these career maps to build real relationships.

Hold Up—What If I Didn't Go to College?

We've focused so far on examples of college and university networks. But what if you didn't go to a four-year school? After all, two in three Americans haven't completed a four-year degree.

Good news: The true power of LinkedIn is that it's not some exclusive old boys' club. Anyone can tap its data to accelerate their career. Here are two other options, no matter your educational background:

1. LinkedIn has the Alumni Tool for almost any school in the world, including vocational programs and high schools—a truly unrivaled data set of career paths to explore. So you can search for and explore any and every school you attended.

2. LinkedIn also offers a similarly filterable solution for companies. Say you're already working somewhere but want to explore the ins and outs of different roles—and the folks who hold them—at your organization. Just search for your company and click the "People" tab.

Bam! You can now explore lots of paths within your current employer (the easiest place to start) but beyond the specific job you're doing today. Then you can also view the paths and required skills of people at other companies where you might want to work next.

Part 2: Test Your Options

You've just taken the critical first step: discovering an entire universe of plausible professional options. This is especially something to celebrate if you've been feeling stuck or overwhelmed up to this point.

Now it's time to test out those options. While it might be tempting to say, "Wow, look at all these philosophy majors working at Nike; that's the path for me," it's an even better idea to talk to those philosophy majors before you take the plunge.

To appreciate why, imagine this scenario: You spend the next few months hustling to land a plum job at Nike. You finally make it in. And then on your first day, your boss says: "Hey, do you mind updating all these spreadsheets by the end of the day?" Which is really too bad, given that spreadsheets are your own personal kryptonite. And the mere sight of all those blank cells makes your eyes start to bleed. And every time someone says, "Pivot Table," you start to break out in hives. . . .

The best way to explore is to talk to the people who actually *do* the job.

Okay, you get the picture.

To avoid this fate, you want to really dig into each possible career path and understand exactly what it entails—what would you *actually* do in this role, is it a good fit for your superpowers, and will it bring you meaning or misery?

The best way to do that is to talk to people who *do* the job—i.e., the alumni you just uncovered in the last step. After all, if you had the choice between reading about a chocolate cake in a cookbook and tasting the cake right here and now, who wouldn't go for the real thing? The same concept applies to career exploration; there's just no substitute for learning from real people with real expertise.

Here's exactly how to start up those essential conversations:

1. Once you run your initial filter(s) on the Alumni Tool to narrow down the pool of users, scroll down to see the alumni doing the very jobs in the very places you're excited about:

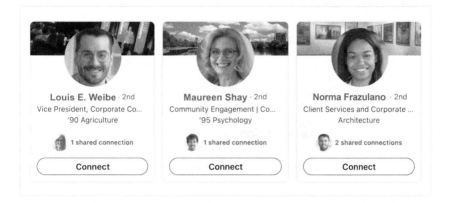

2. Pick one who is doing something intriguing and click the "Connect" button. Then, be sure to also click "Add a note" (since you want to make it clear why you're reaching out):

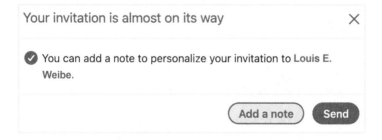

3. Now, here's the most crucial part. Many people blow it by saying something like, "Hey—can you get me a job?" or "Let me tell you how awesome I am!" While you might want both things, neither is particularly appealing to an alum.

In fact, if you're an alum yourself, you might have received at least a few messages like this. If so, you know all too well that no one wants to be so plainly sold to or used in such a transactional way.

Worry not, however, because the vast majority of alumni are happy to help out—they just want to feel good about it. They want a chance to tell their own story or steer the next generation clear of the mistakes they made. But here's what you will almost certainly *not* hear: "Oh, sure, let me serve you up a job on a silver platter just because you happened to be one of the 300,000 other people who went to my school!"

So here's an example of a note that gives the alum the spotlight instead of a sales pitch (you can find a template for this kind of outreach on page 84):

Add a note to your invitation   ✕

LinkedIn members are more likely to accept invitations that include a personal note.

> As a fellow Aggie who's considering a career in Marketing, I was thrilled to come across your profile. I'd love to learn more about your impressive experience in this field -- any chance you'd have a few minutes to chat next week? Many thanks in advance! Sarah

                                              Cancel   **Send**

The key elements here are:

- Playing up your shared affiliation from the get-go.

- Flattery (let's be real, it works).

- Conveying you won't waste their time.

- Next week is always better than this week!

Once you've sent this first request, don't stop there. You want to reach out to at least five alumni, with a goal of having three real conversations (aka "informational interviews") per career path. Why? Well, for one thing, you're unlikely to hear back from every alum. You also want a diverse sample of experiences to help you get focused while making a potentially foundational career decision.

For the alumni who do respond, be sure to keep track of what you learn. Make the most of each conversation by doing the following:

- Ask great questions to accelerate your learning (see Sidebar on the next page).

- Follow up with a great thank-you note. It doesn't have to be long, but it does need to include some of the things you learned. The alums should know that the time they invested in the call was well worth it—and they'll be all the more likely to want to help you again in the future.

After each of your three (at a minimum) informational interviews with alumni who have desirable job titles, work at companies you're considering, or have taken career steps you want to emulate, it's helpful to rate your level of fit. Here's a basic rubric to evaluate what you're learning:

- *3: Great Fit*—I'd love doing this kind of work, it plays to my strengths (but with some healthy "stretch" and learning), and I'd feel good about what I accomplish there.

- *2: Okay Fit*—This work feels somewhat interesting, I could definitely get it done, and I'd have a decent sense of accomplishment.

- *1: Bad Fit*—This work seems fairly boring, I'd have to work really hard just to be mediocre at it, and/or it would give me very little sense of meaning.

Let's look at an example: Say you just interviewed a high school math teacher, who's told you about his days of engaging his students, helping them navigate tough challenges both at school and at home, and ultimately guiding them toward success. If you love to

Great Questions = Real Insights

To make sure you get the most out of your connection with fellow alumni, get ready to ask great questions. Again, you're not pitching yourself or asking for a job—you just need the real, unvarnished truth about what the job is like.

Here's precisely what to ask them during a phone, video, or coffee chat:

- How did you go from school (or a different type of job/role) to your current role?

- How does your job compare to school and tap into what you studied there?

- What do you do all day?

- What do you love the most about your field?

- What's most frustrating about your role?

- What has surprised you most?

By asking these questions, you can get a sense of what it's really like to be in their shoes—what the job feels like, how it compares to your shared experience, and what you might not expect as someone on the outside.

tell stories, have incredible interpersonal skills, and are motivated by making a difference in a young person's life, you might rate that role a "3." If your true love, however, is finding patterns hidden in data, your number-crunching skills are off the charts, and you're most motivated by making sense out of lots of information, this might be a "1" for you.

Either way, your overall list will give you an average rating for each potential pathway. You can then compare the overall ratings across each of the paths to identify the one you should pursue first. Instead of stumbling out of the starting blocks like so many job seekers, you are now armed with a compass pointing you to a clear North Star.

Exploring an Internal Transfer

While many of the methods in this chapter are designed for people entering the workforce or making a significant career change, the same underlying principles apply to current employees considering an internal transfer. Because a great new job—maybe even your dream job—might be just down the hall.

Often, it is.

In fact, roughly half of jobs are filled by internal candidates—it's a whole job market of its own. So if you're pondering (or at least open to) an internal transfer within your current workplace, you're not wasting your time on this chapter. Much of the process is quite similar, but here are a few nuances for the purely internal job search:

- You will likely find that LinkedIn is more useful than your internal employee database, if one exists. In addition to names and titles, the site gives you a career dossier for everyone in your organization. You can find people with shared interests (e.g., the Director of Sales attended your alma mater, or the Head of Facilities volunteers with the same nonprofit) that can make it easier to strike up a conversation.

- Just like you can play the "I'm a student" card when you're in or newly out of school, you can also play the "I'm a colleague" card. This is a very strong "in" that should engender a response while networking. But it is *not* a license to abandon the rules for cold outreach. Don't get too transactional too quickly; try to convey why they're the right person; mention shared connections; flatter them; and don't waste their time.

- Since a potential connection is already in your company, flattery can go even further than normal. They assume, and you can play on, some prior knowledge. Maybe mention something they said in an all-hands meeting, or say that their reputation precedes them.

From Passion to Profession

We first met Andrew Kung while we were all working at LinkedIn. He was a talented recent grad who seemed to have it all: a highly selective job at a fancy-shmancy company with enough compensation to put his instant ramen–eating days behind him.

There was only one problem. Andrew felt stuck.

That's because he was doing a type of job the world expects new grads to do (sales and customer support), not the one that he really craved and excelled at (photography). But unlike many new grads—and frankly, a lot of experienced professionals, too—Andrew wasn't content to just defer his dreams indefinitely. Instead, he started reaching out to professional photographers through his connections on LinkedIn and realized that his dream was completely attainable.

By learning from these insiders, Andrew started to imagine an alternative future that wasn't just pure fantasy, but one that was grounded in the reality of others' experiences. Their stories became the paving stones for a career path that he could start to envision.

Buoyed by his career exploration, Andrew requested a transfer to LinkedIn's New York City office. And within six months, he had networked his

- Start with a lightweight "would love to get to know you and what your team does" ask. Don't ask for a referral in the first call or coffee chat unless it lasts more than an hour and you've said a lot about yourself, *or* you know they're hiring for your dream job. You should instead have lots of nuanced questions and end by asking if they would be willing to be a mentor.

Most companies will have a process for internal transfers. Understand that process. Oftentimes it will include alerting your current manager once you decide to throw in for a new job, which

way into enough part-time gigs that he decided to quit the security of a big company job altogether. Pretty soon his LinkedIn Headline reflected not only his passion, but his new profession:

Within a few years, Andrew had done photography work for Beats by Dre, HBO, and *Esquire*—and had his work featured in the *New York Times* and *Vogue*, and on CNN.

Andrew shares this reflection on his experience: "Before LinkedIn, I always just relied on serendipity to open doors. But with LinkedIn, I realized I could engineer my own serendipity—and my own future."

could potentially be a thorny situation. You must weigh the risks and benefits here, but your HR department and/or recruiting team should be a safe place to help you do so. Also, keep in mind that anyone at your company using LinkedIn's Recruiter can't see that you are open to new opportunities, so there's no way to indicate to them that you want to be considered for an internal move. You can of course make this visible to all members (see page 107), but we don't recommend that unless you're really willing to throw caution to the wind.

Sample Connection Message for Alumni:

Hi FIRST NAME,

As a fellow SCHOOL alum who also majored in FIELD, I was so excited to come across your profile. I'd love to know more about how you built your impressive career—any chance you'd have a few minutes to chat next week?

Thanks for considering!

—YOUR FULL NAME

CHECKLIST: **Exploring**

You did it! Instead of being consigned to wander the earth for all time in search of occupational fulfillment—like some kind of career zombie—you've just given yourself the antiserum: understanding what's out there. And unlike the watered-down stuff that you might find on blogs and social media, you went straight to the source: real people doing the jobs you might really land soon. So give yourself a pat on the back for completing the first major step in the modern job search.

Before we move on, here's a checklist to help make sure you've applied everything we just covered:

- ❑ Explore the career paths of alumni from your alma mater(s). Try applying the following filters to home in on people whose careers excite you:

    - ❑ Location

    - ❑ Employer

    - ❑ Area of study

    - ❑ Skills you possess and can demonstrate (or really want to build)

- ❑ For every career path that intrigues you, reach out to at least five—yielding at least three conversations with—alumni who are in, or have done, the jobs you're most interested in. For each informational interview, make sure to:

    - ❑ Ask great questions that give you a sense of what it's like to be in their shoes.

    - ❑ Follow up with a thank-you note that lets alumni know their time was worth it.

- ❑ Use these paths and informational interviews to assess your level of fit and narrow down your preferred next step.

CHAPTER 4

Think Like a Recruiter: Positioning

Job search success is all about honing your personal brand

> Your story is what you have, what you will always have.
> It is something to own.
> **—MICHELLE OBAMA**

Control Your Own Career Fate

You've just taken the hardest but most important career step: choosing your path. The vast majority of job seekers never sufficiently invest in that first step—and then spend the rest of their search tripping up again and again. Without that compass, their search can become chaotic, unfocused, and reactive. No wonder they don't get results.

But not you.

To reward you for your investment in career clarity, we're now going to take you on a complete step-by-step guide to showcasing your newfound North Star on your LinkedIn profile. With that effective positioning in place, your most important audience—recruiters—can start to discover you for awesome opportunities. Because more than anyone else, recruiters control your career fate.

Imagine, for a second, an omnipotent recruiter scouring the talent universe for the perfect candidate. And no matter how many wishes, dreams, and resumes you lob their way, they remain completely indifferent to your plight—leaving you in career limbo, application after application. Sounds a tad hyperbolic, right? Word to the wise: It's much worse than that! Recruiters don't just crush your dreams by being aloof; they're in fact working hard to stiff-arm candidates all day long. (And, remember, that's *after* their robots have given the Heisman to many, many more.)

To find out why—and ultimately to tilt the odds in your favor—we must peer inside a recruiter's mind.

The Mind of a Recruiter

Okay, okay. Don't get the wrong idea. Lest you think that recruiters are all soulless automatons dead set on the destruction of your hopes and dreams, understand that a recruiter's job is, fundamentally, a mathematical one. They're charged with taking the 250 applicants that the average corporate job receives and whittling that massive list down to THE ONE TRUE HIRE. So, by definition, they need to discard 249 other job seekers along the way. And that's just for one job alone—the average recruiter is juggling an average of 30–40 open jobs at once!

This purely mathematical reality leads to three key insights about how recruiters think.

Insight #1: Recruiters *must* say "No!"

Recruiters need to reject more than 99 percent of applicants by the end of the hiring process, so their antenna is always up for reasons to say "No" to a candidate. And because they're often trying to fill lots of open job requisitions at once, they also need to reject candidates as fast as possible.

As a result, any of the following common problems can be grounds for immediate rejection:

- Spelling errors on your resume

- Mentioning the wrong company in your cover letter

- No headshot photo on your LinkedIn profile—or, increasingly, not a good one

- Not having relevant experience in your background

- Not explaining exactly what you did in your previous roles

- Not demonstrating a clear impact in your previous roles

From simple infractions to serious job search transgressions, recruiters have lots of ways to kick you out of the process. Which means your first rule when dealing with recruiters is: Never give them a reason to ding you outright.

Insight #2: Recruiters are risk-averse.

If recruiters are so hell-bent on saying "No" to more than 99 percent of candidates, how do you get that 1-in-250 "Yes"?

To find this Holy Grail of Job Searching, *really* try to put yourself in the recruiter's shoes: You've got multiple hiring managers breathing down your neck, saying, "My team is treading water over here—I need a new hire ASAP! But they've gotta be good!" And you, all by your lonesome, are drowning in a talent pool full of potentially good candidates.

Even worse, you have no time to investigate that potential. So, with a massive rip current of stress sucking you under, you fill the recruiting funnel with presumable no-brainers. Your life preserver is **The Obvious Candidate**.

And what makes a candidate obvious? Well, if you were a recruiter tasked with finding a Sales Manager, would you want to take a chance on someone who earned a master's degree in art history and has spent a few years fundraising for a human rights nonprofit?

Tips from a Longtime Recruiter

Allison Dietz spent nearly twenty years as a corporate recruiter before transitioning into coaching students and managing tech employer relationships. She was kind enough to share some insights from the recruiter's perspective. In Allison's words:

Be aware that there may be some simple things you are doing that will get you rejected immediately. Before the recruiter even looks you up on LinkedIn or looks at your resume, they are hitting that "So Sorry" button. I'm going to pull back the curtain and share three things that make recruiters reject your application immediately.

1. First in, first hired. First up, fittingly, it is about when you apply. Because even if a job appears to be open weeks after it was first posted, that may just be because a company has a minimum posting policy for their roles. (Specifically, a job may have to be posted for a certain number of days before it can be closed.)

Meanwhile, recruiters usually screen applicants as they come in since they're generally incentivized to hire quickly. So if you see a job is open, do not delay. The sooner you apply, the sooner you can be considered and hired. If you wait until the eleventh hour, the recruiter may not even look at your application and reject you. This is one of those times where the saying really does apply—early birds FTW!

2. Show me the (realistic) money. Another easy knockout question is asking applicants what their salary preference is. Every vacancy has a budget—usually in the form of a range. Thus, you will not be considered if you require a base salary above or even below the budgeted amount. My advice is to do the research ahead of time; know the average salary for the position you are pursuing. There are many resources nowadays: Glassdoor, LinkedIn, and Salary.com are all reputable sites that you can trust.

Be aware that some states and cities prohibit an employer from requiring applicants to provide salary history information (e.g., California, New York, New Jersey, Illinois, and Washington). Salary history bans are designed to narrow the gender pay gap. If you are not required to put down a number, don't. You never want to show your cards first. Instead, always say it's something you're willing to negotiate later. The same goes for during the interview. When it's your time to ask the recruiter questions about the role or company, do not let your first question be about the salary. Otherwise, you are signaling to the recruiter that all you care about is money. If the recruiter asks you this question, my advice is to ask what the budgeted salary range is for this role. Remember, this is just the start of the conversation, so you want to stay flexible. The labor market really is just that—a market. So know your value before you negotiate!

3. The ready candidate is the hired candidate. The last thing that will make recruiters reject your application is how you answer the question, "When are you available to start work?" This question is typically on the application itself because it is easy to screen out applicants who say anything beyond the reasonable two to four weeks' notice. Therefore, my recommendation is always to answer this question with "Immediately" or, if employed, "Two weeks."

If you say it will take longer, you are indicating an insincere interest to the recruiter. You may think you are truthful because you have a vacation planned or want some "downtime" between jobs, but it's not time to worry about that yet. The hiring manager wants their openings filled yesterday—and recruiters are measured on how quickly they fill their jobs.

Similarly, if there are other issues with scheduling and communicating, that will get you rejected. For example, once you are called for an interview and the recruiter does not hear back from you, they will move on. Or, if you are unable to interview for several weeks, that is a sign of disinterest.

Your career may be a marathon, but any specific job search is a sprint. Ready, set, go!

in

Allison (Berger) Dietz

(She/Her) · 2nd
Relationship Builder | Recovering Recruiter | Talent Strategist

Washington University in St. Louis - Olin Business School

Vassar College

Or would you prefer someone who's been a Sales Manager at a firm where you personally know a few people?

Here's the golden rule of recruiting: Don't overthink anything when it comes to identifying strong candidates. It's just like the famous business adage, "Nobody ever got fired for choosing IBM." Recruiters know that they'll never endanger their job security by choosing someone who seems, at first glance, like a natural fit. That means someone who has connected the dots in a purposeful way for the job the recruiter is trying to fill, versus throwing spaghetti at the wall and hoping something sticks. Someone who, usually, has already *done* the job being filled and has the requisite skills. Natural fits are the Obvious Candidates, a recruiter's lowest-hanging fruit.

Which produces a nice corollary for you, the job seeker: Make yourself a natural fit. How? Understand precisely what the recruiter is searching for *and* signal that you match those attributes in the exact places they're looking. If you can show the recruiter exactly why you're a risk-free candidate who can do the job in your sleep (even if it's running a sales team with a master's degree in the humanities!), you've just done them a huge favor. They'll repay that favor by paving your way straight to an interview.

Insight #3: Recruiters need tech tools.

Remember, recruiters aren't stupid. Why would they want to bear the brunt of a massive sorting exercise for every role they're trying to fill? Especially when they recall what their recruiting predecessors had to deal with in the recent past. Just imagine how laborious it was to put a classified job ad in the newspaper in 1969 and get 250 typewritten resumes in the mail. Or to put up an ad on Monster.com in 1999 and get 250 resumes emailed to you directly. Definitely no fun.

This is what makes LinkedIn such a revolution for recruiters; instead of manually sorting through 250 random applications, recruiters can filter them to find the five to ten Obvious Candidates who perfectly fit the bill. After all, nearly a billion professionals have

What About the Nonprofit Job Search?

We couldn't be bigger advocates of the nonprofit sector. After teaching, it's where we both cut our professional teeth. Omar, in fact, wrote about the value of doing so in the *New York Times*; he advises a similar early experience for future career flexibility. So we couldn't write this book without mentioning the applicability of our methods for nonprofits. No surprise: They all apply. And then some.

Take Samir Bolar. He's a former educator, social entrepreneur, and nonprofit leader who had largely ignored LinkedIn, putting it in the ambivalent category of "social media." But when he moved to a new city in a new state, he realized that he needed to optimize his presence and network to get found for new opportunities.

What Samir soon understood is that nonprofits recruit, at every level, just like any other economic sector. They may have less disposable income to throw around, and are often under a microscope for how they spend it, but LinkedIn simply has no peer when it comes to finding the right talent. Nonprofit employers also have special tools and discounts at their disposal. Meanwhile, members can represent their volunteer experience, showcase the causes they care about, and signal that they'd like to be found for pro bono work or nonprofit board service—all features that are especially useful for attracting nonprofit jobs.

Nonprofits, just like other sectors, have their own tight-knit web of connections. So Samir used LinkedIn not only to connect directly with local leaders in his brand-new city but also to offer his time and expertise in order to build a relationship instead of merely transacting about job openings. With a handful of the few organizations he was most interested in, he offered to take on a pro bono project as a way to show his interest and his abilities. It took a few months to bear fruit but eventually led to being seriously considered for several leadership opportunities in the social sector—and ultimately an exciting new challenge straddling sectors running a youth eSports academy.

Samir Bolar (He/Him) · 1st
Executive Director, Training Grounds
Austin, Texas, United States
Contact info

kindly done the hard work of defining themselves online. So why bother letting a wave of uncertain talent wash over you when you can instantly filter that wave for the perfect candidate?

Sure enough, this instant filtering is the main way LinkedIn makes its money; this is its primary value proposition to employers. It's why almost every recruiter in the world—and many a hiring manager, too—pays LinkedIn $10,000 per year to access its fancy, platinum-level version, Recruiter. Because with a single search of this tech tool (which recruiters spend *all day* in, and which two-thirds of them *only* use), recruiters can narrow down their search to just the best-fit candidates.

How Recruiters Use "Recruiter"

Next, to position yourself correctly in the digital job market, you have to understand exactly how a recruiter approaches that invaluable LinkedIn Recruiter product. So let's walk through the main filters in a hypothetical Recruiter search. Then we'll show you the 12 essential steps to pass each of those filters.

Filtering for Keywords and Location

Imagine a recruiter—let's call her Hedley Hunter (clearly no recruiter has ever reached out to us for our comedy skills). She's been charged with finding an awesome Project Manager in Chicago for a small advertising agency. Now, as a rule, Hedley doesn't overthink her searches. She's not getting super-specific, at least not initially. Instead, she goes to LinkedIn Recruiter and plugs those two criteria (Job Title plus Location) into the search engine and lets the algorithm work its magic to find candidates who can 1) actually *do* the job, and 2) do it *there*—not just somewhere around the world. (This isn't hypothetical—we've studied recruiter behavior and been ones ourselves. These two criteria are how they typically start most every search.)

By searching for Project Managers in Chicago, Hedley generates a whopping 130,000+ candidates. That many candidates would be unruly for any recruiter, so a job seeker who wants to get noticed needs to rank highly in the search results. Just like a Google search, any result beyond the first two pages is essentially irrelevant.

When you look closely at these profiles, you'll notice that an interesting—and totally predictable—pattern starts to emerge:

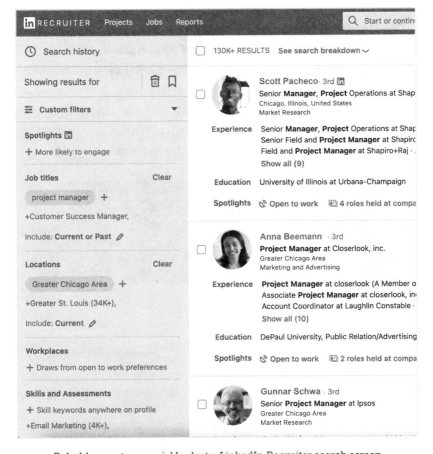

Behold: an extra-special look at a LinkedIn Recruiter search screen.

Sure enough, every single top candidate has listed the same location—Chicago. What's more, each one has something listed in their Headline (the little piece of text that appears beneath their name and, before long, the part of LinkedIn you'll become obsessed with). And no, it's not some Masonic secret mantra or a complicated cheat code. It's simply the *specific job title* that the recruiter searched for in the first place: "Project Manager." Remember, to get a serious look by any employer you need to first be The Obvious Candidate.

Here are the three rules of LinkedIn's search algorithm that you need to know:

1. The Headline is the single most important part of your entire profile—to both the computer and the human. With a 120-character limit, it's much harder to game than, say, the About section, which can hold up to 2,000 characters. That makes the Headline a truer signal of what you're good at than anything else on your entire profile. And thus the algorithm prioritizes it above everything else. So you must optimize it for the *machine*.

A simple, focused headline is catnip to both the algorithm and recruiters.

The Headline is also the one area that a recruiter will quickly skim in the search results page. You need it to pop for them to click through

Does LinkedIn *Really* Matter for New Grads?

Time to acknowledge the elephant in the room for soon-to-be or recent grads: Does LinkedIn *really* matter for you?

A lot of the recruiter psychology we're covering seems focused on candidates with significant experience. So if you don't have much or any, is this section even relevant?

Answer: a resounding YES!

New grads tend to feel the most disempowered by the traditional job search. Without much exposure to recruiters or the recruiting process, applying to jobs online can seem like screaming into the void. But understanding the psychology of recruiters and how they use LinkedIn instantly changes the equation.

Don't just take our word for it. Listen to our trainee Sharissa Sebastiano:

> As a recent graduate, I didn't think that LinkedIn would be such an important tool. But then I realized I had more power and influence in my job search than I thought. . . . I'm able to actively position myself and be a player in the job market instead of passively waiting for my application to be seen and hoping a recruiter will get in touch with me.

So many job seekers—be they twenty weeks or twenty years into their careers—approach their searches passively, hoping to get lucky eventually. Whereas savvy job seekers like Sharissa know that recruiters respond to a carefully constructed profile that puts you in control of your own story and professional brand—one you'll continue to build over time. This proactive attitude landed Sharissa a profile view that turned into an interview forty-eight hours later. It can do the same for you, whether you're a career starter, a mid-career climber, or a final-act pivoter.

to the coveted profile view. So you must also optimize it for the *human* recruiter.

2. Your desired job title is the single most important keyword to put in your Headline. Make yourself an Obvious Candidate by including the exact job you want—Project Manager, Sales Development Representative, ER Nurse, etc.—in your most important section. And yes, that means ditching generic Headlines about your skills (Go-Getter with a Great Attitude) or job search status (Job Seeker Open to Opportunities). But don't worry—putting this job title in your Headline doesn't make it your forever job. You can always change it as your priorities shift!

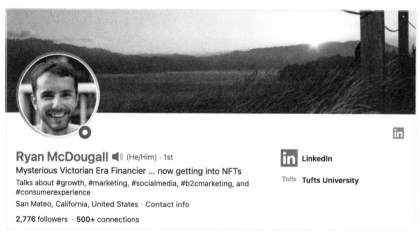

Ryan McDougall 🔊 (He/Him) · 1st
Mysterious Victorian Era Financier ... now getting into NFTs
Talks about #growth, #marketing, #socialmedia, #b2cmarketing, and #consumerexperience
San Mateo, California, United States · Contact info

2,776 followers · 500+ connections

LinkedIn
Tufts University

A brilliant former coworker of ours changes his Headline daily.
Cheeky, but it won't get him found for anything new and potentially better.

3. Your location is like an On/Off light switch for your career. Sure, you might be an amazing Project Manager in Cheyenne. But if you want to land a job in Chicago, you'd better have Chicago on your LinkedIn profile. That's because recruiters normally only want to consider candidates down the block—not across the continent. Even in a time of increased remote work, candidate searches often start with this filter to preserve the option of in-office work, orientation, meetings, and events. So make sure you signal where

Location, Location, Location (Still) Matters

With the rapid ascent of work-from-home arrangements in 2020, it may feel like your location has never mattered less to your employment prospects. As we write this book a couple years later, however, it's clear that the future of work will be all about balance—not just Zoom, Zoom, Zoom all day long.

Take, for instance, a recent McKinsey survey of 100 executives across different industries and locations. While only a small percentage expected their employees to return to the office five days a week, 90 percent expected employees to come in at least one day a week. In other words, feel free to work from home— just so long as we can see you at the office now and then.

So for recruiters looking to hire at one of these firms, location still matters. Yes, they may be willing to consider more remote workers or candidates who live a little farther away, since commuting won't be an everyday affair anymore. But they're not prepared to fly someone in weekly from the other side of the world!

When it comes to time to consider your own location on LinkedIn, know that the old real estate adage still applies. Even so, if you are committed to landing a fully remote job, fear not: We'll show you strategies for both attracting and discovering these roles both in this chapter (flip to page 105) and the next (see page 149).

you want to be—or be prepared to get filtered out in the very first search.

Meanwhile, our hypothetical recruiter Hedley Hunter has narrowed her search from more than 770,000,000 to 130,000—but that's still way too many to sort through. So she moves on to the next filter . . .

Filtering for Engagement

Despite the $10,000 Hedley pays for Recruiter annually, she's limited to just thirty monthly LinkedIn InMail messages (which allows her to reach out cold to a job seeker to whom she's not directly connected). So she thinks, "I need to make sure these candidates are serious." Especially because LinkedIn refunds an InMail credit when a candidate responds. But *how does a recruiter know who's really serious*?

LinkedIn Recruiter is all over it. The product offers three essential engagement filters to help recruiters find not only the best fit but also those most likely to respond:

1. "Open to Work." Imagine Hedley has just found the world's most perfect candidate. They've done the desired job for a decade. They work at the most prestigious firm in the industry. And they've crushed it year after year. There's just one problem: *It turns out they have absolutely zero interest in a new job.* And now her valuable InMail credit is gone forever. That sucks, right? Well, that's why LinkedIn lets recruiters limit their searches to only candidates who are open to new opportunities.

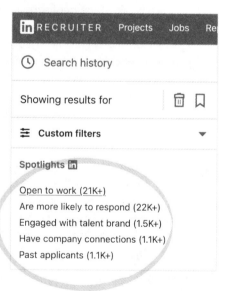

Make sure you pass through these popular Recruiter filters.

2. "Company Connections." Let's say Hedley is considering two rock-star candidates. Candidate A knows three people at the organization, has heard them rave about their experience, and would love nothing more than to join them. Candidate B knows exactly zero people at the firm, has never even heard of it before, and would probably rather gouge her eyes out with a rusty spoon than jump ship to Hedley's squad once she learns about it. Recruiters want to know who's Candidate A and who's Candidate B *before* they reach out next time.

3. "Engaged with Your Talent Brand." (That's LinkedIn-speak for "following your company.") Now, consider the plight of Hedley, who has two strong, interested, and connected candidates but just one InMail left. While she could just flip a coin and take a chance, wouldn't it be nice to know who's not merely looking for any job—but specifically for a job at your company? LinkedIn makes this super easy by allowing recruiters to filter for candidates who've shown clear interest in your firm by following it on the site or engaging with your posts. No quarters required!

Now Hedley is really getting Scrooge-like with her filtering. She's gone from 130,000+ talented strangers to 1,500+ friendly candidates who are worthy of an InMail. But that's still too many to reach out to when you're working on a tight ration of messages and time. So now it's time for the final oft-used filter . . .

Applying the Human Filter

Okay, let's be real. At the end of the day, even with all this technology, no human recruiter is going to pick candidates based purely on some expensive algorithm. Nope, they're going to apply their own human algorithm, based on the way we all size each other up.

One of the clearest places this human bias manifests itself is with profile photos. For example, you'll notice that on Hedley's Recruiter screen, even with all of the objective data we've already covered (Job Title, Location, etc.), photos of each candidate are still featured prominently. Why? Because LinkedIn has found that candidates with photos are fourteen times more likely to be viewed than those who lack them.

In addition, recruiters are likely to lean on other human instincts. Hedley will ask: Does this candidate know anyone I know? Do they use profile visuals (e.g., background photo or work samples) that grab my attention? Do they use language that makes it easy to understand how they fit my search?

So as much as Hedley has been aided by cutting-edge technology to generate this whittled-down list of candidates, her ultimate selection of 5 to 10 candidates to interview will still incorporate age-old instincts. And as frustrating as that may be here in the 21st century, we'll show you exactly how to navigate both these modern and ancient filters in this next section.

How to Win LinkedIn Recruiter in 12 Steps

Now that you understand how recruiters think and use LinkedIn, we'll walk you through everything you need to optimize your profile and get discovered by this critical audience.

Step 1: Get Your Most Important Keyword in the Most Important Place

As we saw earlier, the site's algorithm prioritizes the **Headline** over every other section. And recruiters themselves prioritize the job title over every other keyword.

So let's start by getting your desired job title right into your Headline. Don't overthink it. Just be clear and concise. For example, if you want to be an Accountant, then "Accountant" had better be in your Headline.

But What If I'm Not Already Doing What I Want to Do Next?

Now, we know what you might be thinking: "This feels like a total Catch-22. I want to be an Accountant but I'm not one yet. So how can I put it in my Headline without feeling like a complete fraud?" Good news: Yes, impostor syndrome is real, but we're here to help you fight that battle. That's because you can also list "Aspiring Accountant" or "Future Accountant" in your Headline with absolutely zero penalty.

LinkedIn's algorithm couldn't care less about qualifiers like "Aspiring" or "Future." Instead, the job title itself—"Accountant"— is the only thing it craves. So insert that crucial keyword right where it matters most and don't sweat the fact that it may be a future role rather than a current one. Remember, LinkedIn (unlike most traditional resumes) is more than a mere reflection of what you've done; it's experience plus aspiration.

And, since it's typically more difficult to make 180-degree professional pivots, in your Headline you can also list a highly adjacent (or preparatory) role you *have* held previously. You can do this in such a way that it doesn't appear to be entirely aspirational and yet also still looks super focused.

For instance, try two job titles with a high degree of keyword and skill requirement overlap in your job descriptions. For example, "Project Manager and Aspiring Product Manager" or "Business Development Representative | Future Account Executive" can be more effective for the human recruiter than just "Aspiring Product Manager" or "Future AE" alone. Where job seekers get into trouble and look unfocused is when they include job titles in their Headlines that aren't clearly connected in some way, like "Project Manager | Sales Professional, Engineer | Entrepreneur."

As for other keywords you may want to include in your Headline, let's go back to the focused elements of the job search you put together in the last chapter:

- Did you narrow down your industry? (Example: Energy)

- Did you identify a few essential skills? (Example: Enterprise Resource Planning, or ERP)

If so, you may want to include those in your Headline so they really pop for recruiters. For example: "Aspiring Accountant in the Energy Sector with a Focus on ERP."

If, however, you didn't manage to narrow down your search to those sorts of focused criteria, fear not. Even listing just "Aspiring Accountant" will lift you over all the candidates whose Headlines say "Student at X University" or "Employee at X Company" or "I need a job!"

Step 2: Make Yourself a Local

Location is still key. After all, from the employer's perspective, the downside of searching across nearly a billion professionals is that you're bound to find global talent when you often really want pros down the block.

If you're sitting in San Jose, California, for instance, but you really want to be in Seattle, listing "San Jose" on your profile will prevent you from ever getting to the Emerald City. Make sure you don't get filtered out for your dream job by asking yourself this question: "Where do I *really* want to be next?"

Now we know you're getting ready to pull out those pitchforks and burning torches—"Omar and Jeremy, are you telling me to *lie* about where I am?!?" Well, think of it this way: If a recruiter from your dream organization in your dream city called you up right now and asked you to fly in for an interview tomorrow, would you be on the next plane, train, or bus? Yes! In the context of LinkedIn, it makes

Picking the Perfect Location

I f you're not sure where to focus your job search efforts, consider returning to some of the career exploration strategies mentioned in the previous chapter. That way, you can leverage data from others' careers to guide your own, depending on what's most important to you. Here are a few additional ways to help you decide.

Focus on Function:

If you know the exact kind of job you want, consider focusing on locations with ample opportunities in that space. You can do this rather quickly by searching on LinkedIn. For example, someone interested in sustainability work might discover that there's a spike in hiring in Seattle (since the site lists locations in order of hiring volume):

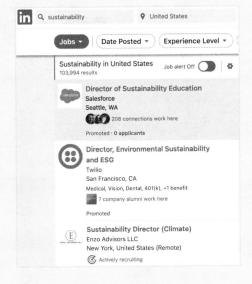

Focus on Industry:

If the exact role is less important than the overall industry, LinkedIn can help you identify hot spots across the globe. For instance, doing a People search on LinkedIn for the biotechnology industry shows that California and Massachusetts are where the action is:

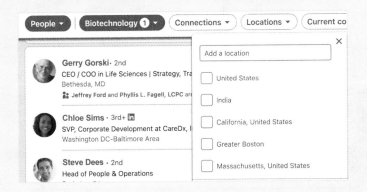

continued . . .

Focus on Community:

You've already seen how powerful alumni can be in opening doors for you. So follow in the literal footsteps of those who've gone before you by filtering your alma mater's grads by location. Just go back to your university's Alumni Tool (see page 66) and check out the top locations:

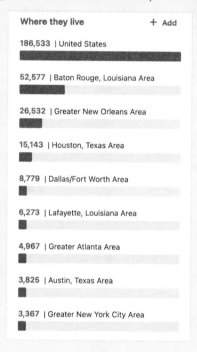

Where they live   + Add

186,533 | United States

52,577 | Baton Rouge, Louisiana Area

26,532 | Greater New Orleans Area

15,143 | Houston, Texas Area

8,779 | Dallas/Fort Worth Area

6,273 | Lafayette, Louisiana Area

4,967 | Greater Atlanta Area

3,825 | Austin, Texas Area

3,367 | Greater New York City Area

no difference whether you're living somewhere now or by the first day of your job.

If you're a student or a new grad, this holds especially true. You shouldn't feel compelled to list your location as the small college town you happen to currently live in when you're more than likely to relocate to a big city next, for example. The same goes if you're truly flexible, no matter your career stage. After all, your current and future location preferences will most certainly come up in your interviews. If so, you might as well "be" in that city already.

Step 3: Shine Your Bat Signal

You're already rising above the majority of job seekers out there who couldn't be bothered to tell recruiters *what* they can do and *where* they can do it. But for the world's most selective jobs, you need to push even harder to rise to the top. To help you stand out even further, make sure to demonstrate your engagement on LinkedIn itself.

That means going to **Open to Work** and shining your Bat Signal to the world of talent hunters. With these preferences calibrated, you get filtered *in* as an engaged candidate instead of being filtered *out*. Let them know that you're in the game for the job titles, locations, and types of work that you're excited about—and to hedge against coming across as overly focused if you're in fact more flexible. Here's how:

1. Go to your LinkedIn profile, select "Open to," and then click "Finding a new job."

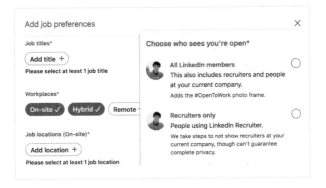

2. Fill in your job preferences. You can list up to five specific job titles. (If you have done the hard work to know the *precise* job title you want next, make sure to repeat it here in addition to being in your Headline.) You can also list up to four additional locations on top of the current one you've set. So if you felt stymied by having to choose a single location in the last step, this is your chance to show off your flexibility—including your availability for remote roles.

But What If I Don't Want My Current Boss to Know I'm Looking?

As you fill out these preferences, just know that LinkedIn has your back across a variety of common scenarios.

If you are truly a free agent, then feel free to share your #OpenToWork signal with all LinkedIn members. That way, your friends, family, and other professionals who come across your profile will know you're on the prowl. It's one more way you can take advantage of all the opportunities they're plugged into—including ones you didn't even know existed.

On the other hand, if you're more of a secret agent than a free agent—i.e., you're looking on the sly while you hold down your current job—then limit your signal to recruiters only. This means random LinkedIn users can't spill the beans to your current boss (hey, it can happen—either purely by accident or for more nefarious reasons). Not only that, but LinkedIn will also apply some clever stealth maneuvers on your behalf; namely, the site will know if the recruiters searching for your talent also work for your current company. If so, they'll hide your Bat Signal to protect you from prying eyes.

Either way, you're getting an amazing deal: Five seconds of clicking buttons could translate into an opportunity that changes the course of your career and your life.

3. Finally, decide how brightly you want to shine your Bat Signal. You can choose to share with all LinkedIn members that you're looking for opportunities (which will add a #OpenToWork photo frame to your profile pic) or share with recruiters only.

Step 4: Get Connected

Getting to the top of the recruiter's list also means boosting your **connections**. That's because, all things being equal, the recruiter would prefer to engage with candidates who are already plugged into their firm, and not deal with total strangers. And, sure enough, LinkedIn makes this distinction easy by virtue of its Company Connections filter on the Recruiter product. So to end up on the right side of this filter, you'll need a large network on LinkedIn. Doing so will increase your odds that, for any given company, you know someone on the inside.

> **Your lack of connections is disadvantaging you every single time a recruiter runs a candidate search.**

Studies suggest that, on average, we each know about 600 people at any given moment. Now look at your LinkedIn connections; if you're like the typical LinkedIn user, you probably have far fewer connections online than people you know in real life. Which might not seem like a big deal until you realize that your lack of connections online is disadvantaging you every single time a recruiter runs a candidate search.

For example, let's say your dream is to work at Nike. And right now, a recruiter at Nike is searching LinkedIn for people with your exact talent. Awesome, right? Well, there are two problems. The first is that there are thousands of people with that same talent, so the recruiter decides to filter by Company Connections. And the second is that, even if a former colleague now works at Nike but you're not connected with them on LinkedIn, then whoops—you're filtered out. That open door of opportunity, which had been cracked open for one shining moment, just got slammed back shut.

To pry this door back open, let's get you credit online for all your real-world connections. While you could pursue this goal one connection at a time, let's instead go for hundreds or even thousands of connections in one fell swoop by importing your address books.

In fact, every time you email with someone or create a new contact in your phone, that person gets added to the address books associated with your email accounts and smartphone, so these are the best digital logs of your personal contacts. LinkedIn can quickly scan them to identify who you already know on the platform. For instance, if you've corresponded with Naomi Sanchez (nsanchez@ example.com) from your email account, LinkedIn will be able to identify her profile by that same email address—and suggest her as a possible connection.

Here's how to import your address book using LinkedIn's Contact Import feature:

1. Click on "My Network" on your home screen.

2. Navigate to "Connections" under "Manage my network."

3. Add your email address to import your contacts. That includes every personal, work, and/or school account you've ever had. You can also import your phone's address book via the LinkedIn smartphone app.

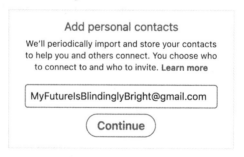

4. Connect with everyone you already know.

Do I Need the LinkedIn App?

We get it! Your phone's home screen is already overflowing with apps you use only once in a blue moon. Do you really need another pretty little icon sitting there, gathering dust?

While LinkedIn's mobile app is nowhere near as mandatory as just using the web-based site itself, there are a few unique benefits you should consider:

- As mentioned, only the app lets you import your phone's address book. So if you store most of your contacts here (vs. your email account), be sure to get the app for this purpose alone. You can always delete it later.

- In addition, the app lets you sync with your phone's calendar. That way, if you've got a lot of upcoming conversations with alumni or employers, you'll get fed intel about them automatically, based on their LinkedIn profiles.

- Finally, if like us, you're always having your name botched, you can even record the correct pronunciation on your app's profile page. Woohoo— fewer awkward intros, FTW! You can also now add a 30-second "video introduction" by tapping your profile picture. Take that, "TikTok Resumes"— it's much easier for LinkedIn to simply add features like this than for a social video platform to build a market for job seekers and hirers to meet at scale!

Now, we know that this advice may cause your Spidey Social Media Sense to start tingling, so let's address a couple of big concerns head-on. First, everyone has been told that connecting broadly on social media is a big no-no. "Keep your Facebook profile private!" "Lock down your Instagram!" "Whatever you do, don't tweet!" These warnings have been around for a whole generation at this point. So we get it: The idea of connecting with as many people on LinkedIn as you can feels treacherous.

But here's the crucial thing—LinkedIn is the social network that breaks all the rules for social networks. Whereas other social media give you sufficient and regular dopamine kicks to be borderline addictive, we'll be the first to admit that LinkedIn can be a total snoozefest—job promotions, professional best practices, yawn. Which means that, unlike other social networks, which are full of outrage, drama, and adorable cat videos, nothing you post on LinkedIn is likely to go viral, no matter how large your network or how exciting your update ("There's a shake-up in the accounting department!"). So the downside of having a broad, diverse network is quite low relative to every other social platform. And if a connection turns out to be sales-y, spammy, or downright inappropriate, you can always disconnect, block, or even report that person.

Next, the upside of a large LinkedIn network is massive. While your all-time greatest Facebook post may have just netted you a lot of likes, wielding a large LinkedIn network and a great profile can alter the entire trajectory of your career.

To understand why, let's review some of the social science research into strong vs. weak ties. Strong ties, in the parlance of sociologists, are the people you know well. Your family, your closest coworkers, your besties—these people are plugged into the same networks as you are. That's part of what makes them such good friends and confidantes, but also what makes them lousy connectors. Strong ties tend to know the same people and opportunities as you do, so they can never introduce you to that new recruiter or hiring manager who will change the course of your life.

Weak ties, on the other hand, are the people you *kinda* know, perhaps from that one class you had together or as a friend of a friend. They are the ones who can really open your eyes to new opportunities. And they're how you get *volume*. Since they sit outside of your established networks, they're like scouts to a whole new universe you never knew existed. They might be able to tell you about an awesome new job at a company you've never heard of, or introduce you to your future boss in a field that you just discovered today.

The upside of a large, diverse network largely rests upon the power of weak ties. While you might already be connected on LinkedIn with your siblings and your besties, it's distantly networked connections who are most likely to get you through recruiters' Company Connections filters and to pave the way to your dream job.

So don't just hope that you connect with the right people one by one—be sure to import your contacts and get credit for all these weak ties, pronto!

Step 5: Be a Follower!

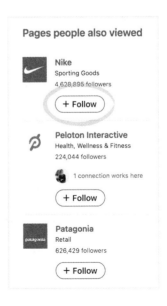

While most of our advice focuses on being proactive and taking the lead on LinkedIn, here's one time you want to be a follower: Always hit the **"Follow"** button for your dream firms.

As discussed earlier, recruiters are stingy with their allotment of thirty InMail messages each month, as they face the mathematical challenge of choosing from among thousands of qualified candidates. So even though it seems like a tiny commitment, having a candidate follow your firm on LinkedIn

How Do I Get Rid of Connections?

While much of this book is focused on growing your network, there might be times when you'll want to prune it back—especially if your connections' messages become annoying or harassing.

Of course, you can always just disconnect by clicking "Remove Connection" on their profile:

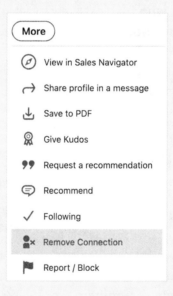

But if you want to make sure they also can't see your profile and updates anymore, just click the "Block" option below that. Now they'll be fully removed from your LinkedIn experience—and won't be notified of the change, either.

can be an incredibly easy way to narrow down your list to just candidates who are qualified *and* interested.

So don't spend a second overthinking what to do here: Follow your dream companies. Heck, follow your better-than-average companies. And maybe even your mediocre companies, too! In fact, you can follow up to 1,000 organizations on LinkedIn. It won't cost you anything, so get started right now.

And when in doubt about the next organization to follow, just consult LinkedIn's handy list of similar companies included on each company page.

Step 6: Get the Most Out of Your Pic

Everyone's heard the famous saying, "A picture is worth a thousand words"—but it's taken on a whole new meaning with the advent of LinkedIn profiles. Why? Well, LinkedIn data is extremely clear that a **profile photo** makes a significant difference in your chances of getting seen.

Not just any headshot photo will do, however. To really make the most of those extra profile views, you'll want to do three things with your profile pic.

Fit Your Future Team

Start by checking out the profile photos of people who have your job already. And specifically, keep an eye on what they're wearing—are they rocking a three-piece suit? Or a nice sweater? Or even some fancy athleisure wear? As small a detail as that seems, it's magnified in the subconscious mind of a recruiter who's looking for fit at the speed of 100 candidates per minute.

So start by mimicking the dress of your future peers. Because as unfortunate as our human biases are, they are real—especially when a recruiter has to choose between multiple qualified candidates in the blink of an eye.

Show a Genuine Smile

Once you've got the right outfit, make
sure you also nail the right expression.
Faces matter even more than fashion. This response is hardwired in us
because it connotes trust (babies, for
example, respond more positively to
smiling faces). So if you're applying
for a job in a Western business culture,
you want to shoot for that culture's
gold standard of facial expressions: the
Duchenne Smile. Named for a French

A Duchenne Smile in action.

neurologist, the Duchenne Smile has an ample research base
demonstrating that individuals are more highly rated when their
smile features all sorts of other involuntary facial features. Those
include wrinkles in the corners of their eyes, and upturned corners
of their mouth.

   In other words, it's a *real* smile that
signals: "I'm excited, I'm friendly, and
I'm genuine." It's *not* a fake smile that
signals, "I'm trying to look excited—
but I actually can't be trusted."
Warmth, not polish.

   So even if the idea of taking a
LinkedIn profile photo scrapes the
bottom of your personal excitement
barrel—yes, a distinct possibility—
then think of something that is gen-

A less authentic smile.

uinely motivating (Kittens! Koalas! Kittens riding on a koala!!!) when
the flash goes off. And that way you can make a genuine connection with the recruiter on the other side of the screen.

What If I'm Considering Multiple Paths?

All of this advice is straightforward if you've already narrowed your focus to a single career path. But what if you're still juggling multiple options? And they each expect different photo looks and positioning?

For example, let's say you're considering sales jobs at both Fortune 500 companies and tiny start-ups. And the profile photos of employees at Hewlett-Packard (last operated out of a garage in 1938) are night and day compared with those of a company that's, well, still operating out of a garage.

Rather than water down your profile in an attempt to appeal to everyone (but really connect with no one), we recommend sequencing your search into two phases:

- Phase 1: Start by focusing on your top-choice path. For instance, if you've got your heart set on B2B sales at HP, check what the current salesforce is wearing in their profiles. That way, if an HP recruiter has to imagine you walking into a corporate boardroom to pitch their products, it won't be such a stretch.

- Phase 2: If you've led with a focus on larger companies for a month and haven't gotten any bites from recruiters, feel free to switch things up. Go for that business-casual look that lets the start-up recruiter know that you can switch between the sales and garage worlds effortlessly.

This way, you get a chance to fully kick the tires on each path, knowing that you've committed to each positioning 100 percent. Compare that to the watered-down approach, where you'll never be sure if your lack of results came from a bad fit or just the mixed signal you were putting out into the world.

One important note: As consistently as the Duchenne Smile performs in Western research contexts, it's completely out of place in certain cultures. Another recent study in *Social Psychology*, for instance, showed that it didn't connote genuineness or authenticity among Gabonese and Chinese subjects. As with everything in life, context is crucial.

Crop It Correctly (and Only Depict Yourself)

Lastly, to make sure that your gorgeous smile doesn't go unnoticed, crop your photo tightly around your head and shoulders. So many otherwise great profile photos are ruined by confusing group shots, or the fact that 100x100 pixels just aren't enough to showcase your winning personality.

Take advantage of LinkedIn's built-in photo-editing tools to crop your photo closely around that attention-getting Duchenne Smile:

a) Go to your profile and click your profile photo.

b) Click the "Edit" button.

c) Zoom in until your head and shoulders fill the allotted frame.

Your profile pic will be your thumbnail across all of LinkedIn (including Recruiter search results), so crop in on that smiling face!

Step 7: Get Even More Photo Goodness

The very first thing you'll notice at the top of your profile is . . . another photo!

Although this **photo background** isn't quite as crucial as your headshot, it is another opportunity to offer recruiters an immediate signal of your positioning (and career seriousness) when they land on your profile—i.e., "Aha, I've come to the right place!"

To make sure that your signal aligns with the one that the recruiter is looking for, go back to those two filters every recruiter starts with: job title and location. Ideally, your background will be branded to amplify one or the other. For instance, as an Accountant, you may want to double down on your job function with a visual signal that's all about data and details:

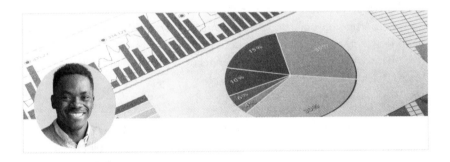

As a Project Manager, you could go with a timeline or project board:

Pictures and Power: Confronting Bias on LinkedIn

Before we go any further, we want to acknowledge the concerns of many job seekers who don't come from the top of traditional power structures. Sharing a profile photo (or video introduction) can seem scary—or the outright wrong thing to do—when this kind of identifying information is known to attract implicit, if not explicit, bias.

Let's get a recruiter's perspective on this difficult issue. Mike Montoya is the CEO and Founder of Stronger Consulting, a recruiting firm that focuses on sourcing

For good measure, Mike approved our use of his profile picture for this book.

and supporting diverse candidates. And his sage strategic counsel for underrepresented job seekers is borne of his own experience as a gay, Hispanic professional. Here's his two cents on what we might call the "Great Photo Debate":

> *People of color often have limited access to networks, which really inhibits their ability to find a great job. As they build those networks with and beyond people who look like them and build their own professional personas, public profile photos are key. I see many people of color not sharing them, and sometimes not even using their names. This is understandable, but I think this is a net detriment to their job prospects, because, more and more, hirers want us to field candidates of color.*
>
> *We are affirmative in our recruitment and doggedly anti-racist in our selection process. I rely on LinkedIn and photos of individuals to give me clues about a candidate's personal characteristics as I work to recruit them for my company or for my clients. And I must say I LOVE professional headshots.*

And as a Foreperson, you could show off a work site:

Or, if location is your primary focus, feel free to lead with that. For instance, as someone who's eager to land a job in Seattle, it never hurts to rock the Space Needle and Mt. Rainier:

Either way, don't spend a cent to purchase a fancy photo (we're all about efficiency in this book). Instead, just head over to a royalty-free image website, like Pexels.com, for access to thousands of beautiful photos.

What If I'm Applying Elsewhere in the World?

Just as there's no such thing as a perfect LinkedIn profile, there's no perfect, universal recipe for profile photos. Instead, every profile and its photo should be developed with a specific audience in mind.

So what to do when you find yourself applying into unfamiliar business contexts, perhaps in a new country? Take that age-old travel advice ("When in Rome . . .") and apply it to the digital age:

- Check out the profiles of people who have the job you want.

- Leverage all the parts of your LinkedIn profile to develop a fit with the patterns you discover.

- When in doubt, reach out—find friendly alumni in that part of the world or that unfamiliar industry and get their take on your new positioning.

Step 8: Sum Yourself Up

Moving southbound on your profile, we get to the **About section**. This section is akin to your professional summary. Don't overlook it like most LinkedIn members; it's of critical importance. That's because it has two major fans.

First, there's the recruiter. Remember, these folks are trying to get through thousands of profiles as fast as possible; their biggest needs are speed, risk-aversion, and InMail scarcity. Recruiters don't want to read about every job a candidate has ever had when they can just skim the CliffsNotes version at the top of a profile. A well-written About section is like a 30-second highlight reel of your career.

Second, there's the algorithm. We've already seen how LinkedIn's search algorithm loves the Headline section. Limited to just 120 characters, that Headline remains the very best source of genuine keywords, since it can't be jammed full of every possible skill under the sun. The second-most important place for the algorithm to mine for keywords, though, is the About section. It allows up to 2,000 characters, which is still fewer than a LinkedIn article (40,000 characters) or Recommendation (3,000 characters).

Let's make yours as effective as possible for both the human and the machine. There are four components to an excellent About section:

1. LinkedIn automatically condenses the About section to 330 or 130 characters, depending on whether the viewer is on their laptop or phone. This works out to about one to three sentences before you're cut off by a "See more" link. So make that first impression count by focusing your first couple of sentences on the key job titles, locations, and skills the recruiter is looking for. Describe who you are and what drives you within a narrative arc (human beings love stories):

> About
>
> As an Accountant with a passion for leading complex ERP projects, I'm thrilled to take my project management and forecasting skills to Seattle to help an amazing Energy firm plan for the future.

2. No recruiter wants to take a risk on an unproven candidate with irrelevant experience, so make sure to then give them the top three most impactful, relevant experiences—especially if you're coming from a different field. For example, here's how a student might make the case that they're ready for an accounting role:

> ▶ Helped manage the Debate Team's budget through careful forecasting and controls, leading to surpluses the last three years
>
> ▶ Created a cost accounting system as an intern with local start-up, allowing company to balance its books for first time
>
> ▶ Provided pro-bono investment advice to Boys & Girls Club, helping generate a 10% return

3. Your initial positioning and your top experiences matter quite a bit since they're likely to be full of rich keywords (e.g., Accountant, ERP, Forecasting). But all that extra verbiage for the benefit of the human ("While volunteering with the Boys & Girls Club . . .") is like so much fluff for a machine that's only hungry for the most important hard skills. So give that algorithm what it craves, through a Specialties line like this one:

> Specialties: Accounting, Auditing, Budgeting, Cash Flow Analysis, ERP, Forecasting, Tax Optimization

When in doubt about which hard skills to include, check out a site we love called Jobscan.co. This site automatically compares your uploaded LinkedIn profile or resume to the job descriptions written by the recruiter. It then identifies and provides you with a custom list of keywords that are most essential to include in your all-important About section. (Of course, be sure to only include skills and keywords where you have actual expertise.)

4. You never want a recruiter to bail on you just because they're running up against their limit of thirty InMails per month. So always include your email to make it easy for the recruiter to reach out:

> Looking for an amazing Accountant? Contact me at jsmith@gmail.com.

Here's what a healthy About section looks like when it's fully optimized for both recruiters and LinkedIn's algorithm:

> About
>
> 1 As an Accountant with a passion for leading complex ERP projects, I'm thrilled to take my project management and forecasting skills to Seattle to help an amazing Energy firm plan for the future.

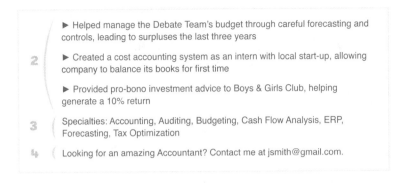

2
► Helped manage the Debate Team's budget through careful forecasting and controls, leading to surpluses the last three years

► Created a cost accounting system as an intern with local start-up, allowing company to balance its books for first time

► Provided pro-bono investment advice to Boys & Girls Club, helping generate a 10% return

3
Specialties: Accounting, Auditing, Budgeting, Cash Flow Analysis, ERP, Forecasting, Tax Optimization

4
Looking for an amazing Accountant? Contact me at jsmith@gmail.com.

Step 9: Work It!

With all the optimizations you've now made to your profile, you might be prepared to phone it in for the **Experience section**. After all, if you already have a resume, do you really need to also include all of that work experience online?

While we totally understand the sentiment, we've got to warn you: The answer is a resounding "yes." A surprisingly large number of LinkedIn members fall into this trap; in fact, the average profile only has one job listed.

It all goes back to our two audiences: the LinkedIn algorithm and the recruiter. Both are hungry for evidence that you're an Obvious Candidate and eager to knock you out for a lack of fit. So don't give them short shrift by leaving your Experience section bare; instead, take these actions to benefit immediately.

Start with the Basics: If you've ever put together a resume, then begin by copying and pasting those resume bullets straight onto your LinkedIn profile. Those bullets might be looked at for a grand total of ten seconds every few weeks on a conventional resume. But when they live on your LinkedIn profile—i.e., your 24/7 resume—they'll be working hard for you every single day, all day long. That's because they're chock-full of keywords that LinkedIn's algorithm is scanning for—and accomplishments that recruiters crave. So even if they're not fully optimized, something absolutely beats nothing at all.

Then, Upgrade: Once you have your basic resume bullets online (or if you're writing your bullets for the first time), think about how you can make the most of them. LinkedIn's algorithm is hungry for keywords, while recruiters are hungry for examples of impact. So how can you give them both? Just follow this time-tested formula:

Keyword + Impact = Amazing Bullet

For example, if you know that "Forecasting" is a critical keyword for your search and you have experience using that skill to drive down costs, you might produce a bullet like: "Developed forecasting model for business, leading to a 10% reduction in inventory overage costs."

Don't Be Afraid to Cut: As much as adding bullets to your LinkedIn profile increases your discoverability, also remember that LinkedIn is all about relevance. So there's no need to have 100 bullets about random projects unrelated to your desired job. Instead, just shoot for one to five bullets per role that speak to the underlying skills you're trying to showcase. For instance, if you're applying for a marketing role and have several bullets from a Peace Corps experience, you may want to cut the ones about agricultural yields. Instead, just focus on the one or two more relevant points about persuading community members to join and build a farmers' cooperative (showcasing your influence and collaboration skills).

Bottom line: There's no need to spend countless hours sweating your LinkedIn profile like you may have already done on your resume. Instead, just start with the bullets you've either developed previously or start fresh and then optimize them for your two audiences on LinkedIn.

The same advice applies for LinkedIn's **Volunteer Experience section**. When we worked at LinkedIn, a study of thousands of recruiters suggested that 41 percent of these talent scouts perceive volunteer experience as on par with paid full-time work experience.

So whether you've worked for a company or volunteered at a non-profit or elsewhere, be sure to get keyword-credit for it on your LinkedIn profile.

And don't just tell recruiters what you've done; show them! As much as algorithms crave keywords, human beings are hardwired to prefer imagery. So consider how you can help recruiters visualize your experience. Try adding:

- Links to an article describing your experience

- Photos of your team in action

- YouTube videos covering your impact

- A PowerPoint presentation summarizing your project

For example, if you helped Habitat for Humanity build 3D-printed houses and got covered in the local news, here's how to add it to your profile:

1. While editing your Experience section, click the "Add Media" button at the bottom of the "Add experience" screen, then "Add a link," and plug in the hyperlink to your desired video:

2. Your visual will now appear right on your profile. It's even more eye-catching than the very best bullet:

Search Engine Optimize . . . Yourself

As you invest in making an incredibly powerful LinkedIn profile, wouldn't it be nice if you could double the power of all this work with just a few clicks? Well, it turns out that you can! That's because there are really just two places where people get searched for on a regular basis: LinkedIn and Google. (PS: There's no shame in admitting that you Google yourself on the regular. Now, if you've got Google Alerts on your own name like us, well . . .)

So whether you're being searched for by recruiters, hiring managers, or potential colleagues, here's how to make sure your LinkedIn profile rises to the top on Google and showcases all the optimizations you've just made:

1. *Make it public.* To ensure that Google can find you, click "Edit public profile & URL" on your own profile. Then switch the "Your profile's public visiblity" button to *On*. Make as many profile components public (and thus indexable by search engines) as you're comfortable with.

2. *Make it easy to find.* One of the major drivers of Google's PageRank algorithm is whether the term being searched appears in the URL (e.g., a search for "men's blue jeans" turns up this result—nordstrom.com/browse/men/clothing/jeans/filter/blue—since all the key terms are right there in the address). So on that same Public Profile page, be sure to claim a custom URL that includes your name.

3. *Make it stand out.* Now, if you've got an uncommon or even unique name, those first two steps are all you need to rise to the top of Google, given that the competition is so limited. (Finally, there's an upside to having an unpronounceable name!) But if you've got countless competitors for your name—especially if some are famous and even more so if they're infamous—then you'll need to work a little harder to stand out. While you may never own the top result, you can definitely own the result for your area of expertise by including it in your custom URL:

🔗 **Edit your custom URL**

Personalize the URL for your profile.

www.linkedin.com/in/ _____

Note: Your custom URL must contain 3-100 letters or numbers. Please do not use spaces, symbols, or special characters.

Cancel   Save

Step 10: School Matters

Depending on when you were in school, it can be easy to overlook LinkedIn's **Education section**. If you graduated ten or more years ago, for instance, that's probably a minor section on your resume. But here's the great thing about a LinkedIn profile: Every single part of it gets scanned by the algorithm. So if you have educational accomplishments that are relevant to your desired role (e.g., qualifications, awards, or even extracurricular experiences that speak to your most important skills), you should definitely include them to increase your chances of being discovered.

But as with every other section of your profile, be sure this section is designed to appeal to both of your audiences:

The Algorithm: LinkedIn's algorithm is on the lookout for keywords, so don't just focus on academics (as great as the Dean's List is, not many searches will focus on that term). Instead, you should absolutely include work-relevant achievements. For example, maybe you did some part-time accounting for the debate team. Don't only talk about your parliamentary gifts (which the algorithm couldn't care less about); mention how you balanced the team's budget. Bam—you now get credit for that critical keyword "budgeting," even if it took place in an extracurricular context.

The Recruiter: Human beings want more than mere keywords—they want to see evidence of real accomplishment. That way they can distinguish between multiple candidates with similar academic pedigrees. There are two easy ways to do that.

First, don't just name-drop an academic accolade; contextualize it. For instance, instead of saying "GPA = 3.5," show them the full picture: "Earned a 3.5 GPA while working full-time to put myself through school." Instead of, "Received the Susan Smith Scholarship," give them the whole context: "Was one of just three students out of a student body of 20,000 selected for the full-ride Smith Scholarship, based on outstanding community service."

Second, treat your Education bullets like Work Experience bullets that include clear examples of impact. While most people will just say something like, "Member, Big Brothers Big Sisters Chapter" (which gives no sense of what you did there), highly attractive LinkedIn profiles will frame it this way: "Volunteer fundraiser and mentor for Big Brothers Big Sisters; helped raise $20K and mentored a struggling student to complete high school."

Step 11: Recommendations > Endorsements

Next up are your **Skills & endorsements section**. Okay, time to fess up—we owe you a big apology here.

As former LinkedIn marketers, we helped to spur a frenzy for Skill Endorsements. You know those approvals where your mom says you're great at "Legal Compliance"? Your childhood friend vouches for your "Excel" wizardry? A former manager says you're skilled at "Nonprofits"? If you had a sneaking suspicion that those were completely bogus, well . . . you're completely right.

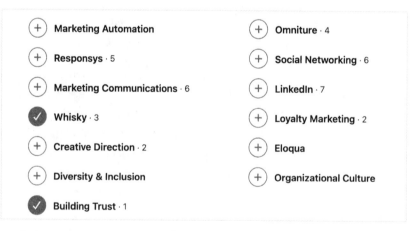

⊕ Marketing Automation	⊕ Omniture · 4
⊕ Responsys · 5	⊕ Social Networking · 6
⊕ Marketing Communications · 6	⊕ LinkedIn · 7
✓ Whisky · 3	⊕ Loyalty Marketing · 2
⊕ Creative Direction · 2	⊕ Eloqua
⊕ Diversity & Inclusion	⊕ Organizational Culture
✓ Building Trust · 1	

Endorsements are a weak signal to recruiters—and the LinkedIn algorithm—because anybody can endorse you for anything.

And LinkedIn knows they're bogus, too—so much so that Endorsements don't show up anywhere in LinkedIn Recruiter. Knowing exactly which skills a candidate is great at would be incredibly useful to a recruiter, but Endorsements are just too full of false positives to be an accurate signal.

So should you skip Skills and Endorsements altogether? Not quite. Endorsements are a weak signal, but Skills are still helpful to list—specifically for the job you want to be found for. (You can reference job descriptions to make sure you've listed the right Skills, or even use LinkedIn's new Career Explorer tool—see page 250). Why? Because Skills—unlike Endorsements—*do* show up in LinkedIn Recruiter. In other words, a recruiter can filter for whether you've listed a specific skill—but not how many Endorsements you got for it. Bottom line: Worry less about getting endorsed for Skills and more about just ensuring they're there.

> The Recommendations section, unlike Endorsements, are surprisingly essential. Third-party validation is critically important.

So with Endorsements hobbled by a lack of legitimacy, that leaves recruiters with a less systematic but more authentic approach to validating your skills: **Recommendations**. Those are the little blurbs that live at the bottom of your profile, with former bosses and colleagues testifying to your experience.

And as manual and old-school as these Recommendations may seem, they're still surprisingly essential in the world of talent hunting. Here's why: 99 percent of your candidacy is based on your own words—your resume, your cover letter, and your interview answers. For a recruiter or hirer, it's a massive decision to base on one admittedly biased perspective. Third-party validation is critically important. So let's make sure you get it using a few easy steps.

What About Skill Assessments?

While Endorsements have failed to generate clear signals about which candidates have which skills, LinkedIn has recently invested in another tactic: testing. You can now take fifteen-question quizzes on a variety of topics and then share your results with recruiters. (To find them, just look for the Take skill quiz button under the Skills section of your profile.)

And most importantly, unlike Endorsements, LinkedIn allows recruiters to filter for them. So, if you're wondering about whether it makes sense to invest time in Skill Assessments, here's your answer, depending on your desired role:

1. *If you're applying for a job that hinges upon a testable skill, absolutely.* For example, if you want a job as a Java Developer, you should be prepared to show off your mastery of Java (both online and in interviews). The downside of *not* showcasing your skill here is that some recruiters might automatically filter you out.

2. *If you're applying for a job that doesn't focus on technical skills, don't sweat it.* Sure, you could take a quiz for Microsoft Word or Outlook, but the reality is that recruiters won't filter for them. That's because a great Salesperson, Teacher, or Project Manager will be expected to know these tools, but no hiring process will rest upon them—at least not compared to the focus placed on leadership, teamwork, and communication. As long as a computer can't adequately test those less quantifiable skills, you're safe from having to take Skill Assessments for now!

Here's how to get started:

- On your profile, go to "Add section," click "Additional information," then hit "Request a recommendation."

- Select your desired recommender and send them a note that shows both gratitude and a clear focus on your desired skill set.

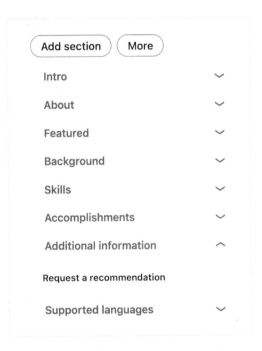

Here's a quick checklist to get the right Recommendations that are in total harmony with your overall story:

- Remember that quality beats quantity. LinkedIn typically only shows two Recommendations at a time—so just focus on two great Recommendations to get started.

- You're looking for the perfect Venn diagram union between two factors: VIPs and People Who Know You Well. Just like with school prestige, recruiters would prefer to hear from a boss or VP over a colleague or classmate. But they also want to know exactly what made you awesome—not just some empty or generic praise. So find someone who's a rock star but can also rep your own star attributes!

- Make an explicit request. Since no one was taught how to give a good LinkedIn Recommendation in school, feel free to fill that void with clear instructions. Ask your recommender to focus on the top three attributes you're looking to emphasize (e.g., Precision, Speed, and Collaboration) and then refresh their memory with a couple of relevant examples (e.g., "You may recall how I balanced our budget in just two weeks, with 100 percent accuracy").

Hi Andréa,
I'm preparing to apply to Customer Success roles and would love to have your expert voice on my LinkedIn profile as someone who knows me well! Would you be willing to provide a short Recommendation, speaking to how I navigated customer challenges at Morpheus? If so, I'd so appreciate it!
Many thanks for your consideration,
William

Send

While finding that sweet spot of a VIP who knows you well, getting a Recommendation from someone is better than no one!

Step 12: Don't Overthink All the Rest

As career coaches, we're firm believers in the 80/20 Rule. In other words, 20 percent of your efforts as a job seeker generate 80 percent of your results. (For instance, think about how much time you spent trying out different resume fonts vs. how many jobs Times New Roman actually landed you!) As such, while we could write an entire book just on the LinkedIn profile alone, we've chosen to focus on the few profile sections that are disproportionately important to the algorithm and recruiter—and to your success.

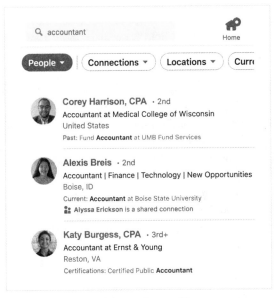

Learn from other profiles.

That said, we know you may be curious about the other remaining sections. (Should I include my SAT score? What about my Project Manager Professional certification?) So here's our 80/20 advice for those: When in doubt, let the algorithm show you what's working for the top candidates right now.

There's no need to pay LinkedIn $10,000 for a Recruiter account. Instead, a similar algorithm is driving your very own LinkedIn searches. So if you want to be an Accountant, search that job title and find out for yourself how the top candidates are positioning themselves, both on the search results page and on their full profiles.

If you run that "Accountant" search and determine that all the top candidates are listing their licenses, including their scores on the CPA exam, and covering all their MAcc coursework, then, by all means, do the same on your own.

The Math Makes It All Work

Now that you know the twelve most important steps toward LinkedIn profile greatness, we wouldn't hold it against you if there's any lingering doubt about whether it's really worth all the effort. After all, your whole life you've probably been told to work on your resume, apply for jobs, and hope for the best. So the idea of spending time on a social media profile may feel like taking a step off the tried-and-true path.

That's exactly what Abhay Sharma, a grad student in Dublin, thought: "I didn't realize that recruiters were searching for people. I thought candidates had to do all the work." But when he decided to give LinkedIn a shot, he was pleasantly surprised: "Having been GIVEN interviews based off my account was an amazing change of perspective! I completely shifted my Headline to add in keywords, which had recruiters reaching out to me over the next couple weeks. It was a very quick turnaround in results!"

To understand why Abhay got such quick results—and why you will, too—let's return to the mathematics of job searching. We opened this chapter by focusing on how recruiters rapidly cut down their candidate pools. Going from 250 applicants to just one hire is math that's always going to work against you.

Applying for more jobs the traditional way can only help so much because it's linear. For instance, maybe you apply for ten jobs a week. Well, with a 0.1 percent chance of getting any of those jobs, you've only increased your odds by 1 percent after a week of hard work. Not so great.

The mathematics of LinkedIn, on the other hand, are positively exponential. Instead of just slowly increasing your odds one application at a time, a magnetic profile exposes you to dozens of searches every day. Before you know it, you're getting seen hundreds of times per week and thousands of times per month—it's almost like compound interest for your career. And just like your investment account, you're getting all that benefit without lifting a finger.

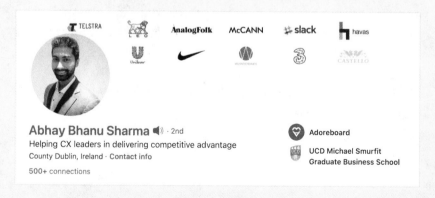

The Bottom Line

Skip all the rumors and hearsay when it comes to job-searching and positioning yourself ("Make sure your handshake can turn coal into diamonds!"; "Don't print your resume on anything less than 90-pound cardstock!"). Instead, keep your eyes on the prize. The only legit reason to have a LinkedIn profile is to gain access to amazing opportunities—not because someone told you it checks a box. The only investments you should make in your profile are the ones that will get you closer to those amazing opportunities.

Life is too short to waste your time on anything else. It's a one-time offer. So keep your eyes firmly focused on what matters most!

CHECKLIST: **Positioning**

Okay, let's recap. You now know more about recruiters, LinkedIn profiles, and hiring search algorithms than 99.9 percent of job seekers. That's a massive advantage in competing for your dream job—not bad. But the only way to truly leverage that advantage is to make sure it shows up on your own LinkedIn profile. So here's a step-by-step guide to make sure every key component is fully optimized:

❑ Put your desired job title in your Headline

❑ Change your Location to where you want to be next (regardless of where you are today)

❑ Turn on your Open to Work signal

❑ Import all your address books to increase your odds of having company connections. That includes the following:

    ❑ Your personal email

    ❑ Your work email

    ❑ Your school email

    ❑ Your phone's contacts via the LinkedIn app

❑ Follow every company you're excited about

❑ Upload a profile photo that nails the three most important criteria:

    ❑ Appropriate attire for your desired employer (When in doubt, search Google Images for "COMPANY NAME office" to see photos of people at work)

    ❑ A genuine Duchenne Smile

    ❑ Cropped tightly around your head and shoulders

❑ Add a photo background that speaks to your functional or geographic interests (drawing upon Pexels.com for inspiration)

❑ Flesh out the About section with content for both the recruiter and algorithm. That includes:

    ❑ An introductory couple of sentences that clearly identify the job titles, locations, and skills you're passionate about

- ❏ Three career highlights that include both important keywords (e.g., Microsoft Excel) and impact (e.g., "saved my organization $11K")

- ❏ A list of skills that are drawn straight from your favorite job descriptions (when in doubt, run a Jobscan.co search)

- ❏ Your email address, for when recruiters run out of InMails

❏ Update your Experience sections to include the following:

- ❏ Your existing resume bullets

- ❏ Both keywords and impact for every bullet

- ❏ Your volunteer work (under the Volunteer Experience section)

- ❏ Visuals where appropriate (e.g., links to articles or YouTube videos)

❏ Optimize your LinkedIn profile for search engines by taking the following steps:

- ❏ Make your profile public

- ❏ Claim a custom URL that makes your profile easy to find

- ❏ Consider adding your area of expertise to your URL, especially if you have a common name

❏ Add school experiences to your Education section, including the following consideration: work-relevant achievements (even if they happened as part of a class or extracurricular)

❏ Add skills that are relevant to the job you want to be found for and consider trying out LinkedIn's Skills Assessments feature to display testable skills on your profile

❏ Get at least two Recommendations with the following characteristics:

- ❏ From someone who has credibility with recruiters— e.g., a boss or executive vs. a colleague or classmate

- ❏ Focused on the key attributes you're looking to portray— e.g., accounting skills focused on ERP projects

❏ Search for the people who already have the job you want and check out their profiles to make sure you've optimized your own in the same way

CHAPTER 5

Find Your Next Gig: Searching

Find the best next opportunity for you

> When you keep searching for ways to change your situation for the better, you stand a chance of finding them.
> **—ANGELA DUCKWORTH**

Time to Go on Offense!

Optimizing your LinkedIn profile is foundational to the digital job search. It helps you get found by recruiters, it's your calling card for networking, and it even gets interviewers excited to meet you. Your profile is really all about playing defense, though. It's a way to shore up your online presence so that no great opportunity (be it a recruiter with a job, an alum with an opportunity—or that darn algorithm) can squeak past you.

Once you've got the peace of mind that comes from having a solid defense in place, it's time for some offense: searching for and applying to the jobs you want. Well, you're in the right place because LinkedIn is now also the world's most trustworthy job board. It scrapes jobs from all over the web, has acquired other job board companies, and includes jobs *only* posted on LinkedIn. (Hirers know this is the best place to get in front of job seekers; they even pay LinkedIn for the privilege!)

You don't have to wait around for a recruiter to come calling—instead, get proactive. You're going to drive the action *strategically* in this chapter.

Here's how you'll do it:

- Understanding how recruiters evaluate applicants and winning over their Applicant Tracking Systems (ATS)

- Uncovering the very best opportunities

- Applying to your desired roles with the most powerful techniques

Beat the Machine: Winning Over the ATS

As mentioned in the Positioning chapter, recruiters often juggle dozens of open roles at the same time, so they don't always have the luxury of discovering the very best candidates by using LinkedIn Recruiter. In many cases, they have no choice but to start with the candidates who have explicitly applied to their job postings. The good news is that you already understand the basic criteria they apply to these applicants playing offense; it's essentially the same as the criteria recruiters apply to the profiles they discover. The recruiter is thinking:

1. My default answer is "No." There are way more candidates than openings so I need to find reasons to reject you right away.

2. If I'm going to say "Yes," I don't want to stick my neck out, since there's a massive downside to risky candidates (you might get me fired!) and very little upside (no one ever got fired for recommending an Obvious Candidate).

3. To help me get through so many candidates quickly, I need to rely on technology—in this case, my ATS.

Now, an ATS may seem like an intimidating new entrant into the Job Search Pantheon of Digital Archnemeses. Upon closer examination, however, it's really just another version of the LinkedIn search algorithm all over again. An ATS is a simple piece of software (separate from LinkedIn) that collects resumes online and then scans them for the right keywords.

But unlike a human recruiter, an ATS will scan thousands of resumes a second. It's no wonder recruiters rely so heavily on this technology to process hundreds of applications before looking at a much smaller sample manually. And, just like the LinkedIn search algorithm, an ATS is incredibly easy to game.

The first thing you should do is to start with a LinkedIn resume template that's built to speak to an ATS. And yes, you still need a resume because even with the rise of LinkedIn, companies often still prefer that you apply with the same format they've grown used to over the decades. Fortunately, LinkedIn automatically generates a downloadable PDF resume for you. Even better, its template includes a few major advantages for winning over your average ATS.

It's focused on keywords, not fancy formatting. Every single ATS craves keywords—after all, words are a lot easier for technology to parse than visuals. (Not even the most sophisticated systems can understand your trendy skills infographic or très chic template.) So LinkedIn starts by giving you ample space for keywords by including ATS-scannable sections that many old-school templates skip (like an About and Skills module), while ditching things that don't matter (like a References section or links to all of your social media).

It leverages the great work you've done so far. You've already optimized your LinkedIn profile for both algorithmic and human review. So instead of having to reinvent the wheel, LinkedIn just plugs all that great keyword- and human-optimized content right into your resume.

It coaches you through the whole process. Every time you start to customize your resume, LinkedIn will guide you through each step, reminding you to focus on all the things we've already discussed: keywords, outcomes, and more. And it will even serve up recommended keywords on a silver platter, like your Robo Resume Butler:

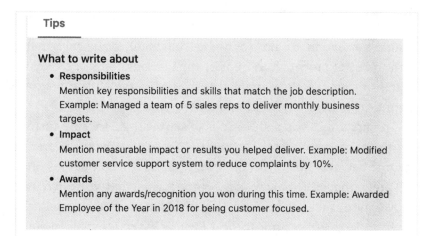

A great LinkedIn profile frames achievements and concrete skills, not merely role descriptions.

Step 1: Get Your Template

Your LinkedIn resume template is hiding out on your profile under the More button. Just click "Build a resume" to get started:

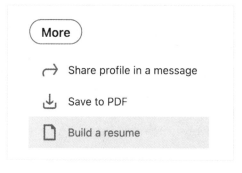

Step 2: Get Focused

We've already geeked out plenty about the many reasons that a LinkedIn profile is superior to a resume (it gets seen more often, isn't limited to a page, and so on). But there is one huge Achilles's heel: Your profile is one-size-fits-all. Unlike a resume created in Microsoft Word that you can replicate a million times over and customize to a specific job, LinkedIn gives you a single URL to contain all your worldly ambitions.

Now, if you really nailed our advice in Chapter 3 and focused your search, that's not such a big issue. Hopefully you've been able to hone your ambitions down to a singular focus based on all the career exploration you've done. If so, your LinkedIn profile has the potential to be a red-hot laser of clarity. But if you haven't quite achieved that level of professional nirvana, fear not. You're not alone. Even if your one LinkedIn profile must cover everything you've accomplished or been interested in, your resume need not—and in fact, it shouldn't!

LinkedIn will help you create a customized version of your resume for any job category you want to pursue.

The right move is to create a customized version of your resume for any job category you want to pursue. Now, to be clear, that doesn't mean you need to create a separate resume for each of the twenty-seven Architect roles

Choose your desired job title
Based on this, you'll get personalized keyword suggestions

Job title

Account Manager

You'll get keyword help every time you build a new resume.

you're considering—those are going to be more alike than different in terms of the skills and keywords required. But if you also want to apply to twelve Graphic Designer roles, you'll definitely want to have a separate version optimized for that world.

And, sure enough, that's exactly what LinkedIn prompts you to do every time you make a resume: Start with the job title you want and focus, focus, focus.

Step 3: Get to the Top of the ATS

Once you've set up your focused resume, it's time to get the right keywords in the right places. Start with LinkedIn's recommended Keyword Insights.

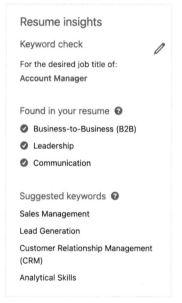

Resume insights

Keyword check

For the desired job title of:
Account Manager

Found in your resume

✅ Business-to-Business (B2B)
✅ Leadership
✅ Communication

Suggested keywords

Sales Management
Lead Generation
Customer Relationship Management (CRM)
Analytical Skills

These are automatically scraped from the profiles of people who have the job you want to get next. To this list, add the keywords you might have discovered via Jobscan.co in the last chapter (see page 124—i.e., the exact verbiage handed to you by recruiters in the form of job descriptions.

Leveraging this combined list, we want you to really go to town all across your resume:

- Include keywords in your About section: "I'm an Account Manager with a deep background in sales management and CRM software."

- Include keywords in your Experience bullets: "Led sales management for a small start-up in the B2B training space, driving my team to a 57% increase in new business development."

- And, of course, include them verbatim in the Skills section: "Sales Management, New Business Development, CRM, B2B."

Voilà! You've got a resume that's ready to rock any ATS in the world. So just repeat these same steps for any other job titles you'd like to pursue and you'll have a full arsenal of customized resumes for every application.

How to Search and Apply, the Smart Way

Once you've got your customized resumes ready to rock, you may be tempted to just start applying for jobs, willy-nilly. And while there's a certain catharsis that comes from throwing yourself out to the world, please resist that temptation. Because unlike the classic job seeker who applies everywhere, gets nowhere, and then goes home and gives up, we want to make sure you use the right techniques to go the distance.

Here's a complete, data-backed *system* for turning your application process into a science. This is not a mad scramble or a desperation lunge, but rather a simple guide to making the most of every possible opportunity.

Use "All Filters" and Alerts to Access the Best Opportunities

The first step is to make sure you're getting regular access to the best job postings. And while you could manually search LinkedIn's job board every five seconds, it's just so much more efficient (and less painful!) to let LinkedIn's search alerts do the heavy lifting for you.

So let's now get your search (and alerts) up and running.

1. Just start by typing the name of your desired job title right into the LinkedIn search box. Don't worry about picking out the perfect title. LinkedIn is great at coming up with similar jobs, even if they don't all use the exact same title. Just be sure to choose the "Jobs" option from the drop-down list:

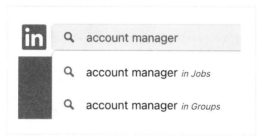

2. Once you have a basic list of opportunities, click the "All Filters" button. Bam! You've just accessed the extremely useful Advanced Search filters. You can now slice and dice your way to the perfect roles:

3. To make sure you're looking at the right set of jobs, use the Industry, Job Function, and Title filters. For instance, if you know from your career exploration that you want to do sales in the tech industry, feel free to focus on that.

But if you're open to different kinds of roles across multiple industries, that's perfectly fine, too. There's no need to be overly limited at this stage when you're flexible anyway.

Filter only Jobs ▼ by   ✕

☑ Computer Software   ☑ Information Technology and Services

☐ Financial Services   ☑ Internet

☐ Marketing and Advertising   ☐ Hospital & Health Care

☐ Construction   ☐ Insurance

☐ Staffing and Recruiting   ☐ Retail

+ Add an industry

Job Function

☑ Sales   ☐ Marketing

☐ Business Development   ☐ Product Management

☐ Information Technology   ☐ Management

☐ Project Management   ☐ Customer Service

☐ Other   ☐ Health Care Provider

+ Add a job function

Title

☐ Product Manager   ☑ Account Manager

4. The same is true for Location. You can absolutely choose just one. But you can also select multiple destinations from the Location filter. Or even look specifically for on-site, remote, or hybrid opportunities:

Easy Apply

Location

☑ New York, NY   ☑ Chicago, IL

☐ San Francisco, CA   ☐ Atlanta, GA

☐ Los Angeles, CA   ☐ Austin, TX

☐ Boston, MA   ☐ Seattle, WA

5. Of course, make sure it's the right Job Type for you:

6. Finally, with your filters applied, show your results, then easily turn on Job Alerts from the same results page:

7. Of course, if you see any great job postings right here and now, by all means apply to them. But now you've got daily job matches coming straight to your email inbox, instead of stressing about catching every single great job as it's posted!

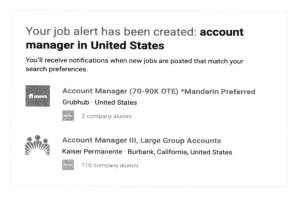

Alerts help you jump on a great job as soon as it comes open.

Goodbye, One-Page Resume

When you export your resume as a PDF from LinkedIn, you may be in for a shock:

"Oh no! A two-page resume!!! I might as well renounce all work and live in a cave. . . ."

Well, before you check Airbnb for Neolithic dwellings, here's some heartening news: A recent study revealed that recruiters—GASP—actually *prefer* two-page resumes. In fact, they preferred them almost three to one over one-page resumes for mid-level and managerial candidates. And here's the real shocker: This finding even held up for entry-level candidates, where you'd think everyone expects and prefers brevity.

So even if you've always been told to restrict your entire life to an 8.5-by-11-inch piece of paper, don't believe the hype. Take that second page if necessary—and then make the most of it!

Hiring Rate: Two-Page vs. One-Page Resumes

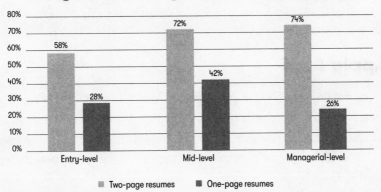

When asked to choose resumes for a potential hire, participating recruiters selected two-page versions at a higher rate (y-axis) than one-page versions across a variety of career stages.

A few notes:

- You'll notice that there are lots more filters available here in "All Filters"—and we'll cover many of them shortly. But for now, start with a basic search, just to get a sense of what's out there.

- Make sure to set up separate searches for each of the job titles you're excited about by repeating these steps. That way, no rogue opportunity escapes the gravitational pull of your job search system!

- We know this idea of relying upon automated alerts may feel foreign, especially if you're used to searching for jobs every few days or so. But know that it rests upon sound psychology—we humans just aren't good at dealing with the ups and downs of job searching. For example, how many times have you looked for a job, found nothing, and just decided to give up? Let LinkedIn's job search algorithm do the work for you.

- You can *trust* LinkedIn's sophisticated algorithm to deliver not only the right matches but a comprehensive list of them. Job alerts will catch everything relevant that's out there!

Apply ASAP

Once you've set up your job alerts, set aside time in your schedule to review the newest postings every day. Ideally, do so in the morning; recruiters tend to review candidates earlier in the day. Tempting as it is to hit the snooze button on your search, that's not how recruiters think.

Just imagine a recruiter who's spent the last two weeks going back and forth about an Account Manager job posting with the hiring team. After all the debate and editing of the post, they've finally launched their job description to the world. Are they going to sit back and wait a few weeks for the applications to roll in?

What About Other Job Boards?

Just like with other social media companies, it turns out that LinkedIn's professional networking has strong "network effects." In other words, the fact that LinkedIn has hundreds of millions of professionals makes it highly attractive to employers across the world, which makes it that much more attractive to professionals. It's a virtuous cycle. So it just becomes inevitable that the vast majority of jobs will end up on LinkedIn—which means it's a great place to launch your search. There are a few instances, however, in which you may want to look further afield.

- **You're focused on a specific niche:** While LinkedIn has broad coverage of just about every industry, there are certain fields where companies tend to cluster on industry-specific sites. For example, some of the earliest-stage start-ups may post exclusively on AngelList. And by the same token, Idealist is a thriving community of nonprofit opportunities.

- **You want to take advantage of specific features:** Although LinkedIn has come to match the job-scraping abilities of other job boards, there are sometimes features that just can't be found anywhere else. For instance, Indeed lets you use Boolean syntax in searches (e.g., *title: "product manager" -hardware* will find all the PM jobs that aren't in the hardware space). And Glassdoor will let you filter your results by company rating so you can watch out for less-than-desirable places to work.

- **You want peace of mind:** If you're dreaming of a job at a specific company, setting up search alerts on their own job board can give you psychological insurance that you're not missing out. Plus, you'll get access to custom filters designed for that firm. For example, if you're set on landing a job working on the next Disney masterpiece, you can get tailored alerts for Animation roles at jobs.disneycareers.com.

Heck, no! They're going to be like a kid on Christmas morning who can't wait to sneak downstairs and check out the presents under the tree—i.e., the applications on the ATS. (Yes, this is like Christmas to some people.)

"I set up daily alerts for new product management jobs in Toronto. I used LinkedIn to network with Product Managers, and when roles opened up that were affiliated with them (i.e., at their organization), I reached out to them for a referral as well as advice and tips. It works!"

This recruiter is going to give special attention to the first few applications that roll in because those are the bright, shiny presents they can't wait to unwrap after all that patience. The applications that show up two weeks later, however, are like the decaying fruitcake from Aunt Ruthie. Sure, it was a nice gesture. But at this late date in the holiday season, recruiters are more Scrooge than Santa and can't wait for this whole thing to just be over.

Sure enough, recruiters are eight times more likely to grant you an interview when you apply in the first ninety-six hours. (Don't worry, however, about applying within the first hour, since that doesn't make much of a difference—save your lightning-fast reflexes for your *Jeopardy!* audition!) So avoid Fruitcake Syndrome and get your applications in ASAP.

Apply Broadly

Not only should you apply quickly, but you should apply broadly. Here are the guidelines for doing so.

Don't worry about being underqualified. Lots of candidates won't apply for a job unless they meet all the criteria. But that's a huge mistake, given that recruiters generally want or expect candidates who meet only 50 percent of them. Why is that? From a recruiter's perspective, someone who meets every single one of their twenty-seven job description bullets is likely to be overqualified; pursuing them might just waste time when they either decline an offer or, worse yet, bail right after starting. Whereas someone who meets half the criteria has enough skill to come in, learn on the job, and make an impact—but not so much that they'll be bored and decline the offer. Bottom line: Don't let impostor syndrome dissuade you from going after your dream job.

Don't put all your eggs in the same basket. We'll talk in the next chapter about how to get a massive advantage over other candidates through networking. But for now, let's assume that you have about a 1 percent chance of winning any given job listing just by applying online. What that should immediately tell you is that it's pure madness to pursue only one at a time. Instead, let your dreams expand a bit. Not only is any given job hard to get, but we humans are notoriously bad at predicting what will make us happy (Exhibit A: bling). So instead, embrace a diversified portfolio of 100+ applications, even to jobs that may not seem dreamlike on their face.

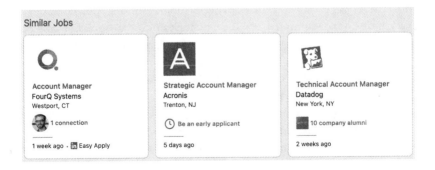

Browse "Similar Jobs" to diversify your application portfolio.

One of the best ways to do that is through LinkedIn's algorithm. No, not the one that screened you out in the last chapter—but instead, the one that plugs you into new opportunities on every single job listing. Just scroll down to the bottom of your desired listing and you'll find a dozen or more similar opportunities just waiting to be filled.

***Do* apply systematically.** As mentioned earlier, one of the most common job search pitfalls is the tendency to start strong, then fade

The Paradox of (Job Search) Choice

As a rule, we humans tend to prefer more. More food, more pleasure, and absolutely more choice: Fifty brands of blue jeans are better than five, 100 kinds of Starbucks drinks are better than ten, and, of course, 1,000 job opportunities are better than a mere 100. We're a culture of maximizers. But what if it turns out that all this choice is in fact . . . hurting us?

That's the counterintuitive argument that psychologist Barry Schwartz makes in his groundbreaking book *The Paradox of Choice*. He argues that having more brands, more options, and more of everything makes us less, not more, happy.

It turns out the same is true with applying for jobs. Because sure, while you'd rather live in a town with more opportunity than less, you can only do one job at a time. Being faced with thousands and thousands of jobs can be detrimental if it leaves you with paralyzing fear of missing out (FOMO). It's a classic case of "the grass is greener on the other side of the fence" or in this case, "the gig is a little sexier on the other side of the cubicle wall!"

To beat back this feeling of missing out when you do a LinkedIn job search, return to the investment you made back in Chapter 3—exploring different career paths and narrowing down your focus to just the one or two that are right for you. Now leverage that investment by being ruthless in weeding out the jobs that don't fit. Because, yes, there may be some sexy-looking jobs out there. But like those fifty pairs of blue jeans, will all of them look sexy *on you*?

quickly. We're hardwired to seek immediate gratification. (Fun fact: There's a direct line from hunter-gatherers pursuing the instant calories of fruit to casino-goers pursuing the instant reward of slot machines.) Our DNA just doesn't favor long, hard slogs. Applying for jobs can be a tedious pursuit, given that you may not see the fruit of your labor for weeks or months at a time. So just like our recommendation to outsource the search process to LinkedIn's job alerts, so do we recommend outsourcing the application process

Don't just take our word for it. Joel Abramson, one of our MBA clients and now a Senior Director in the finance industry, shares his top tip after taking our LinkedIn course: "Don't be discouraged by the overwhelming amount of companies/jobs/posts out there—leverage advice and filters to narrow things down!"

In Joel's case, he was able to talk to alumni from his alma mater and winnow his list of target roles. Then by rigorously limiting his search to those roles through filters and search alerts, he quickly landed an interview for one of his target opportunities.

So when the sheer volume of jobs on LinkedIn starts to loom a little too large, feel free to embrace the counterintuitive—but wise—philosophy of "less is more."

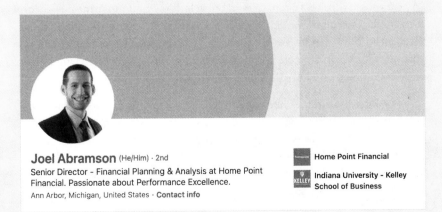

Joel Abramson (He/Him) · 2nd
Senior Director - Financial Planning & Analysis at Home Point Financial. Passionate about Performance Excellence.
Ann Arbor, Michigan, United States · **Contact info**

Home Point Financial

Indiana University - Kelley School of Business

to an accountability buddy. Here's how to set up a foolproof application system:

a) *Find a really good friend*—not just someone who cheers you on, but a person who's not afraid to call you out on your BS. (And yes, you could choose a romantic partner—although just be warned that this level of candor may take some of the romance out of your relationship!)

Should You Apply with a Cover Letter?

Given this premium on speed, what should you do when facing every job seeker's Hamlet-like dilemma: To write a cover letter, or not to write a cover letter?

To answer this eternal question, as always, put yourself in the shoes of a recruiter: You've got to find just a few great candidates; you've got a mountain of applicants; and you've got barely any time to conduct your search.

Given those conditions it's hardly a surprise that only an estimated 26 percent of recruiters claim to read cover letters—and that's most likely an overcount. (Recruiters would probably prefer not to admit they're shirking their duty!) What's more, even if just one in ten recruiters read cover letters, you never know which recruiter that is ahead of time. So here's a simple rule of thumb to help you make the most of what we do know:

- *For jobs that you're not truly in love with, feel free to skip the cover letter.* This will enable you to get your application in quickly, thereby reaping the massive benefit of applying in the first ninety-six hours. You'll also avoid the analysis paralysis that sinks many job seekers, in which you spend so much time stressing over the cover letter that you become tempted to give up on your entire search.

b) *Give them access to your LinkedIn account—*specifically, they should plan to check on your Applied Jobs page every week:

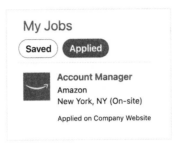

- *For jobs that you must have, write a cover letter—but keep it focused.* Even if there's a 74 percent chance (or higher) that your cover letter will never be read, submitting one gives you psychological insurance against future FOMO. That alone makes it worth the time and effort. In other words, if you end up not getting the job, at least you can content yourself with the knowledge that you did everything within your power to win it. You won't be haunted by the idea that you were just a cover letter away! That said, you still need to protect yourself from the quicksand that is cover letter overload (e.g., "I promise to have my cover letter in soon, I just need a few more days to add a bibliography . . . "). Limit yourself to the handful of things that recruiters care about:

    a) Keywords: Do you have the skills to do the job? Prove it by giving an example or two of similar work you've already done.

    b) Engagement: Are you seriously interested in this job? Make your case by expressing clear enthusiasm for something specific about the role or company.

    Voila! Nail the key points in a couple of paragraphs and you're golden. Move on and get back to winning the more important game: getting a great job! (See page 164 for a sample cover letter.)

c) *Set a weekly goal for job applications*—ideally, at least ten per week. Why that number? Well, if we stick with our 1 percent chance of getting hired per application, then you'll have a pretty sound chance of landing a job after several weeks of applying at this rate. Even if these applications don't lead to offers (and one eventually will), just getting more interviews along the way will give you both positive feedback and valuable experience to sharpen your interview skills.

d) *Have your friend hold you accountable*—by empowering them with a shared goal. For instance, maybe you plan a weekend getaway together, but make it contingent upon hitting your weekly application targets. That way, each time they check up on you, they can remind you of what's at stake—for both of you!

Do apply strategically. Now, just because you have to apply to ten+ jobs per week, it doesn't mean you should apply randomly. To increase your hiring odds beyond 1 percent for any given job, consider adding these "All Filters" parameters for your search:

- *Under 10 Applicants:* LinkedIn keeps tabs on how many candidates have applied to each job. By clicking this filter, it will steer you to opportunities with less competition. This is a huge advantage because, keep in mind, your fractional chance of winning any given job is defined by this simple equation:

$$\frac{Your\ Strength\ as\ a\ Candidate}{Your\ Competition} = Probability\ of\ Hire$$

So while most of our strategies are focused on boosting your numerator, it never hurts to minimize your denominator, too!

- *In Your Network:* Here, LinkedIn looks specifically for jobs where you know someone on the inside. This is an incredibly powerful way to search because a referral from a company insider increases your chances of getting an interview by a factor of ten. So definitely click this filter to boost your odds—and check out the exact steps on page 173 to convert an insider into a referral.

Actively recruiting: Have you ever spent weeks pursuing a dream job, only to hear crickets after all your effort? And when you checked six months later, you discovered the job was never even filled? These "ghost postings" are incredibly frustrating; they're also incredibly common, given that recruiters often won't bother to take down jobs if the hiring manager changes their mind or resources shrink. Fortunately, LinkedIn now has a way to protect yourself from the wrath of these unfriendly ghosts, by letting you know exactly who's "Actively recruiting." You'll only see this tag for jobs for which the recruiter is logging into LinkedIn to actively review applications and proactively reaching out to new candidates on LinkedIn Recruiter. So try to prioritize jobs with this green bull's-eye symbol when completing your weekly quota:

Specific Filters for Specific Situations

So far, we've approached the search/application process mostly as if you were a generic job seeker. But the reality is that we all have unique challenges and needs when it comes to finding the perfect fit. There are some positive and useful aspects of LinkedIn that can speak to more specified circumstances.

First, LinkedIn has a truly diverse set of jobs. Whether you want to work for a giant multinational corporation or a tiny, mission-driven NGO, chances are strong that LinkedIn has a job for you. That's because LinkedIn dropped a cool $120 million on a search engine that does nothing but scrape the internet all day for newly posted jobs. The result is that the site often features more than 10 million jobs across the world on any given day—a whole ocean of opportunity.

Second, the platform has gotten way better at supporting diverse needs. Not only does LinkedIn now have nearly all the jobs in the world, but it also has so many new ways to slice and dice them. For example, here are just a few more filters you could apply:

- *I'm a student/recent grad.* Sick of searching for entry-level jobs and coming up with roles that require 5+ years of experience? Try filtering your search specifically by Experience Level. Just remember the research we cited previously: You don't need to be 100 percent qualified in order to have a good shot at landing a job.

- *I need a specific benefit.* Expecting a new child? Need to pay off your student loans? LinkedIn lets you filter for the Benefits that matter most by scanning job descriptions for these exact keywords:

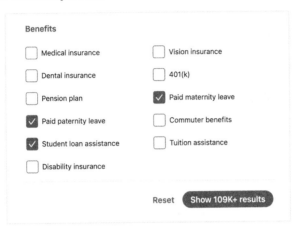

- *I need help getting my career restarted.* Seventy million Americans have a criminal record that could potentially disqualify them from getting a fair shake in the job application process. Under LinkedIn Features, you can focus on the best opportunities by filtering for employers who have pledged to hire people, regardless of record:

Keep Going

As we close out the chapter, let's reflect on the criticality of the Searching step. Now that you've achieved more clarity of focus on what kind of role you want to be in, this step has been all about pro-actively finding—and laying seeds for—an actual opportunity that will bring that vision to life. Things are getting real! But don't stop now—it's time to keep up that proactivity, put yourself out there, and ramp up that super-important step of networking.

Sample Cover Letter:

Dear Sir or Madam,

I'm thrilled to be applying to the Account Manager role at 3M. That's because:

1. I've discovered that serving customers well is a true calling. For example, in my current role, I built out our first CRM database, just so we could keep track of our clientele's needs and wishes more efficiently. And the result is that we've decreased churn by 27 percent while increasing account size by an average of $5,000.

2. I'm so impressed by the way that 3M has built a culture of continuous innovation. From the invention of the Post-it Note to the firm's current cutting-edge work in solar, that spirit of never resting on your laurels just deeply appeals to me—and those are the exact kind of products I'd love to represent.

As such, I'd love the opportunity to discuss the role further at your convenience.

Thanks for your consideration!

—Shanice Wells

CHECKLIST: **Searching**

To get your own high-powered application system up and running, here's a recap of the most important next steps:

- ❑ Once your LinkedIn profile is optimized, build a resume based on it so you have a consistent personal brand and story

- ❑ Create a separate version of your resume for every function you want to pursue (e.g., Sales Representative, Customer Service Representative)

- ❑ For each version of the resume, focus on the keywords that LinkedIn and Jobscan.co recommend, embedding them in your About, Experience, and Skills sections

- ❑ Search for the jobs you want based on Industry, Function, Title, Location, and Type—and then set up alerts for each search and review the newest postings each day

- ❑ Make sure you've connected an email address *you actually check* so you get those postings sent to your inbox

- ❑ Apply within the first ninety-six hours to every job that's appealing to maximize your chances

- ❑ Include a simple cover letter (e.g., here's the similar work I've done and clear evidence of my enthusiasm) for the jobs you're most excited about— and skip it for the rest

- ❑ Set up an accountability system where a good friend tracks your applied jobs and holds your feet to the fire on a weekly basis

- ❑ Consider also setting filters for your unique needs (e.g., Experience Level, Benefits, and Fair Chance Employers)

When choosing which jobs to apply to, consider these criteria:

- ❑ Apply for jobs where you match about 50 percent of the job description bullets, since that's the sweet spot between woefully underqualified and annoyingly overqualified

- ❑ Aim for ten+ jobs per week to increase your odds of building momentum early in your search

- ❑ Apply for jobs where you'll have an advantage—e.g., you know someone on the inside or there are few applicants already

- ❑ Look for jobs that are Actively Recruiting to avoid getting ghosted!

CHAPTER 6

Get the Ultimate Edge: Networking

Get in the door by putting yourself out there

Connection is why we're here; it is what gives purpose
and meaning to our lives.
—BRENÉ BROWN

Networking, Demystified

Halftime status check: You've done your homework to identify
the right jobs for you. You've built an incredible LinkedIn profile to
attract recruiters. And now you've started applying systematically
and strategically to the best—and best-fit—jobs. You're already several steps ahead of most job seekers.

But awaiting you is *the* biggest advantage you can grab in the
entire job search process: networking your way to a referral from a
current employee. Think of a referral as the most efficient route to
getting seriously considered for a job you really want. Rather than
having to trick the algorithm, all you have to do is get a single person on the inside to validate you. Preferably the *right* person.

In this chapter we'll cover the critical and often-confusing topic
of networking. We'll show you how to do it on LinkedIn so you can
earn a referral at any organization in the world. Then we'll look at
networking with hiring managers themselves, and how job seekers
can use these techniques to mitigate the effects of systemic inequi-
ties in hiring. Now let's dig in.

Referrals:
The Biggest Advantage

We've already explored how recruiters use technology to hunt for the proverbial needle in the haystack of applications. But at the end of the day, technology can only take you so far. Would you marry someone based solely on the recommendation of a Match.com algorithm? Or buy a house because it was at the top of Zillow's list? Nope, you'd want something a little more, well, human to buttress your decision. And that's precisely what recruiters do. Before deciding on a candidate, they always look for human input—from their teammates and fellow recruiters, from hiring managers and interviewers, and from internal referrals.

Savvy job searchers know that who gets picked isn't a meritocracy. They also know that the shortlist of people under consideration consists of those who are already in the inner circle—because search results are ordered by connection proximity *to the person doing the search.*

The most important of these human inputs to hirers is the referral. Getting someone on the inside to both vouch and advocate for you turns out to be the single best way to get an edge in the whole job search process. Just sense the power of referrals in raw numbers:

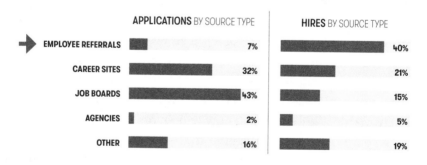

Referred candidates account for a whopping 40 percent of hires.

This data, culled from a leading ATS from the website Jobvite, is nothing less than the Rosetta Stone of getting your dream job. That is, it's the purest translation of how recruiters prioritize candidates, sorted by where they come from. And it turns out that the source recruiters value most is totally attainable for any job seeker, with strategic networking and a little hustle.

Let's unpack it bit by bit. Starting with the left-hand column, you see that a full 75 percent of all applications arrive via Career Sites (typically an employer's "Jobs" page) and Job Boards (e.g., Indeed, ZipRecruiter, Monster, Idealist, and LinkedIn itself). This likely comes as no surprise, given that online applications have become the default job-search strategy in the 21st century.

However, when we move over to the right-hand column—actual hires—we find that those online applications account for only 36 percent of the job offers. Wait a second . . . if three-fourths of the applications are only leading to one-third of the jobs, where are the offers *really* going?

Sure enough, when we track Employee Referrals and Agency hires from left to right, we discover that two application strategies used by fewer than one in ten job seekers are accounting for nearly half of all hires. Wait . . . what???

That's right, getting a referral from a current employee or getting introduced to the hiring manager by an agency leads to massively outsize results. And what do these two strategies have in common? You guessed it: actual relationships. With, you know, actual humans.

Agency: a job placement firm that job seekers may pay. Or, an executive search firm or headhunter, who will work for free on a job seekers's behalf because companies tap them to source hard-to-fill and/or senior roles—especially in start-up industries or niche industries (like fintech or hospital administration).

Timing Your Referral Right

As powerful as referrals are, it often takes a long time to earn them—especially if you have to develop new connections first. With the extra priority given to the earliest applicants, this timing lag can become a serious issue. So here's a quick rule for negotiating any tricky timing:

- If you already know someone at the company, have them refer you right away. Since their referral counts as an application in the ATS, you'll get the benefit of applying early along with the power of a referral.

- If you don't know anyone yet, apply immediately and then seek a referral. That way, even if you don't get one for a week or two, you won't miss out on the bonus associated with being an early applicant.

To understand what's driving this phenomenon, let's return to our hypothetical recruiter. Yes, they've worked hard to find some great candidates both on LinkedIn Recruiter and in their pile of applications. But now imagine that someone inside the organization comes to them and says, "Hey, I know this candidate—they would be amazing!"

If you were in their shoes, who would *you* pick for your final interview slot? Pick one:

- The outside candidate who has awesome keywords and checks all the right boxes—but who remains a total stranger and could be an axe-murderer for all you know?

- The insider candidate whose keywords are so-so—but whose former boss just happens to be BFFs with your boss's boss?

Riiiiight. Yeah, us too. That's the power of human relationships, for better or worse. And that's exactly why you need them on your side.

For hirers, relationships de-risk candidates. It's not quite that a referral will always trump qualifications; it's that hirers almost always have to choose between several solid candidates, so relationships become the differentiator. And a referral gets you not just a serious look but a look in the first place. Many companies, in fact, have a policy that *any* referral will at least get a phone screen or first interview. Depth of connection to the employee, or others at the firm, isn't really a criterion; the mere act of a referral is all the validation they need.

Indeed, the professional world is an interconnected web. In most industries and markets, the web is smaller and tighter spun than you might think. But the upside of this reality is that you're always just one connection away from a totally different future! In a zero-sum world where your victory almost always means someone else's loss, referrals are a rare win-win-win. To more fully grasp the power of a referral, just look at it from the perspectives of each key stakeholder:

Company: According to the same Jobvite study referenced earlier, referred candidates cost less to recruit, perform better, are hired faster, and stay on the job longer. As such, it's no wonder that 86 percent of recruiters and employers said referrals were the number-one source of high-quality candidates.

Referrer: Because companies value referrals so highly, they usually incentivize their employees to make them; and most companies, even hot start-ups with funding out the wazoo, aren't in the business of throwing away money. Successful referrals typically generate a bonus from $1,000 to $5,000—all for simply going into the referral system and plugging in the job seeker's name, resume, and desired job title. Not too shabby for a few minutes of work!

Job seeker: And, of course, the biggest beneficiary is you, the applicant! That's because a referral takes you from a random outsider to a preferred insider. Which means your chances of becoming an employee instantly skyrocket.

Employee Referrals Have the Highest ROI

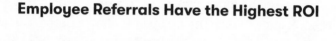

*Referrals are much more likely to be hired and stay
on the job longer. Every company knows this.*

In essence, employee referrals are treated almost the same as internal transfers: as easy-to-validate and "safe" candidates. You do yourself a massive disservice by not doing everything you can to secure a referral for a role you're pumped about. So now you know *why* referrals are the Midas touch of job-seeking, turning everything they grace into gold. But *how* do you manage to get one? Especially if you don't know anyone on the inside?

How to Get a Referral

Good news: We're going to get you a copy of your dream company's employee directory. And no, you won't need to break into the HR department, *Mission: Impossible* style. LinkedIn gives you a completely searchable and filterable directory for most every organization in the world. Just search for your desired employer's Company Page and click the number of employees (aka "potential referrals" for you, the savvy job seeker).

With your employee directory in hand, let's take a tour of six different ways to get a referral—no matter how small or selective your desired firm is.

Option #1: Get a 1st-Degree Referral

As with everything in this guidebook, we recommend beginning your referral search with the absolute lowest-hanging fruit: Who do you already know at your target employer? The very best referral comes from someone who sits at the Venn diagram intersection of people who *can* help and who *want* to help. People you already know are well positioned to fill that sweet spot!

1. Apply the 1st-Degree Connection filter. To find your peeps on the inside, click the 1st-Degree checkbox under the "Connections" filter.

But Networking Is So . . . Sketchy!

If you're anything like us, you probably dreaded this chapter most of all. So many of us have grown up with this image of networking: guys with slicked-back hair and red power ties glad-handing over drinks while they pass out their fancy, embossed business cards. In other words: the "old boys' network" brought to life. And if you're not part of that world—i.e., most people!—you're basically out of the game before it even starts.

That's exactly what we expected as former elementary school teachers making our first forays into the business world. But as introverts who had absolutely zero desire to go to mixers and randomly glad-hand, we're here to tell you that networking on LinkedIn is the polar opposite of the traditional concept. This is a big part of why we think of it as The Great Opportunity Democratizer; the old boys' network cannot be replicated in such a ubiquitous and public professional community.

In this community, what you find is the best of networking: People who are open to new connections, cutting across the old socioeconomic, racial, and educational dividing lines. LinkedIn users want to help others connect to better opportunities because they may return the favor someday. (There are even stories about couples who met while networking on LinkedIn!)

Here are a few ways the game has changed for the better:

Traditional Networking	Networking on LinkedIn
You have to know the "right" people (e.g., the people who work at the "right" companies or who went to the "right" schools).	Everyone you know is the right person! Second-degree connections allow you to plug into just about anywhere.
It's all about being lucky. Did you happen to run into someone at the random happy hour who can help you?	It's all about making your own luck. Identify the exact right people and pursue them logically.
Introverts need not apply. If you can't press the flesh like a pro, don't bother showing up.	This is networking for all. By democratizing access to the world's talent pool, anyone can network (even from behind the comfort of your computer screen).

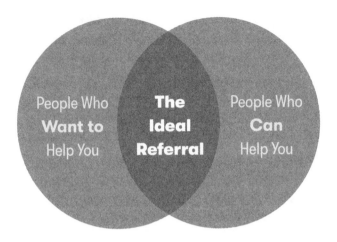

2. Reach out to your 1st-Degree Connections. If you know some-one on the inside, great! (It could be literally anyone, though gen-erally speaking, the more senior, the better.) Don't overthink this step—just reach out and ask for a referral. You're already connected, so you can and should message them directly on LinkedIn.

Feel free to use a message like the following one, starting with a reminder that you know each other. Remember, you're not asking them to do anything untoward or even particularly onerous. Rather, you're inviting them to act in their own best interest by potentially earning a referral bonus (and getting an awesome new colleague).

Hi Leena,

Long time no talk! Hope all's well. I just came across this role at Disney [insert URL here] where I think I could be a great fit. Any chance you'd be willing to refer me for
the role?

If so, I've attached my resume here. Thanks for considering—it would mean so much to me!

Truly appreciated,

Daria

With a 1st-degree connection, this kind of direct approach is best. You are making it easy for them to respond, and frictionless to refer you by including the job link and your resume. Even so, you should expect that many people will want to discuss the position and/or company with you before putting in the good word. That's totally reasonable, and you should view it as an opportunity not only to vet the role but also to prepare for possible formal interviews; it's insider knowledge!

You should also expect that some people, despite the lure of a referral bonus, will be unresponsive. Don't take it personally, and don't assume they're ignoring you; they may just not have seen your message. When we worked at LinkedIn, the entire company could see a dashboard showing how frequently visitors came to the site and how long they stayed.

Don't worry if a connection doesn't respond. It happens.

Members are most engaged on LinkedIn when they're doing one of three things: looking for a job, looking to fill a job, or looking to drum up new business. Your contact may not be doing any of those things, so you may need to grab their attention by other means; next, try email. You will already have their email address if you connected with them initially via the Contact Import tool (see page 110). Just search their name in whatever email service you use.

3. Reap your reward! As soon as your contact refers you in the ATS, you should get an email notifying you. You'll likely hear from the recruiter about an initial interview in the first seventy-two hours, when the first tranche of interviewees is usually selected. If you don't hear back within a week, however, be sure to reach out to your contact. Even if the recruiter has missed your referral in the ATS, your contact can follow up with them directly and flag your application—which is often an even more powerful way to get on that exclusive radar.

Option #2: Get a 2nd-Degree Referral

Okay, but what if you don't know anyone directly? Are you out of luck? No way—remember that stat from the beginning of this chapter: *Only 7 percent of applicants are able to get a referral.* But the same thing that makes them hard to get also makes them incredibly powerful—and worth every ounce of your effort. So keep on pushing by moving to 2nd-degree connections.

Second-degree connections are LinkedIn users who know someone you know—basically, friends of friends. Some quick math shows the massive reach of this 2nd-degree network. Say you have 100 connections and each of your connections also has 100. Assuming you don't all just know the same people, you're likely to end up with around 10,000 2nd-degree connections. And assuming you imported your address books and have way more than 100 connections, well, you can just see the power of this secondary network start to explode.

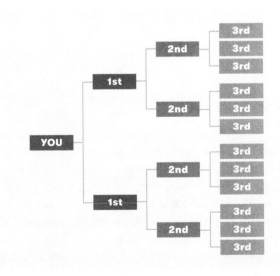

Second-degree connections are your ticket to a broader, healthier network.

Here's our threshold for reaching out: I know you (i.e., we've met, either IRL or virtually) and/or you've given me at least one good reason to connect with you (i.e., what you do is interesting, I want to work where you do, or you've sent me a personalized connection request).

Now that you understand the exponential forces underlying your 2nd-degree network, let's tap the power of it, step-by-step.

1. Apply the 2nd-Degree Connection filter. Just like with your 1st-degree search, head over to the "Connections" filter and search for 2nd-degree connections at your desired employer:

The Follow-Up

People tend to be more invested in people for whom they do favors. It's sort of like how we get attached to the sports teams we spend time watching, or to the stocks we buy. So don't only *ask* for referrals, introductions, and recommendations; be sure to *follow up* and let the person know what happened. This is a networking best practice no matter the outcome. If you didn't get the job, maybe they can help you get feedback so you can nail the next one (or keep you in mind for a future role); if you did, then you're the bearer of good news!

Even if you don't know anyone directly, once you start turning on the networking spigot, chances are strong that someone you know will know someone. Since you're going after people you don't already know (i.e., 1st-degree connections), it's good to be a bit more targeted now. Specifically, we recommend finding a 2nd-degree connection who really nails both sides of the "Ideal Referral" Venn diagram, based on some quick network- and profile-sleuthing:

- *People Who Want to Help:* If possible, it would be great to have someone who will really advocate for you. So look for 2nd-degree connections in which your mutual connection is someone who knows you well and will be excited to go to bat for you.

- *People Who Can Help:* Assuming you have at least a couple of 2nd-degree connections to choose from, go after the ones who have the functional fit and seniority to help you most. While any referral is better than none at all, some referrals do count more than others. First, if the insider is on the specific team you want to join (e.g., a Disney Imagineer), they'll hold more sway than someone who's distantly related (e.g., Pixar Animator). Second, if they're a well-respected leader on that team (e.g., a Manager or above), they'll have more say than someone who merely interned there for the summer.

2. Start with your mutual connection. Don't make the rookie mistake of immediately reaching out to the target employee. As tempting as that might be, think about how it would feel from their perspective: "Who's this random person reaching out?!" We all have an innate wariness when it comes to dealing with strangers. But there's one other human phenomenon that's even more powerful: social proof. This is our tendency to trust anyone or anything when it's recommended by our friends. (It's the reason why politicians ask people to put signs on their lawn, or why Facebook incessantly shows you what your friends like.) And it's the reason why an introduction from your mutual connection almost guarantees you'll get through. You are leveraging your contact's credibility to help build your own relationship with the target. So always start with outreach to that shared connector when plugging into your 2nd-degree network!

3. Ask for an intro. Once you've identified the very best mutual connection, send them a message like this:

> Hi Himanshu,
>
> Hope all's well with you. Might you be willing to introduce me to Selena Zhang? I'm thinking about applying for a job on her team at Disney but want to make sure it's a good fit.
>
> Thanks so much in advance!
>
> —Daria

Let's first assume this person knows you well and likes you. In this case, they'll be able to make an intro that's the digital equivalent of a red carpet ("Daria is one of the very best people I've ever worked with—any team would be lucky to land her!").

But what if you're unable to find such a perfect mutual connection? Perhaps your connector has only known you for a little while, knew you a while ago but not recently, or has never worked with you at all. In that case, do a little more of the heavy lifting yourself to ease the weight off their possibly reluctant shoulders. Try sending a message like the following:

Hi Himanshu,

Hope all's well with you. Might you be willing to introduce me to Selena Zhang? I'm thinking about applying for a job on her team at Disney but want to make sure it's a good fit.

If you're okay to do so, I've included a message below that you can just forward over and cc me on.

Thanks so much in advance!

—Daria

<<<Message to Forward>>>

Hi Selena,

I recently came across your profile on LinkedIn and was so fascinated by all the incredible things you've done. In particular, I'd love to learn about your experience in Imagineering at Disney, as I'm considering applying for a role on the team.

That said, I know you must be incredibly busy right now. But please let me know if you have even ten minutes to chat in the next week so I can learn from your expertise.

Thanks for considering!

—Daria

Now your mutual contact need not compose a world-class introduction. Instead, she can spend just five seconds brokering the connection with a tight and focused pre-scripted message. And she'll still get all the karmic glory of doing a good deed for both you and her friend (by potentially helping them fill out their team)! Easier for her, helpful to the target contact, better for you—what's not to like?

4. Convert an intro into a referral. Even with a warm introduction, it can be a bit much to ask your new contact for a referral right off the bat. So it's best to set up a quick chat, as we saw with alumni in Chapter 3 (see page 78). Be sure to ask questions that get them talking about their experience. A convo can also help you understand the opportunity and confirm your own interest.

You might ask:

- *How did you make the decision to join this company?*

- *What do you love about it?*

- *What do you hate about it?*

- *Would you make the decision to join again if you had it to do all over?*

If you like what you hear, follow up with this natural segue into referral mode. You might say:

Thank you for sharing your very helpful insights. Based on them, I'm excited to apply for a job here! The way you described the camaraderie and focus on excellence resonated with what I'm looking for. If you were in my shoes and wanted to get the best shot at an interview, what would you do?

This question will frame your burgeoning relationship positively by demonstrating that you were listening and learning from their expertise. It also shifts the relationship into an even higher mentoring gear (i.e., "if you were in my shoes . . . "). That in turn opens the door for them to be both generous and candid about the importance of a referral. If they don't bring referrals up directly, you can always prompt them to think about it by saying:

That's awesome advice! One last question: I've heard that referrals matter a lot to recruiters. Is that the case here? How does that process work at your organization?

The second question is meant to directly probe at the company's specific referral policy, since they can differ firm to firm (some even disallow referrals if you've already applied online).

And now, without being pushy or rude, you've found an internal ally who is ready to go to bat for you and boost your chances of an interview tenfold!

Behold, the Power of Two Degrees!

Putting 2nd-degree connections at the center of your purposeful networking efforts can pay off in a major way. The best way to appreciate the enormous potential of such an approach is to see it in action.

Our trainee, Emily Park, had previously been reluctant to make any asks of her connections. She didn't particularly enjoy in-person networking and lacked a playbook for doing so as a PhD researcher of intracellular cancer drug delivery. But she eventually got over her hesitation and got big results:

> *"I found a company on LinkedIn whose work was really interesting to me, so I looked up their employees to see if I was connected with any of them. I found out that the CEO of the company was actually connected with my former colleague. So I got introduced to the CEO via LinkedIn message [from our shared connection]. And after a few days, I received a reply from the CEO and was invited for an interview!"*

Way to go, Emily! Where traditional relationship-building methods can be intimidating, LinkedIn opens up a world of new methods and possibilities. Her experience goes to show how 2nd-degree networks and a bit of bravery really can empower anyone to access opportunity. As Emily says, "Don't be afraid to reach out to LinkedIn members who you aren't connected to. There are so many people who are willing to help—you've just got to give it a shot."

Option #3: Get a Referral from an Alum

If you don't have any 2nd-degree connections at your desired organization, fear not—alumni referrals are the next best thing. After all, many an alum received help from someone who came before them. If so, they'll be much more likely to want to return the favor. It's one of the most important parts of higher ed: You're part of a lifelong community. We always respond to lend a hand to students and alumni of any age and sub-school within our larger alma maters. So let's tap into that alma mater love to turbocharge your career.

1. Apply the School filter. First, select your target company to identify current employees, then click the "All Filters" button. You'll be using these search filters in ways that surprisingly few users know about (and that don't require LinkedIn Premium or Recruiter to utilize). But now *you* do, so let's make the most of them.

Scroll down to the School section, where you can specify your alma mater(s). If you've attended more than one school (even for a short amount of time or for, say, a certificate program), be sure to check off all of them to guarantee full coverage of your multiple alumni networks. Even if you attended just a single school, check to see if there are multiple school listings (e.g., Texas A&M and Texas A&M Mays Business School) and then select them all. Just begin typing "Texas" and LinkedIn's type-ahead will suggest other affiliated schools to add. While LinkedIn counts these listings as separate

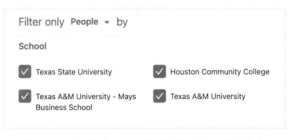

Be sure to include every institution you attended, and every sub-school within those, in your search.

schools (and we know this is a bit confusing), you should feel open to reaching out to any alum across the board, no matter which degree or which department is printed on their parchment!

2. Identify the perfect alum. You may have even more alumni to choose from than 1st- or 2nd-degree connections, so selecting the right person to target is that much more important. As noted previously, the ideal referrer is someone who works on the specific team you'd like to join because they will have far more sway with the hiring manager. Alternatively, they should at least have connections with several of those team members, indicating that they may work closely together. So here's an extra search hack to find the exact right person:

a) Go back into "All Filters."

b) Scroll down to the Title box.

c) Enter your desired team/title (e.g., Marketing, Imagineer):

Title

Imagineer

Just like that, you now have a list of people who *want* to help you (i.e., alumni), filtered for people who *can* help you. (Our trusty Venn diagram, back in action!)

3. Get their email. So far we've focused on reaching out to people you already know. Whether you send them a message on LinkedIn or to their email address, there's a pretty darn good chance you'll hear back. But now we're about to reach out cold to total strangers, so let's use some more advanced techniques. Specifically, you should understand that LinkedIn messaging is an imperfect channel. Following the outreach templates in this book—particularly those that emphasize shared affiliation and connections, flattery, and a request for an informational interview—will increase your odds of garnering a response. Still, your message might not have its intended impact for any number of reasons.

For instance, your contact might have signed up for LinkedIn with a company email address—but has since left that company and so no longer gets notified about messages. Or perhaps they only check LinkedIn a few times a year (members are most active on the site when they're job-seeking or job-filling). Finally, your contact— mistakenly, and to their own professional detriment—might paint all of LinkedIn's emails with a broad brush and mark them as spam, or has altered their settings so messaging notifications don't get sent to their email.

Here's some extra motivation from college student Joey M. to aggressively reach out to alumni:

"Don't be afraid. You'd be surprised by how many people are open to have a conversation with you and connect with you, especially alumni."

So your contact's LinkedIn inbox may not always be the ideal venue for your message, but which inbox do you think is a total slam dunk? That's right, the one they check 100 times per day and stay on top of like their life depends on it: their work email inbox. The only one they're paid to check!

There's only one problem—how do you find it? Here are a couple methods:

- Look up their email address in your school's proprietary alumni directory. If you're not sure how to access that, just contact your Alumni Office.

- Check out the website Hunter.io. Their Email Finder tool scours the web to identify the right email pattern for every organization in the world and can even give you the address for a specific person.

4. Send a message. Once you've found the perfect alum *and* their email address, here's the kind of message you want to send them. Focus on what you have in common and how much you can learn from them (aka, good old flattery):

Subject: Advice for a fellow UCF grad?

Hi John,

Hi from a fellow UCF grad! I came across your profile and was amazed by all the impressive things you've done. In particular, I'd love to learn a bit about your experience on the Imagineering team at Disney, as I'm considering applying for a role there myself.

That said, I know you must be incredibly busy right now. But I'd love to pick your brain for just ten minutes in the next week or two.

Thanks for considering!

—Daria

Then you're off and running to build a rapport and relationship with this alum, planting the seed for a future referral. (And word to the wise: *Next* week is always better than this week!)

Option #4: Get a Referral from a Former Colleague

At this point, it should be abundantly clear that the referral game is all about commonality: What do you share with people on the inside? Here's yet another linkage to explore. Consider other groups of which you've been a member—for example, your past employers.

As powerful as a shared alma mater is, a connection based on shared experience—on "Hey, I know what it's like to be in the trenches back at X organization"—can often be just as effective. And luckily, LinkedIn makes it super easy to find these former colleagues who are now at your dream employer. (It's a common occurrence if you're looking to stay within the same industry.) Here's how.

1. Apply the Past Companies filter. Again, once you've clicked the number of employees from the Company Page, click on the "All Filters" button. This time, scroll down to the Past Companies section and choose all the organizations where you've worked in the past.

To be clear, this search will produce people with whom you have a shared *former* employer. Just like with schools, this is another blast from the past that can serve as connective tissue. You're tapping into two strong parts of the human psyche: team-signaling and nostalgia.

2. Send your perfect contact the perfect message. Just like before, pick the ideal contact based on proximity to your dream job and then send them a highly targeted message:

> Hi Mia,
>
> Thank you for your service. I recently came across your profile on LinkedIn and, as a fellow National Guardswoman, was so impressed by all the incredible things you've done. In particular, I'd love to learn about your experience on the Imagineering team at Disney, as I'm considering applying for a role there myself.
>
> That said, I know you must be incredibly busy right now. But I'd love to pick your brain for just ten minutes in the next week or two.
>
> Thanks for considering!
>
> —Daria

Option #5: Get a Referral from a Fellow Volunteer

What if you're new to the workforce? Or perhaps you don't have an alma mater? What kind of commonalities can you possibly identify? Well, as with all referral efforts, don't be afraid to think big: What other kinds of meaningful pursuits matter to people outside of their work and school?

Research shows that people often see their volunteer experience as even more meaningful than their paid work. Hirers are no different. When we worked at LinkedIn, we interviewed recruiters and hiring managers; more than half said that they evaluate and consider both kinds of experience as *the same*. If you can find employees who volunteer for similar organizations or causes as you do, you're likely to find something deeply important in common. Here's how:

1. Search for your volunteer organization. Plug in an organization where you volunteer (or even where you *might want* to volunteer and are a genuine fan of) and click the number of employees. LinkedIn's search engine scours a user's entire profile—including the Volunteer Experience section—so it can help you track down like-minded peers on the inside.

2. Reach out with a values-focused message. In addition to picking a contact based on how close they sit to your desired team, be sure to engage them with a focus on your shared values:

> Tyreke,
>
> Hi from a fellow Habitat for Humanity volunteer! I found your profile and was so impressed by all the amazing things you've done. In particular, I'd love to learn about your experience on the Imagineering team at Disney, as I'm considering applying for a role there myself—and am curious how Disney's values align with the ones that have drawn me (and you!) to Habitat.
>
> That said, I know you must be incredibly busy right now. But I'd love to pick your brain for just ten minutes in the next week or two.
>
> Thanks for considering!
>
> —Daria

A View into Profile Views

" **I** 'm afraid that people can see I've viewed their profiles." This is something we hear often with our clients. We get it . . . sorta. Here's the thing: LinkedIn is not a social network. It is a professional platform that happens to layer on social elements in ways that are truly helpful. Mutual profile-viewing and cold outreach are vital parts of network-building and LinkedIn's relationship economy. This is accepted and common practice and adheres to site etiquette.

If someone from your target employer, especially a potential hiring manager, has viewed your profile for a job you've already applied to or been referred for, that's a signal of their potential interest. (Or, if it's been a week of radio silence since they viewed it, you may want to ping them.) But you'll never know they did so if you don't allow others to see that you've viewed *their* profiles. (Here's how: In your "Settings & Privacy," click on "Visibility" and "Profile Viewing Options," then select "Your name and headline.") It goes both ways!

So try your best to quiet your fear around the visibility of profile views—it's the new norm.

Option #6: Get a Referral from . . . Anyone!

Now, you may be thinking, "Omar and Jeremy, these are all great tips for a company the size of Disney. But my dream organization only has fifty staffers. How am I ever going to get a referral when there are so few people to give 'em?"

No worries! An enterprising student taught us the following method when we worked at LinkedIn. As you'll see, it allows you to strike up a conversation with any employee at any organization, no matter the size:

1. Start with the company directory. Just like before, begin by pulling up the list of all the employees at your dream employer. But this time, avoid the temptation to start reaching out cold.

2. View profiles. Skim the Headlines of people in the search results and start clicking on the profiles of everyone you're interested in connecting with. While this may feel like pure professional voyeurism, trust us that your recon mission will pay dividends shortly.

3. Wait—then check. Having completed your initial round of profile views, sit back and wait to harvest the fruits of your labors. LinkedIn is unique among social networks in that it lets you see who's viewed your profile. By viewing others' profiles, you're professionally winking—and are therefore much more likely to be viewed by them in turn. This is the most popular feature on all of LinkedIn for a reason! So wait for forty-eight hours to give your "clickees" time to see you've viewed them, then click on "Who viewed your profile" from Your Dashboard. You can then identify any employees at your desired organization who've viewed your profile.

> **Your Dashboard**
> *Private to you*
>
> ## 830
> Who viewed your profile

4. Reach out. Now that you know who's intrigued by your profile view, send them a connection request with a message:

> Hi Raj,
>
> Just noticed that we checked out each other's profile this week! I know your time must be tight but would you ever be up for a quick conversation about your experience? I'd love to learn from the decisions you've made in your impressive career.
>
> Thanks!
>
> —Daria

And then, just as we saw in the previous sections, once you have them on the phone, on video, or sitting across from you in a coffee shop, you can build the relationship that naturally evolves into a referral opportunity. That's truly a win-win; not only do you get a shot at your dream job, but your referrer gets internal accolades and a juicy bonus!

Networking = Finding Commonality

One note before we go any further: We've covered the concrete ways that custom-built LinkedIn search tools help you forge connections. But zooming out a bit, let's acknowledge that there's infinite fodder for personal connection.

Networking is all about finding or creating commonality, and we've really only scratched the surface. There is no substitute for a thorough profile review when you find a person worth connecting with, whether as a potential referral or just someone to learn from. Their profile might contain all sorts of other information—from stuff they've written to awards and achievements they've won, from posts they've created or engaged with to "interests" (companies, groups, and influencers they follow) and even their horizontal background image. All of these are possible ways in—to your network, a conversation, and ultimately, an authentic connection.

Here's Omar's longtime background image. It's a values-indicator. If you were reaching out to him, how might you customize your message to make sure it lands?

Become Your Own Headhunter

You now have the techniques to get a referral at any organization in the world, irrespective of whom you know personally. Next, let's look at another key focus for your network: reaching out to hiring managers themselves. This is a next-level technique to *really* take matters into your own hands. And how do you do it? By becoming your own headhunter.

To truly grasp the power of headhunters, let's break down that illuminating chart from page 168 some more. You, our eagle-eyed reader, may have noticed an outlier: agencies. How

HIRES BY SOURCE TYPE

EMPLOYEE REFERRALS	40%
CAREER SITES	21%
JOB BOARDS	15%
AGENCIES	5%
OTHER	19%

are 2 percent of applicants using them to land 5 percent of all the jobs? That may seem like small potatoes, but whereas most other application channels like job boards are highly inefficient, agencies seem to be doubling your odds.

The answer lies in the same phenomenon that drives the success of referrals: *People like to hire people they know.* And just as referrals turn an outside candidate into an insider, agencies turn a random applicant into a hand-picked heir apparent. So how do they do that? Well, here's what agencies really are: headhunters. In other words: finders and poachers of talent. And while that label may have negative connotations, hiring managers sometimes turn to headhunters to solve their problems. These outside talent scouts can track down great talent, pronto (since they're not juggling dozens of other searches like internal recruiters). So even if it means paying them a sizable commission of 15–20 percent of a new hire's salary, their ability to deliver solid results can be totally worth it for the employer.

Now this is all well and good from a highly experienced candidate's perspective. And if you followed our profile optimization tips in the Positioning step, your profile will stand out to headhunters just as much as it will for internal recruiters. But headhunters won't give you the time of day if you're not an *Ultra*-Obvious Candidate. That's because they're ultrarational—they only get paid if their hiring manager client chooses one of their candidates. No headhunter is going to waste even a second pursuing non-obvious candidates when they could just put forward slam-dunk candidates who can do the job in their sleep and who are a guaranteed path to getting paid.

So if you're just starting your first career or looking to change paths, are you totally out of luck? Nope! You'll just need to make your own luck—by becoming your own headhunter.

Think about the essential function that a headhunter plays: reducing the applicant noise for a hiring manager and helping them focus on just the best candidates. Could *you* also do that for a hiring manager? You bet. All that's required is a little boldness—and a direct outreach. Let's look at two paths to make it happen.

Getting in Touch with a Specific Hiring Manager

After first applying to a job (ideally one that was posted recently), you need to identify the specific hiring manager for that role. Luckily, with your superior LinkedIn sleuthing skills, you'll be talking directly to your future boss in no time. Here's how.

1. Understand the hierarchy. Just like a headhunter, you need to figure out who's in charge of hiring before you can make your case. So start by pulling up a list of the people on your desired team. For example, if you're pursuing that Imagineer role at Disney, you'll want to check out everyone who has those terms on their profile using "All Filters" in Advanced People Search:

Title	Company
Imagineer	Disney

2. Find the right person. Once you have a list of insiders on your desired team, check out their titles to get a sense of who's in charge. In our example, while there might be lots of individual Imagineers, there may be only one Principal Lead (or whatever leadership verbiage your target company employs). While those other folks may be involved in interviewing and deciding who gets hired, the Manager, Director, or Lead will likely be the hiring manager.

3. Reach out with a painkiller. With your future boss identified, try to snag their email address via the Hunter.io technique outlined on page 186. When you're ready to reach out, avoid the trap of focusing on *your* own needs ("I'd love to work for Disney!"). Instead, put yourself in the hiring manager's shoes and empathize with *their* needs ("I have so much to get done and so few people to do it!").

Now, don't just try to guess what those needs are. They've already done the hard work of listing them out for you right on the job description! Although reviewing these ten to twenty bullet points might sometimes feel like deciphering hieroglyphics, they're actually a cry for help: the pain of the hiring manager, converted into the specific skills and responsibilities they crave.

So take those pain points and make yourself the painkiller, the Advil to your hiring manager's existential headache. For example, imagine that you saw these two bullet points on your desired job description:

- *Generate new creative ideas based on a deep understanding of audience desires and insights*

- *Work cross-functionally with engineers, designers, and programmers to bring ideas to fruition*

In that case, here's the kind of email you might want to write to the hiring manager:

Subject: Prospective Imagineer with Insights + Engineering Experience

Hi Luisa,

I just came across your job listing for a new Imagineer—and know that finding someone who can understand both audiences and engineers is a tough combination.

That said, this is exactly what I've done throughout my career! For instance:

As a psychology major at UCF, I've conducted three separate studies into consumer satisfaction—including what audiences crave and how to deliver massive delight. And I shared these with a friend who works at Universal Studios as they were planning their annual calendar of events.

As the Head of Fundraising for our Habitat for Humanity chapter, I was responsible for organizing our biggest charitable event, the Let's Build a Home Golf Tournament. This meant collaborating with a team of engineers from our College of Engineering + Computer Science to develop mind-blowing special effects. Working closely together, we designed seven new experiences that raised more than $20,000—a new record.

So I'd love to apply those same skills to Imagineering—both to understand Disney's amazing customers and then to translate those insights into incredible new experiences.

Of course, I know you must be very busy right now. But I'd love to pick your brain for just ten minutes in the next week or two on how I can support your team's needs.

Thanks for considering!

—Daria

Can you spot how Daria has woven in specific examples aligned to the job requirements in the posting?

Why You and the Hiring Manager Should Be BFFs

We know what you're thinking: "Fellas, wasn't it enough for me to win over the recruiter, the LinkedIn algorithm, and the ATS? Now you're telling me there's *someone else* I also have to worry about?"

Yeah. Sorry about that. But among all the gatekeepers standing between you and a great job, the hiring manager is the one who's the most likely to fight for you. Here's why.

Recruiters, unlike hiring managers, may be the "face" of the hiring company, but they're ultimately mercenaries. Instead of being committed to a specific role, they work to fill multiple roles simultaneously. And then as soon as they help staff fill a given role, they skedaddle—meaning that even if the new hire ultimately is a disaster, they're long gone by the time the truth emerges. They simply have less incentive to find a truly perfect candidate, which is why they're happy to settle for someone who merely looks like an Obvious Candidate and then move on.

The hiring manager, however, bears all the consequences of the hire. Remember, this person would be your future boss. They're the one who will have to train you, cover for you if you ramp up slowly, put you on a probation plan if you underperform, fire you if you can't turn it around, and repeat the entire process to find your replacement. In other words, your success or failure on the job has a tremendous bearing on their own—and frankly, even affects how much they like their own job!

That perfect alignment of incentives between their need for an all-star employee and your ability to deliver is why a hiring manager can be your best friend in the selection process. So as daunting as it may feel to reach out to yet another stakeholder, just know that if there's a single insider you truly want to win over, it's gotta be the hiring manager!

4. Close the deal. If the hiring manager responds, take a moment to consider what an amazing coup this is: You've just gone around the formal, mass application process that most others go through (those job boards and career sites with low rates of return), the ATS, *and* the recruiter! Instead of battling your way through those gate-keepers, you now have a clean shot on goal—you'll be communicating directly with the person who holds your fate in their fingertips. That's a *massive* advantage.

Now that you're corresponding with the person making the decision, keep them interested with a light-touch response about your eagerness to chat. When you get the interview (even an informational interview is an interview!), make the most of it by first emphasizing your competence. Always focus on how you can come in and hit the ground running. No hiring manager has the time to fully train or hand-hold their reports. So the more you can pitch a specific vision of what you could do on Day One

> Always project competence and warmth when communicating with a hiring manager.

(e.g., "I'd love to start with a study of Disney World visitors reporting a negative Net Promoter Score"), the more you'll be perceived as capable of alleviating the hiring manager's pain.

At the same time, project warmth; you'll want to make it clear that the hiring manager will *like* working with you. And the best way to do that is by asking good questions (e.g., "What have your best reports had in common?" or "What does success look like to you?"). Then demonstrate that you've been listening (e.g., "I love that your top teammates have been focused on building bridges to other teams—that's exactly what I did in my internship this summer . . . ").

Getting in Touch with Any Hiring Manager

As smooth as your LinkedIn job search skills become, there may still be a great role or two that slips by. To make sure that you're getting first dibs on *all* the very best jobs out there, there's one more search you'll want to run. But it's not for jobs—it's for hiring managers.

After years of hiding in the shadows behind recruiters, hiring managers are starting to raise their hands on LinkedIn. Why? Well, for the same reason that they choose to engage with headhunters in the first place: "Good enough" isn't enough. Sure, their internal recruiting teams will eventually find them someone decent. But now that LinkedIn has democratized the search for talent, opening nearly a billion resumes to anyone, hiring managers aren't content to sit on the sidelines anymore. Instead, they've started getting savvier about using their LinkedIn Headline space to fill their needs:

Erin (Fenton) Casale 🔊 · 1st
Head of Education Customer Success @ Qualtrics - I'm Hiring!

The great news for job seekers is that any info on LinkedIn is both searchable and totally fair game. (While some of this hiring-manager behavior may be mere chest-puffing, they can't be upset if you reach out—they're inviting that!) So here's how to take advantage of this awesome new signal to find your future boss:

1. Search for the signal. Start with an advanced People search for "hiring." While this may turn up some false positives, it will also give you access to all the variants that hiring managers use to signal their interest (e.g., "I'm hiring!" or "We're hiring").

2. Filter for function. With millions of results, you want to start by filtering for the specific roles you're excited about. You can do this via the Title search under Keywords in "All Filters." For example, if you want to pursue a marketing role, plugging in "Marketing" will turn up hiring managers from "Marketing Manager" and "Director of Marketing" to "VP of Marketing" and "Chief Marketing Officer":

3. Filter for fit. Now you've narrowed your search to just hiring managers who align with your professional interests. But feel free to cut the list further by other considerations, including Location, Industry, and even Company. Just click those filters, also under the "All Filters" tab, and then slice and dice away:

4. Get more info. Once you've found the exact right hiring managers, check out their individual profiles to learn more about them and identify the specific roles they're looking to fill:

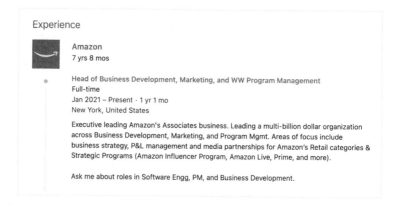

Hiring Managers: Cheat Codes for the Job Search

When you're getting nowhere with applications and recruiters, reaching out to a hiring manager can instantly change the course of your career. Check out Alfred Sogja's story:

> "As a first-generation college grad, I didn't realize that the odds were stacked against me when I applied to consulting firms. However, I discovered that people on LinkedIn are willing to help if you reach out with a strong interest in learning, first and foremost.
>
> In my case, I found people at my dream company, Deloitte, and reached out cold with a really targeted message. The person I reached out to turned out to be a hiring manager at the firm—and he ended up hiring me!"

Alfred G. Sogja · 2nd
Aspiring Strategy and Operations Professional | Passionate about Entrepreneurship + Human Capital
New York, New York, United States · Contact info

Try to see job-searching for what it really is: a really, really hard game. While you might run into a ton of obstacles, be a savvy player and find those smart strategies for success. And one of the smartest is to avoid those obstacles altogether by going straight to the hiring manager!

5. Make your case. Once you know about the specific role, it's time to put everything you've learned together to make your case. Grab their email via Hunter.io, send them a personalized painkiller note, and be sure to mention anything you have in common (e.g., a shared connection, alma mater, past employer, or even similar volunteer experience). When in doubt, check the Highlights section at the top of their profile for a quick summary of what you share:

And just like that, you've skipped those two common job-seeker complaints:

- "Getting hired is all about luck."

- "I feel like my career is basically out of my control."

Instead, you can manufacture your own luck and take control of your own career destiny.

Networking Amid the Inequities of Hiring

As much as we believe in (and have witnessed) the power of LinkedIn as The Great Opportunity Democratizer—namely, by allowing you to connect with just about anyone around the world—the sad reality is that hiring processes are still rife with discrimination.

Take something as basic as your name: Research has shown that just having a "white-sounding name" on your resume makes one 50 percent more likely to get an interview versus a perceived Black candidate with the *exact same* credentials. And here's an even more sobering stat: A meta-analysis of studies like the one above now shows that there's been absolutely no reduction in discrimination against Black candidates since as far back as 1989.

Of course, discrimination isn't limited to race. Other real-world experiments have shown that LGBTQ+ applicants face similar levels of resume discrimination. And women face discrimination at the resume-and-profile review stage in general—recruiters are on average 13 percent less likely to click a woman's profile in LinkedIn Recruiter search results. (It's even worse in traditionally male-dominated fields, like sales and STEM.) In fact, the effect is so pervasive that resume reviewers rate female candidates as deserving of less mentorship and lower salaries. And then there are the many, many job seekers who intersect across these and other identities, adding layers of uncertainty.

With such ferocious headwinds, it's no wonder that many job seekers who feel like outsiders throw up their hands in frustration. But if this describes you, there are three things you can do to wrest some power back in a flawed and unfair system.

Shaheen Sharif, a successful sales leader, fears the consequences of not "fitting in":

"The sales profession is a white, male-dominated profession. In my experience, the social atmosphere revolves around drinking and I am a bit of a lightweight. As a candidate and at times an employee, I'm also afraid I'm being judged and discriminated against because of my Muslim religion. There's a lot of fear and misconceptions about Islam."

1. Take advantage of every possible advantage.

Discrimination is infuriating because it puts you at a disadvantage before you even get to the starting line. While unfair hiring practices (and society itself) will take time to improve, there are clear things you can do now to gain an extra advantage. They include the key techniques of this chapter:

- *Get that crucial referral.* As the Jobvite data from the start of this chapter shows, you're more than ten times more likely to get hired as a referred candidate than by applying cold through a job board.

- *Get in direct touch with the hiring manager.* An agency-introduced candidate is more than twenty times more likely to get hired than someone who applies through a job board. Connecting directly with a hiring manager, as an agency would, can yield similar results.

And what do these two approaches have in common, especially as it pertains to discrimination? While hiring discrimination often operates at the knee-jerk, subconscious reaction level (e.g., reading names on a resume) where candidates are quickly stereotyped and dismissed, receiving a referral or getting to know the hiring manager forces employers to see you as a full person. Which is how hiring *should* work!

Sure enough, not only does a referral significantly increase your chances of getting your foot in the door, but it can even help open more doors down the line. For example, a Cornell study shows that Black candidates who are referred into an organization are 20 percent more likely to be promoted later, possibly because a recommendation by a trusted colleague works against some of the discriminatory tendencies that continue after being hired.

2. Be the change.

While individual candidates should advocate for themselves with every means available, we should all be advocates for more open networking and fairer hiring processes—no matter our political persuasions. Simply put, enabling equitable access to meaningful work *must* be a part of *everyone's* personal and professional mission.

So if you're currently employed (even, perhaps especially, if you're trying to leave) or on good terms with a previous employer, push your organization to adopt hiring practices that are actively antibias. LinkedIn, for its part, is putting a renewed focus on tools to help companies do just that, but it can't do it alone. For example:

- The drop-down search box in Recruiter now uses gender-neutral job titles to promote gender inclusivity:

- Anonymous resume and profile review is an important measure to mitigate the snap-biases we mentioned, and it's catching fire across industries. In LinkedIn's Recruiter settings, company administrators can now hide candidate photos and names for anyone (often hundreds or even thousands). The idea is to nudge evaluations more in the direction of merit, not optics:

- LinkedIn also now allows members to add demographic information—including race, gender, disability, military service, and more. The company says that it will protect privacy around this data. We have every expectation that, while this information may not be viewable by every member, it will at some point be viewable by recruiters, who will then be better equipped to directly search for more diverse candidates. Recruiters and search firms have been begging LinkedIn for this particular data set for years.

Knowing that is the likely future of how this personal info may be used, you can decide for yourself whether the potential risks outweigh the benefits. Our two cents: Employers writ large aren't going backward on diversity; it's only going to grow in import to them, especially as LinkedIn—their default tool—makes it easier to focus on it. So on balance, we recommend sharing this information on your profile.

3. Do something today.

Advocate for any and all organizations you are currently or have been a part of to utilize these tools. And don't stop there. Push them to bake equitable practices into their hiring DNA by focusing on what candidates can *do* and perspectives they bring—not just who they *are* (or appear to be).

We all benefit when networking and hiring is fairer and more meritocratic, and there is plenty of data proving that diverse teams perform better. But system-level change requires vocal and persistent champions. To that end, we also want to mention two anti-discrimination bills that deserve your backing:

- The CROWN Act prohibits hiring and workforce discrimination based on hairstyle and hair texture— again, like names, a tacit way of discriminating against specific groups. At the time of writing, the bill (or similar legislation) has already passed in fourteen states—an encouraging reminder of the inexorable march of progress. Help bring it to other states by signing the petition at thecrownact.com.

A Change Agent's Words of Wisdom for Job Seekers of Color

While writing this book, we got to meet Kirstyn Nimmo, founder of GOOD WORX, a consultancy that develops brands, campaigns, and workshops for companies that want to embrace diversity and inclusion. We greatly value her perspective and experience. Here is her advice for job seekers who are people of color:

- **Take up space.** Remember that you deserve the spaces you occupy, and that you are not responsible for creating environments that support your success.

- **Bring your full selves to work.** The world has been missing your perspectives and contributions for centuries, and they have tremendous potential to transform industries.

- **Break the system.** Remember that many of the infrastructures that currently exist were not created with people of color in mind, and some were created to intentionally exclude people of color. Some of these systems can be reformed into inclusive structures, but others are beyond repair. You have the opportunity to rebuild those systems into inclusive models that support the future.

- **Pitch the ideas or work that you feel is important if it doesn't yet exist.** You can accomplish this by leveraging the case for people, purpose, and profit, understanding that in many cases you are expanding a company's consumer base by better serving people of color, and stepping into your role as a catalyst for necessary change.

- **Be you.** No one else in the world can offer exactly what you bring to the table. Be confident in your ability and perspective, and don't be surprised if you literally change the world.

Kirstyn Nimmo · 1st
Founder & Managing Director at GOOD WORX Social Innovation
Consultancy, Public Speaker & Facilitator
Brooklyn, New York, United States · Contact info

GOOD WORX

**American University -
Kogod School of Business**

- The Equality Act would extend antidiscrimination laws that already protect people on the basis of race, sex, and religion to also include sexual orientation and gender identity. Learn more about the legislation and how to support it at hrc.org /campaigns/equality-act.

Combating Ageism in Hiring

It is illegal for American employers to discriminate against someone—an employee or an applicant—on factors such as appearance, race, color, religion, sex (including gender identity, sexual orientation, and pregnancy), citizenship, disability, and more. And the Age Discrimination in Employment Act also forbids age discrimination against anyone age 40 or older.

Less favorable treatment based on these factors—or even asking about them in interviews (e.g., "Do you plan to have kids?")—is impermissible. But does it happen anyway? Absolutely.

Ageism isn't sufficiently top of mind given how rampant it is in the workplace. Worldwide studies show that workers ages 45 to 60 are the "most overlooked" segment of the workforce—they rank the worst in the eyes of hiring managers on readiness and prior experience, driven largely by a perceived hesitation to learn new technologies and skills.

Every employer must lean much further in to combat ageism. But you can take steps to protect yourself. You might remove the year of graduation and scrub early jobs (especially if not relevant) from your profile; refine your story and achievements to ensure resonance; network aggressively; and get validated by peers. We want you to know that not only does your experience matter, but it is valued and needed. At times, you may just have to do a little extra convincing.

CHECKLIST: Networking

To make the most of the incredible power and reach of networking, here are the key activities to focus on.

For any job that you're serious about, get a referral by pursuing these options in order (ranked from most surefire to most risky):

❏ Search for 1st-degree connections at your most desired employers and ask someone you already know for a referral

❏ Search for 2nd-degree connections, ask your mutual contact to introduce you, and make it easy for them to do so by drafting the message

❏ Search for alumni from all your alma maters, filter by Title, and then track down their email address via your alumni directory or Hunter.io

❏ Check for connective tissue with current employees—such as schools, past companies, groups, or interests/causes

    ❏ Search for current employees who used to work where you've worked

    ❏ Search for current employees who volunteer where you've volunteered

❏ View the profiles of current employees, then see who views your profile in return

To get an extra relational edge and go right around the traditional gatekeepers (recruiters and the ATS), consider reaching out to hiring managers directly via these options:

❏ If you have a specific job in mind, try to identify the hiring manager by looking for senior staffers on your desired team

❏ Send these likely hiring managers a painkiller message focused on what they need

❏ If you just want to connect with hiring managers in your chosen field, search for "hiring" on LinkedIn; then filter down based on Title, Location, Industry, and/or Company

CHAPTER 7

Seal the Deal: Researching

Build your knowledge to land the job offer

Research is formalized curiosity.
It is poking and prying with a purpose.
—ZORA NEALE HURSTON

You've Gotten This Far . . .
Now Get Prepared!

Hopefully your networking (and all that exploring, positioning, and searching) has already paid off in the form of a referral—or even an interview. If so, congrats! But now you've got to turn that interview into a job offer. So . . . how do you prepare?

Well, it's time to do your more-than-due diligence. Adopt the mindset of a PhD researcher to get as much insider information as possible (and LinkedIn has a *ton*). This is your time to shine.

Kudos if you've managed to stand out to a recruiter as a potential fit. You're making progress, but it's still just *potential*. After all, recruiters and hiring managers make their selections based on a candidate's knowledge. Here's why: When multiple candidates have similar prior experience, education, skill sets, and connections into the firm—often the case in the final round of the interview stage—knowledge becomes your differentiator.

In this chapter, we'll first summarize *what* you need to know. Then we'll dive into *how* to attain that knowledge by employing specific strategies. We'll add some seriously useful advice on crushing a job interview and finish with bonus knowledge on vetting an employer once you've finally scored an offer.

And we should note, while we're talking primarily about real interviews here for an actual job, many of the same strategies apply for purely informational interviews, as well. And doing your research is also very useful in the exploration phase, as you focus— and vet—your list of target roles and companies. There's lots to gain in this Researching step, even if you're still feeling your way toward your dream job.

Three Types of Knowledge: Company, Industry, People

The most fundamental thing you must possess to win the job is knowledge of the role itself—and of how your own story fits into it. As you know well, employers assess candidates based on their skill sets, developed through work, volunteer experience, or coursework.

Sure enough, demonstrating this kind of specialization via "hard" skills (like those you show off through Skills Assessments on your LinkedIn profile) is a common way in, especially at entry- to mid-level positions. It's why there are many efforts to teach kids how to code, and online courses and boot camps that laser-focus on thoroughly marketable and employable skills.

But that's just a part of the equation—a minimum threshold to allay questions about whether or not you can perform the basic job duties. Indeed, there's a growing argument for generalization that focuses on the "soft" skills necessary to lead teams and organizations. Namely, those skills include continual learning and communication (both written and oral). So to nail your interview and land your dream job, you have to demonstrate your ability both to meet the job requirements *and* to tackle new and as-yet-unknown responsibilities. And you have to cite specific examples that show, not just tell. It takes solid knowledge to do just that.

So how did the world of work get here?

With the uncertainty and constant fluidity brought on by technology, automation, and globalization, the best employers increasingly want versatile, future-proof "chess pieces." Sure, they seek out candidates who know the requisite amount, but also those who can flex and grow as an organization's needs do. No one can say for sure what skills will be required of a Product Marketer in 2030, for instance, but they'd better be able to add value that algorithms can't (e.g., staying on top of industry trends, deeply understanding customers, and building real relationships with coworkers).

> **To nail your interview, it takes knowledge to show you can both meet the job requirements and tackle new responsibilities.**

In an interview, what this boils down to is articulating your own experience, your orientation toward constant growth, and your passions—all in tight alignment with the job description. First and foremost, you want to be seen as an Obvious Candidate with the knowledge to do a job for which there is an acute need. But you also have to show that you understand a hiring manager's unique pain points both now and looking forward—you can fill in a missing piece no matter what the puzzle ends up looking like.

Think of all this knowledge-building as *requirements* in a job description—they're that crucial! So we've categorized them for you:

Knowledge of the company *and* the industry: You speak the lingo and have a strong grasp of the company's and industry's cultural norms. You take pains to understand company strategy, and to show you can think bigger—and take on more—than the specific role you're interviewing for. You learn industry trends and competitors, and stay on top of their implications for the business.

Translation: Your goal with company and industry research is to convey that you are in fact not *really* an outsider. It's a bit squishy, but there's a vibe that every interviewer knows when they see it: It's a positive feeling a strong candidate imparts when they understand what the firm is all about; can articulate what makes them unique; and, most importantly, convey that they can hit the ground running without requiring significant ramp-up time.

Knowledge of the people: You get the team. You understand the players, the roles, and how they all work together. And you don't get asked to communicate and collaborate; you do so proactively. At every turn, with every level and department, you seek to make authentic human connections.

Translation: Recall that recruiters are risk-averse and want to get candidates in the funnel who seem to be a perfect fit. But once you're in that funnel, beyond showing you have the industry- and company-specific knowledge to look like a member of their team, you separate yourself from other serious candidates with human connection.

As we've said time after time, we must embrace—and use to our advantage—the reality that the new job search is not a meritocracy. (Don't get it twisted, it never was; it's just that now you can *do* something about it.) We speak from experience as hirers, coaches, and job seekers: A shockingly large part of the decision on who gets hired comes down to perceived fit with the team. This cements confidence—often even if a candidate is a stretch on the job requirements.

Fit comes from intimately understanding the people, before you even have a first conversation, and asking the right questions of them when you do. This "People Knowledge" starts with researching the recruiter and the interviewers, and finishes with frank conversations with others who know what it's really like to work there once you crush the inter-

A shockingly large part of the decision on who gets hired comes down to perceived fit with the team.

view and get an offer. (It's been said that you can't dislike someone once you know their story. This is true for interviewing as well!)

Now you know *what*. Time to learn *how*. So first let's look at the tools to really understand the employer you're in talks with.

Know the Company

What's the number-one mistake employers say candidates make? It's not a weak handshake or poor responses to interview questions. It's knowing embarassingly little about the company. But good news: That's completely avoidable. Here are a handful of great methods for understanding any company you want to work for.

Create Targeted Job Alerts

As we outlined previously in the Searching step, you should set up LinkedIn Job Alerts for the company, specific office location, and team or function that you're pursuing (see page 150). If you didn't do this already for the company at which you're interviewing, do it now! It will keep your fingers on the pulse of the company's priorities and needs.

Monitoring these alerts each morning in your inbox, even after you've secured an interview, will help you understand where the company is investing and what its biggest opportunities for growth are. This can be great stuff to drop in your interview responses or to sound more informed in the Q&A portion. For example, you can say, "I've noticed the company seems to be hiring a lot in marketing (or in Cincinnati) relative to other teams (or locations). This is interesting because in the last three years I've built a strong network of marketing connections here that could really be useful for a push like this."

Ignorance Isn't Bliss: A Cautionary Tale

Don't do what Omar did during his first two rounds of interviews at Apple: not knowing the (in this case storied) company well enough to realize that wearing a suit and tie was cultural anathema. Apple proudly started the casual work attire culture in Silicon Valley, and Omar—less than two years removed from his MBA and dressed to the nines—simply looked like an outsider. Luckily, the hiring manager liked him, and advised him to leave the tie at home (and throw on some jeans!) for his final round with the VP. He got the job.

Omar's lack of knowledge about the company continued into his first two weeks: After diligently taking notes in a four-day leadership meeting, he blasted those notes out to the entire team of dozens. Though that was a cultural norm at his previous employer, it wasn't at Apple—which is infamous for its secrecy. He got called into the principal's office (the boss's boss), got a stern reprimand, and promised to . . . fit in better.

You can avoid such mistakes. Research the company beforehand, not on the job; the time to learn to surf is when the tide is low, not when there's a tsunami! Indeed, conformity is not always pleasant, but it's often necessary to get hired. An essential purpose of researching a job is to determine for yourself whether that sort of conformity comports with your own values and expectations for a workplace. Don't blame yourself if a company's culture doesn't feel like the right fit for any reason; if that's the case, maybe it's time to cross that job off your list.

Review the Company Page

Here's a handy tip from an international MBA student whom we worked with on how to sequence your company research: The LinkedIn Company Page is invaluable in the research phase. Nearly *every* employer of all sizes and sectors, from start-ups and nonprofits to huge multinationals and government agencies, has a Company Page presence on LinkedIn. This is your new hub for learning company-speak; information on culture, hiring, and strategy; researching the latest jobs; and connecting to real people. Spend some time reading and getting a feel for things here. It will help you understand their identity, articulated in their own words (which will soon be *your* words).

Start by doing a simple search in the top navigation bar. As you search for any organization, suggested (standardized) options will appear in the type-ahead:

Our trainee Stehly is all about Company Pages:

"I use LinkedIn as a starting point when I am doing research on a company I will interview at. I browse through all the information on their page and then I navigate to their company website outside of LinkedIn."

A LinkedIn Company page is essential for employers to build their "talent brand." Know it well.

Now that you've landed on the Company Page, there are four things to do:

1. Read through it in its entirety. Your goal here is to get a working knowledge so that you'll move beyond the basics in the interview. Keep a close eye out for how they talk about themselves and their key messages to both customers and prospective employees. Many an interviewer—especially the most senior—gets frustrated if they have to explain things about the company that are publicly available. (That's a quick way to end up in the "outsider" box.)

Click through every tab—especially the "Life" one. This is the primary place that LinkedIn instructs companies to market themselves as employers; believe it or not, firms pay to create and post this content to help them attract top talent. Check out the "People" and "Videos" tabs as well—they will give you inside looks into the culture and values.

Lastly, the "Jobs" tab shows openings, which are often listed first on LinkedIn before they're syndicated (i.e., pushed to other job boards around the web). And you can also sign up for company-specific job alerts while you're on the Company Page, if you prefer.

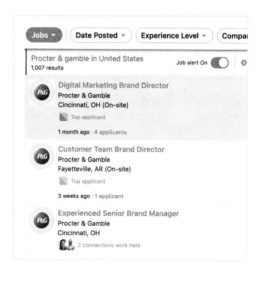

2. Find connections who work there (and, of course, can provide a referral). Part of what makes LinkedIn so helpful (and so widely preferred) is that it's not simply a job board or a place for employers to talk about themselves; it's the definitive *social layer* on top of the professional world. For instance, notice that when you're on a Company Page, LinkedIn makes it easy to find employees who work there. Just click the "People" tab. (It will look familiar to you if you've played around with the Alumni Tool, as we advised earlier.)

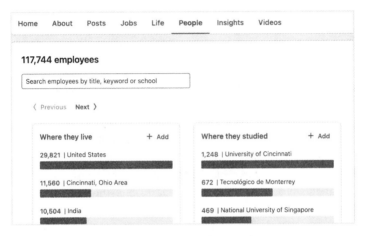

You can easily slice and dice employees of any company—just like you can with alumni—to focus your outreach.

You are using this information to find connections—or those invaluable 2nd-degree connections—to give you a sortable lead list of people who can get you in the door and/or provide insider expertise ahead of your interview. On the "People" tab, for example, why not filter by the school you attended for the people most likely to connect with you out of the blue?

And if you're still in informational interview mode, you can use this opportunity to work toward (and maybe even earn) a referral. As we saw in the last chapter, the referral system can differ by employer, so your target referrer may have different incentives. Therefore you must learn the unique referral processes for the places at which you most want to work. Make this a question you ask during informational interviews—as these folks may also end up being the contacts you are trying to "warm up."

Researching Workplace Diversity

Mike Montoya, whom we heard from previously on the topic of profile photos (see page 120), shares advice borne of being on both sides of the job market—as a hirer of diverse candidates and being one himself. In Mike's words:

My Experience as a Recruiter

As a national recruiter in the education sector, I have worked with thousands of candidates and hundreds of clients to find and hire exceptional individuals.

I often ask them to define what a diverse pool will include in their eyes. This is where this discomfort begins, and where a client's actual awareness of what diversity and inclusion means for their organization reveals itself. Advanced organizations have already done the hard work of looking inward at their history of hiring and retaining employees, uncovered their shortcomings, and are taking action. A fairly simple analysis can reveal where their organization excels and where they are lacking; it comes through in routine employee engagement surveys. If a client doesn't have one, that says a lot about where they are on the journey toward establishing and maintaining a diverse workforce.

During negotiations for a job you are a serious contender for, I recommend asking your prospective employer about the findings from their most recent employee engagement survey, and what the organization is doing to address any diversity and inclusion concerns that exist among current employees.

My Experience as a Job Seeker

Before I'm a professional recruiter, I'm a human—one who has been employed by a variety of organizations with varying degrees of inclusivity. Ultimately, I only want a candidate to accept a job with a client if they feel like it's in their best interest and they will be happy for at least a year, hopefully five. I have the same aspiration for myself. This has not always been the case for me. In fact, I spent five years doing work I loved in an organization whose judgment was that being gay was totally incompatible with all their core values. After this, I became much clearer and more conscious about the bare minimums that any future employer must have in place for me to even consider them as viable.

Here are my tactics:

- For large companies, check out the corporate equality index to learn more about their practices that support inclusive hiring and advancement.

- For smaller companies and nonprofit organizations, look for clear policy statements about equal opportunity hiring on their external position announcements that include protections for race, religion, sexual orientation, and gender.

- Look at employers who hire search firms for their senior-level hiring; I found it easier to suss out an employer's intentions with this third-party conversation.

- When I was twenty-six (circa 1998), I updated my resume to include my volunteer involvement with LGBTQ and Hispanic serving organizations. If an employer never asked about these activities, I didn't take them too seriously regarding their interest in inclusion.

"But it's 2022!" you might be saying. I agree, times are changing, and employment opportunities are improving for minorities. I encourage candidates to take some time and determine what they really want out of their employment experience.

- Do they want a very inclusive environment, where they may be one among many?

- Do they mind being, or is it exciting to be, a pioneer and a poster child for inclusion in an organization that is early in its journey?

- Do they want to wear their differences on their sleeve, or do they prefer more privacy and separation between their personal and professional life?

The summer of 2020, with all its unrest, opened the eyes of at least some employers. It all feels like they are a little late to the party, but I'm optimistic about the good intentions. As an employee, I would want a willing employer. That is: Willing to go on the journey of becoming more inclusive. Willing to learn and invest in and support their employees. Willing to see employees as people and as "talent" worth attracting, developing, and keeping long term.

3. View model profiles. Being able to sort employees also makes it easy to find people who are *currently in* the role you want (or at least a similar one). Viewing their profiles is super helpful because you'll learn more about what the job entails. Their own descriptions of their responsibilities and accomplishments will provide real-world suggestions for how to frame your own experience and skill set.

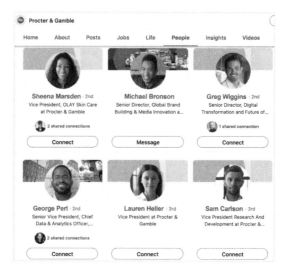

4. Let recruiters know you're serious about their company. Yet another separator of candidates is that they're truly passionate about the firm. Head over to your Settings, click the "Data Privacy" tab and then "Job seeking preferences." Toggle on the "Signal your interest to recruiters at companies you've created job alerts for" button:

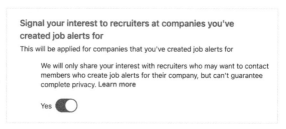

This is a little-known way to not only raise your hand to recruiters at a specific company, but to raise your whole arm.

After spending some time on the Company Page, be sure to check out the company's website (linked at the top of the page) and then sites like Glassdoor. Too many job seekers invert this sequence, failing to recognize that LinkedIn is the main place where HR departments give regular love to. (That's because they'll typically manage a LinkedIn Company Page whereas the company website will be the marketing team's responsibility.) This is the recruiting team's home page, so it should be your home base as things start to get hot and heavy.

Scour SlideShare

SlideShare.net is a company that LinkedIn acquired in 2012, and then sold off to Scribd in 2020. We like to describe it as "The YouTube for PowerPoints." It can be a rabbit hole, but skilled job seekers know to engage with it purposefully. You can find presentations, often compiled by consultants or MBA students, for tons of companies. They typically analyze the firm and sometimes their industry, espe-

Here's how Miguel, a job seeker in Europe, taps this resource:

"I use SlideShare to get brief summaries on the company, then gut-check it when I find profiles of insiders to talk to there."

cially in tech and consulting. Just search for the company at the top. It can help you quickly prepare and empower you with super-savvy insights. Other smart people have done the work for you!

One note of caution: Before leveraging (i.e., pawning off) these insights as your own, check the date when analyses were posted. It's an archive, so as you browse the site, make sure the information is current (within the last few years, depending on the industry)—or at least still relevant.

Search (and Get Fed!) Helpful Content

Here's another benefit of following a company: Company posts will start to show up in your news feed. Once using LinkedIn becomes a daily habit (do it!), this can be a helpful way to get the latest and greatest on the organization where you want to be. (In the next section of this chapter, we'll cover some other ways to train your news feed to serve you useful content for landing your dream job.)

Researching the company with these methods is how you begin acquiring the knowledge you need to impress your interviewers. When you combine it with research on the industry and the people, all that's left is to ace the interview and ensure it's the right fit once you do. Read on!

Know the Industry

Once you've gotten to know the company inside and out, it's time to expand your knowledge. Even if you're an industry veteran looking for bigger and better opportunities (or new job functions within it), landing an interview should be the strongest possible motivator to immerse yourself within the industry zeitgeist.

Remember, the more you can make yourself a safe choice, the more you improve your chances of getting the job. You do that by signaling, in every conversation, not just that you *want* to be a part of their industry—but that you already *are*!

Business author Seth Godin writes in his bestselling classic *Tribes: We Need You to Lead Us*, "A tribe is a group of people connected to one another, connected to a leader, and connected to an idea. . . . A group needs only two things to be a tribe: a shared interest and a way to communicate." In an interview, that shared interest is something you are passionate enough to be well-versed in. But communicating this interest effectively is heavily shaped by the industry and its unique lingo.

Surprise, surprise: LinkedIn is your go-to place for getting neck-deep in these industry waters. As you jump in, your main task is to teach LinkedIn's algorithm what kind of industry content is most useful to you. Teach it what you want to find and the algorithm will display more of it.

Let's look at how a well-curated feed can help you prepare for an interview.

Curate Your Feed

LinkedIn's algorithm will give you personalized industry-related information based on the content and people you choose to follow. To curate the content you'll need, start by using hashtags. For instance, define the industry as both the economic sector in which you want to work (e.g., "Finance") and the skill set ("Analytics") you need to do so, and follow as many hashtags as you can reasonably stay on top of. Just scroll down on your LinkedIn home page and keep your eye peeled for "Followed Hashtags."

You should also follow *every* market-leading company in the industry you're targeting—even if you don't want to work there, whether it's for geographic, fit, or work culture reasons. (Remember, you're permitted unlimited company follows, so don't be shy!) In part this is to show you're serious about the job transition, as these companies all appear at the bottom of your profile. But more importantly, for interview preparation, these firms share interesting content that's useful to absorb. These companies are the innovators (or simply the best-resourced) that both understand and shape industry trends.

A quick way to do this is to let LinkedIn help you. At the bottom of the aforementioned "Followed Hashtags" section, click "Discover More." You'll land on a page that consolidates suggested companies—and even people—to follow based on your other recent follow actions. (A tad creepy, perhaps, but useful—and we're all used to way creepier stuff with Amazon, Google, and Netflix reading our minds.)

You can also curate your feed based on the people you follow and connect with. (FYI, connecting with someone by default also follows them.) These are the folks online who can most help you build your knowledge of industries and job functions. It's all about what they share, react to, or reshare from a connection you don't (yet!) have.

Followed Hashtags

\# nowhiring
\# education
\# law
\# legalissues
\# lawandlegislation
\# data
\# bigdata
\# analytics
\# datamining
\# businessintelligence
Show more ⌄

Discover more

Following hashtags is indeed quite useful.

Naysayers sometimes knock LinkedIn for being an overly self-promotional place. But most of the time, the content that people share isn't noisy or boastful—or at least not *only* that. Posts often provide practical and varied insights into navigating the world of work—from trends in your space to opportunities that could accelerate your career.

The LinkedIn algorithm places extra import on certain types of content. First, it favors job postings that your connections share; if the job is interesting to you, you should definitely engage with that share to teach the algorithm to give you more of the same. (A simple "like" will do, and a click or reshare is an even stronger cue.) LinkedIn will also prioritize a piece of content that more than one of your connections have shared. Keep mental tabs on whether the site is regularly sharing from someone specific; this is probably an influential person you will want to follow yourself and potentially find a way to connect with directly.

In its tireless effort to lay claim to being the default location for professional content on the internet, LinkedIn has tapped thousands of "influencers" to author content on a variety of topics and industries. Some of these influencers have built massive followings on the platform, so they're motivated to continue sharing their unique insights. These insights are seldom republished elsewhere, so you can get an extra edge if you use LinkedIn to keep a finger on the pulse of what the innovators are saying. *Especially* as you prepare for interviews in a new industry or job function, we recommend spending a bit more time on the site perusing this kind of content regularly. Start by clicking the "Follow" button for those industry influencers, company leaders, or even the hiring managers whose minds you most need to peer inside.

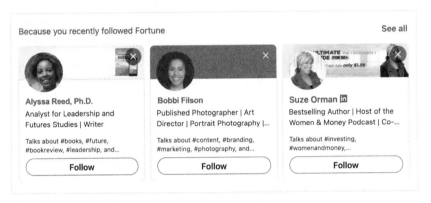

Following the right influencers is a good way
to shape the news you get on your home page.

Join Relevant Groups

LinkedIn Groups are communities where people with shared affinities (usually industries, industry associations, or alumni) can congregate online. To find Groups relevant to you, just start by typing a term in the search box (such as "Nonprofits Social Media" or "Women in Tech")—and then selecting the filter for "Groups."

It's also good to view profiles of people currently *in* the job you want, as well as the hiring managers for those jobs. Check which Groups they're in (at the bottom of their profiles under "Interests") and join them, too. You can see all the Groups you're a member of under "Work" in the top navigation bar.

Here are a few reasons why Groups are valuable to research-minded job seekers:

- **The Groups you join also show up on your profile.** It's an indication of seriousness—and a particularly good one if you're pivoting or trying to cement your experience.

- **Groups immerse you in the digital dialogue of your desired industry or function.** There are topical Groups that focus on skill-building; others skew toward identifying trends and sharing original opinions. Many focus on strengthening shared identity (i.e., alumni groups and companies). While not all Groups are equally useful or even active, start by joining the largest by member count for the industries and/or functions in which you most want to work. Then add a handful that are a bit outside or adjacent to your immediate interests (e.g., Product Managers vs. Product Marketing Managers). But if there's regular content being shared, no need to go too wild! You now have a valuable signal of membership on your profile.

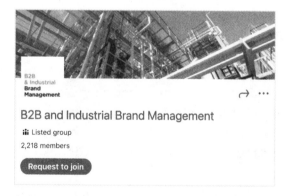

Niche groups can help you trend-spot and learn lingo.

- **Groups can be great connective fodder.** They're a quick way to identify specific people you should follow, give you profiles to browse, and even provide you with the rationale for a connection request ("I see that we're both a part of the Brand Manager group . . . "). There is also an element of exclusivity to some Groups. Most are public, but some are private; if you want to join the latter, just send a message with your request saying you're already either in this industry or trying to break into it.

To be sure, Groups are useful, but know that they're not nearly as valuable as they once were. Since its inception, LinkedIn has had a bit of a, shall we say, haphazard relationship with its Groups product. In its first decade of existence, Groups served as an "office watercooler" featuring broader and more diverse voices. It was one of LinkedIn's most active areas, with moderated discussion boards for users to share relevant content, keep tabs on what was happening, post job openings, and network together. Over time, though, Groups have been eclipsed by the more purpose-built tools that you've been mastering throughout this book. But Groups still serve a unique and helpful purpose in the Researching step!

Know the People

In our own experience as hiring managers, this cannot go without screaming from the mountaintops: You must review the LinkedIn profiles of every person on your interview panel *before* your interview! And if you weren't provided with this information, get scrappy. It's totally okay to ask the recruiter or HR contact—or whomever you *do* already know or have had any communication with—for the names of the expected interviewers. And even if you're only given titles, you can often identify your interviewers ahead of time just by searching for the specific title on LinkedIn (e.g., "VP of Operations at Tesla").

What About All That LinkedIn Spam?

We'll fess up: We're partially responsible for the, umm, bountiful number of emails you get from LinkedIn. Like any other marketer in the world, we wanted to drive eyeballs and clicks to our specific products, and . . . we got a little carried away. LinkedIn has since gotten better about coordinating these email sends so as not to overwhelm its members. For many, though, it can still be a lot.

In fairness, much of what LinkedIn pushes to you isn't spammy at all. You *want* to receive these kinds of notifications frequently: inbound messages sharing interest from recruiters, job alerts, and updates from companies you want to work at. Make sure you have an email address connected to LinkedIn that you check regularly rather than some old account gathering dust. In fact, LinkedIn may even block you from receiving new recruiter messages if you *don't* respond to recruiter messages within a certain time period, or turn off your "Open to Work" Bat Signal (see page 107).

As for the more spammy stuff, there's a lot you can do in LinkedIn's privacy and communications settings to change the what, where, and when of your notifications. You can, for example, toggle off certain kinds of communications completely, like birthdays and other network updates. Or set a preference to receive them weekly instead of daily.

Finally, a lot of the perceived noisiness of the platform comes from users themselves. If you find that specific contacts are constantly trying to sell or spam you (or worse, harass you), there's always the option to disconnect, unfollow, or block/report them. They'll disappear from your inbox and your feed. Bam! Instant spam-reducer.

So many candidates clearly fail to perform this most basic of steps. And yet it's the absolute bare minimum for interview prep in the digital age. You're seeking to understand the specific experiences and interests of your interviewer(s), with the goal of finding connective tissue on both a professional and human level.

Once again, put yourself inside the mind of a busy hiring manager. From their perspective, nothing is more maddening than an interviewee not checking out your LinkedIn profile. They don't want to have to go over the basics of their background when it's all readily available online. While an interviewer will usually start with the "tell me about yourself" question, they'd rather not waste precious time answering that question themselves!

It bears repeating: You MUST review your interviewers' LinkedIn profiles.

As a candidate, you should instead come prepared to demonstrate your knowledge of your interviewer's work and volunteer experiences, shared connections, passions and interests, schools, original articles, and group memberships. Be ready to ask intelligent and nuanced questions that cater to that manager—and show you've gleaned a sense of who they are.

You can dig even deeper into how they think and what's top of mind for them by reviewing their activity on LinkedIn: all their likes, comments, and posts. (Okay, it's perhaps just a *tiny* bit creepy, but remember that all this stuff is meant to be seen, after all.) These next-level insights aren't necessarily stuff to bring up in the interview itself—"I saw that you liked a post by your coworker . . . " may fall a bit flat—but it can give you Jedi insight on where their heads are at and what they find interesting. This is especially true for the hiring manager.

So for whom should you do this interviewer due diligence? Answer: everyone! This includes recruiters before a phone screen, or if an "interview" is purely informational or something you requested. Every interaction is a chance to impress. Informational interviews are, well, information-gathering, but they're also laying seeds for a referral and a "real" interview. Making that happen requires that you *know* an interviewer just as you would in an official interview. (In fact, while our focus in this chapter is on formal job interviews, in reality the lines are blurry. We make little distinction between "real" vs. "fake" interviews, or unofficial vs. official—they're *all* interviews!)

Priming an informational interviewer for a future referral also requires that the conversation feel substantive, not transactional. You're not relying on them to tell you things you can learn on your own about the people, the company, or the industry. Your goal is to establish an expectation of reciprocity. Once you make a connection, always be thinking what you can do for them and when. (Maybe being your referral ultimately *is* that thing; it'll get them a nice little bonus.)

While you're at it, especially when researching the hiring manager, don't just stop at LinkedIn! Google them, too. You may well land on talks they've given or articles they've written that will yield additional insights you can reference (with a dash of flattery!) and discuss together.

Crushing the Interview

Now you've researched your interviewers. Next up, let's investigate how to ace the interviews themselves. We'll draw upon seven interview fundamentals that stand the test of time:

1. Prepare for the "tell me about yourself" question. It will start most every interview in some version or another. So there is *zero* excuse for not having a concise and pointed answer to it. Do not wander.

Yes, it's a lazy question for an interviewer to ask. But it's a starting point, and you cannot be lazy with your answer. Interviewers are ascertaining your overall narrative and whether you can be crisp and compelling. From there, they'll jump as soon as possible into specific experience on your profile or resume, or perhaps get your thoughts on business problems they're facing. Don't expect the interviewer to ask you about all your best skills and experiences; the onus is on you to paint a beautiful picture they want to buy from the gallery. Even if—*especially* if—that artwork is a mosaic. Connect the dots for them right from the get-go.

2. First impressions matter. Did meeting your significant other's parents for the first time ever feel like a job interview? Yeah, there's a good reason for that. According to a study of 2,000 bosses by Undercover Recruiter, a third of interviewers know in the first ninety seconds whether or not they're going to hire a candidate. We humans tend to make rapid determinations of competence, whether right or wrong. Sadly, at the same time, many interviewees lack confidence. And that self-doubt is only amplified if you're interviewing via phone or video, when it's harder to read reactions or gauge if you're connecting.

The way to combat this is twofold. First, demonstrate your competence by being purposeful. Your narrative should be directed. When you talk about what you have done, use examples that are highly relevant for the job—everything else is noise. Second, exude warmth to make a human connection. As you prepare for an interview, think about the stories and pieces of your work or academic history that are most compelling *to you*: That passion will come through. These interview snippets will be like your emotional home base. Even if an interviewer keeps a stern poker face, genuine passion and excitement are irrepressible and contagious.

3. Avoid overly generic responses. A common interview pitfall is failing to litter your answers with concrete examples that show, not just tell, what you're capable of. Before the interview, think through how to make these examples malleable so you can insert them into the conversation almost irrespective of the question.

For instance, arm yourself with a few go-to stories in the "Problem-Action-Result" format that help shift a vague response into the specific. Focus your examples on the two most common types of interview questions: 1) a success/achievement you're particularly proud of (bonus points if it includes collaborating with or influencing others), and 2) a roadblock you overcame or tough decision you made. Again, you're aiming to bring up these examples even if you're not asked specifically to do so (i.e., "Tell me a time when . . . "). They hammer home that you can and already have performed the job duties.

These examples will also help you describe your experience so that you focus less on your past job responsibilities (what your role was) and more on your accomplishments (what you actually got done). Remember that this framing of achievements, not just duties, is vital on your LinkedIn profile, too.

4. Be deliberately—but not overly—self-promotional. An interview is only partly about making sure you're answering the specific questions you're asked. A savvy interviewee knows it's also an opportunity to drive home the right points in order to stand out and maximally strengthen their candidacy.

Indeed, an interview is not the time to be too humble. Don't stretch the truth, but when you give examples or talk about previous jobs, try to use "I" statements more than "we." If you don't, it can be difficult for the interviewer to discern your role within a team. After all, that's what they're trying to assess: you, not your coworkers.

5. Look for common interview questions online. They're often just a Google search away. There are shared documents and wikis that interviewees contribute to, and Glassdoor is also a solid source. LinkedIn also indexes a list of the most common interview questions (look under "Jobs," then click "Interview Prep").

And do not forget the irreplaceable value of an insider: Once you've built a relationship with someone on the inside, especially if they're in the same job function or part of the company you want to be in, it's fair game to ask them for general parameters on what you might expect in an interview. Or, depending on the depth and comfort level of the relationship, you might even ask for information on the interviewer themself.

6. The questions you ask can be as important as the questions you answer. The best interviews feel more like a conversation than a quiz show. Don't be so deferential that you're paralyzed to jump in with a well-timed, well-formed, or genuinely curious question for the interviewer if it feels appropriate. But sense the vibe—some interviewers just want to get through the list of questions they've written or have been given.

Remember, the discussion is not over when they turn it over to you to ask questions! This section of the interview is crucial to the overall impression you make. Like the "tell me about yourself" question, don't approach it lazily. Have ten solid questions in your back pocket, ranked by priority, in case some get addressed during the course of the interview.

Having made sure your questions are tailored to each interviewer by looking into their backgrounds, you should also prepare questions that show your ability to think critically about the company, the team, and the challenges they're facing. Speak from wherever you derive your authority; for example, maybe you haven't worked in a comparable company or role yet, but you know what it's like to be a customer or user of their products.

Like job seeker Aseem, know your interviewers:

"I use LinkedIn to check what the interviewer has done for that particular organization. This helps me get to know them and shape portions of my interview. It also heavily shapes the questions I ask them, as I can encourage a more in-depth conversation."

The Muse, a career advice site we like, also suggests asking these three rather bold questions:

- "Do I have the job?"

- "Is there anything we discussed today that makes you feel that I am not the one for the job?"

- "What can I do to convince you I'm the one for the job?"

These are not necessarily recommended in every situation, nor even most. But if you feel like you're reading the room well, and you're either slaying it or believe you have nothing to lose, then you might give 'em a try.

7. Don't forget the (speedy) follow-up. After the interview, you need to thank the interviewer in a short but substantive and authentic way. You can do so by sending a message on LinkedIn (if you're already connected or have an InMail to burn on Premium), or through a personalized connection request. Some HR departments have a policy of not sharing contact info in the interview stage, but if you really want to make sure the note gets to the recipient, try looking up their work email address on Hunter.io. Or infer it from the email of the recruiter with whom you've been interacting. (If it ain't right, it'll bounce back to you as undeliverable anyway!)

Our experience has been that many a job seeker, especially those in the first half of their careers, don't make a habit of this all-important step. The truth is, many of today's hiring managers— including your two authors—are pretty old-school. We expect a prompt thank-you note. (Believe it or not, we used to *handwrite* thank-you cards and snail-mail them.) If that note never comes, we may take it as a sign of disinterest.

The other problem is that the job seekers who *do* send thank-you messages are often too late. The days of a personalized card arriving four days later are long gone, and speed of follow-up is key. Hiring decisions can be made almost immediately. The higher up you go,

LinkedIn Tools for Interview Practice

S ince this is a book about the *digital* job search, we hasten to add that LinkedIn also has tools that can help you with your interviews. Under the "Jobs" tab in the top navigation bar, you can go to an area all about Interview Prep. It includes crowdsourced practice, in which you answer questions and submit them for feedback from your connections. There's also AI-powered practice for feedback on things like pacing, too many "umms," inflection, and tone. Finally, LinkedIn Learning also has hundreds of short modules on how to rock your interview (learn more on page 275).

Like most things in life, practice makes perfect. Before you get the job offer, you'll most likely have to pass through several interview rounds (four on average). You want to practice as much as you can before those conversations, not *in* them!

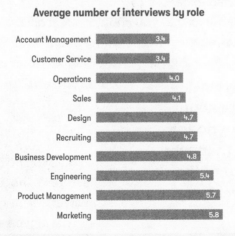

Average number of interviews by role

Account Management	3.4
Customer Service	3.4
Operations	4.0
Sales	4.1
Design	4.7
Recruiting	4.7
Business Development	4.8
Engineering	5.4
Product Management	5.7
Marketing	5.8

Certain roles tend to require more interviews than others.

especially, interview panelists are texting with the hiring manager, and the hiring manager is texting with their manager to gauge gut reactions. If you successfully slip in a meaningful message during that window in which the decisions get made, you increase your odds of landing the job.

Explaining Employment Gaps

Nearly all of us experience periods—from gap years to leaves to times of professional or personal difficulty—when we're not employed. Let's dig in to how we should think about employment gaps, how recruiters think about them, and what we should say about them in an interview context.

We often get these questions from job seekers, especially those who are mid- or late-career:

"How do I explain gaps in my career?"

"*Do* I need to explain gaps at all?"

"Will employers notice or care if I took time off to raise children? To go back to school? To deal with health issues? Because I was in a bad situation I had to get out of?"

The general rule is that you shouldn't feel obligated to spotlight these gaps. Most employers care more about what you can do for them today than why you were out of the workforce three years ago. So there's absolutely no reason to lead with a focus here. That said, it pays to devise a plan just in case you do get asked. And while there's no one-size-fits-all answer, having a clear and honest narrative ready can allay

Most employers care far more about what you can do for them today than why you were out of the workforce years ago.

potential concerns. The best way to prepare for all this is to write out your talking points and rehearse them before your interview.

The truth is that most employers aren't so interested in exhaustively, ruthlessly interrogating your work history. They understand that people have myriad reasons for work gaps. They'd rather find out if you have the requisite skills, fit well into the company, and can think on your feet—the past is only *part* prologue. An interview is mostly an opportunity for you to shine the spotlight on the relevant and compelling parts of your experience and dim the light on everything that isn't. You get to choose. So how?

Have you ever seen a politician or a savvy CEO giving a spiel on TV and found yourself asking, "Uhh, wait, *what* was the question?" That's no coincidence! It's because they've been thoroughly trained on "bridging." They're using the simple "ABC" technique that works in job interviews, as well:

A: Acknowledge. This is the most important part. You will lose them at the outset if you're not at least *pretending* to respond to their actual question and attempting to answer it. An acknowledgment might be, "Great question. I'd be happy to discuss that period in my career."

B: Bridge. Redirect the substance or scope to the point you *actually* want to make or the example you want to cite. For example: "It was definitely a tough time, but there was a silver lining—I got a chance to take a few data visualization classes online that I never had time for before."

C: Control or **Contribute**. Deliver your key message: your best strengths and the go-to examples that are your most compelling proof points. For example: "And having now mastered those techniques, I feel like I can add even more to your team. Which is why I'm so excited for this role in particular."

Here are four more pointers on the topic of employment gaps:

1. Create titles that fill in the gaps. We once heard a recruiter joke that a title on a profile or resume of "Independent Consultant" is sometimes code for "Unemployed." But this is by no means a universal sentiment, so it might be something to consider including. Look at it this way: You're always doing *something*, right? Pick up a project or think back to those you completed during the time that's under a microscope, even if it's an hour per week or unpaid.

2. Err on the side of transparency. If there's a glaring gap (longer than a few years and otherwise unexplained), you can use the About section of your LinkedIn profile to address that head-on, knowing most interviewers will at least skim it. For example: "After a fast-paced first part of my career, I decided to take seven years off to build a family and a new skill set. I engaged in many pro bono projects during this period and am excited to re-enter the full-time workforce." (Note: We do *not* universally recommend this! Use discretion and maybe bounce it off a friend or former colleague; you don't want to set off unnecessary alarm bells.)

3. Read the tea leaves. In the unlikely event that a hiring manager is interrogating an employment gap that you feel is defensible or just don't want to be asked about, take that as a potential sign that this may not be a person you want to work for. Sometimes a manager's own insecurities come up in these processes and it's something to pay close attention to. We had a saying at Apple: "'A' players hire other 'A' players. 'B' players hire 'C' and 'D' players."

4. Remember we're in it together. If you were let go during an economic downturn, don't stress about going out of your way to explain it. We're confident you will even find extra compassion among employers if you were, say, affected by the layoffs of a recession or the COVID-19 pandemic.

How to Handle a Firing in Your Job History

Here's a painful but extremely common question we hear all the time: What if you've been fired?

According to Alison Green, who writes the popular *Ask a Manager* blog and has published books on management and hiring, there are three steps in this case:

Step 1: Don't Lie

Trying to cover up or misrepresent your firing is a recipe for ruin. It's unlikely to end well; the employer will probably find out in their reference checks. Green points out that "if that happens, the lie itself would be a deal-breaker—whereas an honest explanation often wouldn't be." Stretching the truth of what happened may even burn bridges that could impact future employers.

Step 2: Keep It Brief

"Saying too much will make it a bigger deal than it needs to be, and generally you'll come across as pretty defensive," writes Green. "Typically all you need are a few sentences explaining what happened."

Step 3: Follow the Script

Explaining a firing is less about what happened and more about what you learned from it. Green suggests a calm and non-defensive response like: "Actually, I was let go. The workload was very high and I didn't speak up soon enough and ended up making mistakes because of the volume. It taught me a lesson about communicating early when the workload is that high, and to make sure I'm on the same page as my manager about how to prioritize."

Bonus Knowledge: Know What You're Getting Into

If you received a job offer, congratulations! Pat yourself on the back for passing through the discovery, application, and interview gauntlets; that's no small feat.

But we hate to break it to you: Your work is not quite done. Do yourself a solid and avoid Jeremy's fate of lasting just a few weeks at a company that was super desirable . . . but only on the surface. You must backchannel and do your *own* check to make sure you know what you're *really* getting into.

Run Your Own Background Check

The most effective strategy here is to add a filter for Past Companies (which you can find under the "All Filters" button on the advanced search screen). We used this same filter on page 188 to find contacts with whom you might have a shared prior employer (and who are doing cool stuff now)—it's also a great tool in this due diligence step.

Why? Because reaching out to these contacts will help you get the real scoop on what it's really like to work there, warts and all. That employer is no longer paying their salary, so they don't have the same vested interest in putting a shiny veneer on the company, a team, or even a specific manager.

Rachel, a Brand Manager in Kenya, endorses this tactic for post-offer research:

"I use LinkedIn to engage former employees on specific roles and understand actual challenges that the company had and their own reasons for leaving."

For more focused results and people more likely to offer unfettered takes, apply additional filters for your alma mater(s) and specific job titles. Remember, company cultures are more fiefdoms than monoliths.

Arm Yourself for Salary Negotiation

You've also got to know your own value when it comes time to negotiate salaries. LinkedIn has a Salary tool that will provide estimates for many types of jobs across markets and seniority levels.

These can be helpful data points, but don't rely on them alone. (LinkedIn often extrapolates their salary data from employer job listings, which don't usually give salary ranges unless they're required.) Glassdoor takes a slightly different approach: They work from the bottom up, asking employees themselves to report their salaries if they want to use other parts of the site (like viewing *other* salaries). Of the two platforms, Glassdoor has the better data set—both more

Search LinkedIn's salary database using filters like location, title, and years of experience.

comprehensive and more accurate. Use both sites as gut checks against each other. And, like Glassdoor, you now have to share your own salary to be able to view others (or if you're actively negotiating, you can just trial Premium for free for 30 days).

If you happen to have built a great relationship on the inside, it is not inappropriate to ask if they know rough salary bands and what's in range by level. Typically, the recruiter will convert to playing this role for you once you get to the offer stage.

Research Reaps Rewards

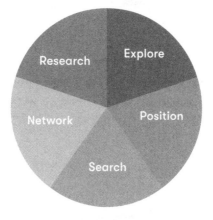

You've now completed the Non-Trivial Pursuit wheel of the new job search!

Here's one last thought to close out the chapter: The candidates who land great jobs seem to do all of these steps early and often. It's almost infused into their process from the very beginning; they don't wait until the end to research the company, industry, and people. They've already been able to acquire a sense of fit, understand company culture and lingo, and know whether this is the right place to try to score an interview and ultimately work at. Recognizing that they're interviewing the firm, as well, is an emboldening confidence-builder to boot. And you can get there, too, by being a tireless, leave-no-stone-unturned researcher.

You knew already that the modern job search rinses and repeats each part of the five-step framework. But now you're armed with the basic tools and skills you need to jump into each of them, then jump out and into another. In the next chapter we'll cover more advanced strategies to hack into the recruiting and hiring process in each step so you can really level up.

We end this chapter with some wise words from tennis great Arthur Ashe: "One important key to success is self-confidence. An important key to self-confidence is preparation."

CHECKLIST: **Researching**

Candidates separate themselves with their knowledge of the company, industry, and people. Then, they use that knowledge to put their best foot forward: speaking like a true insider, having concrete examples that will resonate, and being able to have a nuanced (and authentic) exchange with interviewers. Here are the key steps to focus your research and be as prepared as possible to seal the deal.

Know the Company:

❑ Create LinkedIn Job Alerts for the company, specific office location, and team or function that you're interested in

❑ Review the Company Page in-depth, especially the "Life" tab

❑ Find at least three current employees who can help you get in the door

❑ Find model profiles of people in the job you want. Pick up on the nuances of how they describe what they do and use this insight to inform how you position yourself

❑ Signal your interest to recruiters at companies you've created job alerts for

❑ Check out the company's website (linked at the top of the page) and sites like Glassdoor to glean more information

❑ Scour SlideShare.net for primary research on companies you might want to work for. Consultants and MBA students may have done the prep for you!

❑ Stay up to date on company content that appears on your news feed, especially the kind you want more of

Know the Industry:

❑ Teach the algorithm to curate your feed by following and engaging with select hashtags

❑ Follow the largest and most innovative companies in your desired industry. They tend to shape industry norms and priorities.

❑ Follow industry influencers, company leaders, or even hiring managers to go directly to the source of the knowledge and get a feel for what innovators are saying and thinking

❑ Join a handful of the largest LinkedIn Groups for the industry or job function you want to be in. If they are relatively inactive, join another.

❑ Check out which groups people currently in the job you want (and people who hire for that position) are in, and join them, as well

Know the People:

❑ Review profiles of every interviewer in advance, as well as posts and shares they've made and their broader web presence

❑ Prepare for "informational" interviews as you would for "official" interviews. Both are a chance to impress and ultimately get a referral and the job.

Know How to Crush the Interview:

❑ Practice your answer to "tell me about yourself" so it's crisp and purposeful

❑ Demonstrate competence by showing why what you've done is relevant for this job, and demonstrate warmth through your passion and energy to foster human connection

❑ Develop several concrete examples that put your best achievements forward and take answers out of the generic and into the specific

❑ Make sure you're able to talk about what makes you the most compelling candidate and speaks to your unique strengths, even if the questions don't directly do that. Be ready to bridge.

❑ Look for common interview questions, by role, for the company you're interviewing with on the web, including the company's own site as well as Glassdoor

❑ Prepare thoughtful and customized questions for your specific interviews, and try to level the power dynamic by having a conversation

❑ Follow up with any and every interviewer, speedily but genuinely

❑ Try out LinkedIn's interview practice tools, to get feedback both from the machine and from your network

Know What You're Getting Into:

❑ Background check: Do a "Past Company" search, coupled with a title and maybe even a shared school, to make a connection who will give you the lowdown on what it's like to work there

❑ Know your worth and leverage by researching salary estimates on LinkedIn and Glassdoor

CHAPTER 8

Leveling Up: Advanced Methods

Keep learning and iterating

When you want something,
all the universe conspires in helping you to achieve it.
—PAULO COELHO

Add to Your Tool Kit

With the five basic steps of the new job search now complete, you've earned a Job Search Hacker black belt. Now let's help you level up your skills one more time. Trust us: You're ready to have some more tips and tricks thrown your way. They're each organized in terms of the five steps you know (and maybe even love?) by now.

So let's clarify how to use this chapter: These are advanced tools for more seasoned job seekers. Use them as you see fit. How much should you focus on them relative to the strategies laid out previously in the book? Think of them this way: They are vitamin supplements (nice-to-haves), not aspirin (must-haves). Which do you take when you're in acute pain? Exactly. The five-step framework is your aspirin; this is a chapter of supplements.

And just like vitamins, these strategies are especially effective when you get them through your diet. So instead of viewing these methods in separate bits and pieces, feel free to integrate them into the other more foundational steps as you get more comfortable with them. Now let's get started!

Pro Tips for Exploring

Try Career Explorer

Many job seekers struggle to know what type of work to look for in the first place. For that type of exploration, LinkedIn now offers AI assistance with their skills-based Career Explorer tool. (Note: This tool is so brand new that it's not even on the main LinkedIn site yet. But here's a shortcut to get you there, no matter where LinkedIn places it in the future: thejobinsiders.com/explorer)

In a nutshell, Career Explorer allows you to explore which types of positions might be a good fit based on the jobs (and skills needed for them) you've already had. Then, you can search for new positions based on those skills, not just by job title or location (as is the case on most job boards). Career Explorer uncovers the *overlap* between skills typically required for what may seem like very different jobs.

For instance, let's say you're a Project Manager in Atlanta who's sick of being stuck in the office all day. Is there some way that your existing skills could lead you to a new job that's a better fit?

Well, by matching the skills you already have with those across thousands of other professions, Career Explorer can help you find roles you didn't even realize were related, like Construction Manager. The tool will give you a percentage match between roles, as well as other data showing levels of skill overlap and how popular the transition has been for other workers.

In addition, it outlines the skills you need to build so you can fully cross the chasm, including LinkedIn Learning courses you can take to close the gap (learn more on page 275). Plus, in the spirit of fully exploring careers by learning from insiders, it makes it easy to find connections on LinkedIn who can help you kick the tires on this potential role.

Career Explorer shows you a variety of paths to build upon your existing skills—or even new skills to build next.

So if you ever find yourself stuck in a role that feels like a dead end, just know that there are any number of paths leading from there to your next opportunity. Career Explorer might help identify those pathways.

Don't Just Apply to the Economy— Graph It!

While your alumni network is a massively powerful tool, it still reveals just one set of potential paths for career exploration. What if you could move up a level higher to see the full range of opportunities across your country or region?

Try using LinkedIn's Economic Graph reports (economicgraph .linkedin.com) to get that bird's-eye view of the whole labor market. You don't have to decipher complex Treasury Department jobs reports or economics think-tank policy pieces to learn these trends—just let LinkedIn scan its massive database to show you who's hiring in your area.

Here's an example of how you might use them:

- Let's say you're a current student who's interested in the construction industry and wondering whether you can land an internship next summer. Start by pulling up a report on hiring trends in the industry:

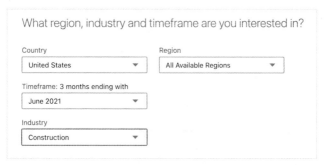

- Next, check out the *Top Trending Employers* graph and take note of employers whose hiring rates are growing quickly so you can explore those companies for internship opportunities.

- Then take a look at the *Top Trending Jobs* graph and jot down the specific job titles for which people are frequently hired.

- Finally, view *Top Trending Skills* to get a sense of the skills that are important for these kinds of roles.

- Armed with this macro view of your desired industry, you can now vet these opportunities in the same fashion described in the Exploring step in Chapter 3—by identifying and reaching out to existing professionals. For example, you might reach out to a Project Manager to get a sense of their work and whether it might be a good fit for you.

And now, when it comes time to launch your internship hunt, you're not limited to building off the paths of the alumni who happened to attend your alma mater. Instead, you're being powered by the trends and data shaping your entire industry!

A Word About Buzzwords

Some professional buzzwords are anathema to recruiters; they're far from the recruiter catnip that way too many people assume them to be. We've seen plenty of job seekers, both young and old, overusing meaningless and generic shorthand like "extensive experience" on their LinkedIn profiles and resumes. Studies show that younger job seekers tend to use these more often, usually in an attempt to signal that they fit in. But employers don't see the signal so much as . . . the trying.

During the 2010s, LinkedIn compiled an annual list of the buzzwords recruiters hated most. These stand the test of time:

Rank	All Buzzwords Since 2010
1	Specialized
2	Experienced
3	Leadership
4	Skilled
5	Passionate
6	Expert
7	Motivated
8	Creative
9	Strategic
10	Successful

We're not saying to never use these words and phrases. (For instance, maybe a descriptor like "passionate" really is an appropriate and useful differentiator for you; if so, try gut checking that with coworkers or friends by asking how they would describe you.) We are saying that you use buzzwords at your own peril, especially in your Headline and the beginning of your About section.

When In Doubt: Explore In-Demand Jobs

If you're just not sure where to focus your search, you can always start with a list of the most in-demand jobs. And sure enough, LinkedIn has already crunched the data for you. Inspect the list and learn about each job type at: opportunity.linkedin.com /skills-for-in-demand-jobs.

Specifically, LinkedIn has identified the top ten roles that:

- Have the most job openings

- Have shown steady growth for four years

- Pay a livable wage

- Leverage skills you can develop online (so you don't have to invest in a whole new degree)

At the time of publication those jobs were as follows:

- Software Developer

- Sales Representative

- Project Manager

- IT Administrator

- Customer Service Specialist

- Digital Marketer

- IT Support/Helpdesk

- Data Analyst

- Financial Analyst

- Graphic Designer

Each of these jobs feature hundreds of thousands or millions of openings—which means you can feel confident that you're going where the action is. Before you take the plunge into any given role, however, be sure to talk to insiders. That way, you can find a role that is not just in-demand, but that's also a genuinely good fit between employers' needs and your unique skills.

Pro Tips for Positioning

Frame Your Active Candidacy

Recruiters typically segment candidates into two main categories: active and passive. Active job seekers are more urgently looking for a new job, while passive ones are employed but open to new opportunities. Passive candidates include "tiptoers" on one end of the continuum (those who are thinking about making a move but aren't yet applying) and "super-passive" candidates on the other end (those who wouldn't consider anything short of the world's greatest opportunity).

So why do these categories matter to an active job seeker? Well, it means you're not only competing with other active applicants. In fact, research shows that the majority of "candidates"—roughly 73 percent—are passive job seekers.

More consequentially, many recruiters and hiring managers view these passive candidates as highly qualified and desirable—especially for more senior roles. There are a few reasons why. Passive candidates are usually employed by a competitor or other known entity in the space. They've passed through any number of LinkedIn Recruiter filters, so their keywords and experience are likely quite strong. And they're often connected to people on the inside (i.e., an employee thought of them and is trying to "sell" them on applying for the job).

Given that there are recruiters out there who value passive candidates more than active ones, you should be thoughtful about how to broadcast that you're on the market. For instance, we definitely *don't* recommend wasting valuable characters in your LinkedIn Headline saying that you're searching. Not only can it be off-putting, but those characters are better used to focus on the keywords that recruiters *do* search, like your desired job title. The job seekers we work with, especially those with more previous work experience, get the best results by toeing the line: *appearing* to be a passive candidate even if they're actively seeking a new role.

That said, a more spray-and-pray strategy like adding the #OpenToWork photo frame can be valuable at specific moments. One time is just before expanding your 1st-degree connections with the Contact Import tool. Those hundreds of new people you're adding will see you're #OpenToWork when they inevitably check out your profile to see what you've been up to—it may very well pay dividends.

William Lewis
Project Manager
San Francisco, California, United States

This #OpenToWork photo frame is useful only at specific moments.

Another time is when you've written an awesome original article. As it gets distributed throughout LinkedIn, a hiring manager could think not just, "Wow, this author is impressive," but also, ". . . and I might even be able to hire them!"

Show, Don't Just Tell, with Posting

Posting an article on LinkedIn—strategically, not indiscriminately—can be gold. In the platform's efforts to be sticky and social, however, parsing what matters from what doesn't sometimes gets confusing. There are all sorts of posts, like status updates, pictures and videos, events, notices for work anniversaries or new jobs, endorsements for others, and original long(er)-form content—but one of these things is not like the other. Big hint: It's that last one.

Writing and posting articles is sort of like blogging, only with a built-in platform for distribution (i.e., your connections and

Jedi Mind Tricks for Job Seekers

Humans share fundamental traits that you can tap into to really level up your job-seeking game. Let's look at a handful of those traits.

1. **Reciprocity:** We're wired to support people we trust. You can foster this expectation when providing informational interviews or making referrals or introductions. When someone thanks you for helping them out, don't cheapen your effort with something like, "no problem" or "no big deal." Instead, say, "you would do the same for me!"

2. **Social Proof:** Most of us don't really know what we want. This is exacerbated by "choice overload," the reality that people can't handle the many choices they think they want. So what do we do? We wait to see the outcomes of our peers' choices before making our own. That means when you reach out to a new contact, be sure to reference your mutual connections (e.g., "So great to meet a friend of Chanelle's!") Even if the mutual contact is fairly new to you, their existing relationship will grease the wheels of your conversation ("Well, seeing as you're friends with Chanelle, too, I'd love to chat!").

3. **Sense of Urgency:** We're all procrastinators. We take a ton of mental shortcuts every single day to ease our cognitive load. For example, when that interesting-but-not-pressing connection request comes through, we decide not to prioritize it in the moment—and often we never come back around to it. Instead, create urgency, even if it's a bit artificial, when you need a response or a serious look at your application. Make it seem like time is running out on your candidacy or interest in connecting.

4. **Lower the "Activation Energy":** This term, borrowed from chemistry, describes the effort required to get something done. Lowering activation energy is a key part of creating new habits (e.g., if you want to run first thing in the morning, sleep in your favorite running clothes). As a job seeker, you want to make it as easy as possible for the person on the other side—a desired connection or referrer, an interviewer or an applicant-screener—to say "yes." Spend time thinking about the quickest way to move them along the decision journey and reduce their cognitive load. Little things like having your email address right on your profile (in the About section) or starting off your interview with a line like, "I know I'm perfect for this role" can sometimes be all that's required.

connections of connections—so, probably better than a traditional blogging site like Medium). This is the only social media share that *actually matters* for job seekers on LinkedIn. Why? Because it's an opportunity to show that you have an original thought and can think critically, as opposed to merely resharing someone else's posts—which might help *them* get hired, but is less useful to you.

Your written posts are attached to your profile and remain viewable for anyone who's skimming it, including prospective employers or connections. This is especially valuable for career switchers—you're putting yourself out there for the industry or function you want to be in, and demonstrating skill and competency even without the relevant job experience.

Aim for 500–750 words and add an image to entice clicks. Consider including prompts for readers (like responding to a key industry- or company-specific challenge), reacting to a recent news story or op-ed, or offering key takeaways from an event you attended. Make yourself a thought leader!

Here are some examples, based on different industries and career levels:

- *Nonprofits:* "7 Ways to Increase Donor Engagement"

- *Manufacturing:* "What Will Supply Chain Management Look Like in 10 Years?"

- *Tech:* "How I Helped My Start-Up Raise Its First Seed Round"

- *Consulting:* "How Majoring in English Prepared Me to Be a Consultant"

A medium- or long-form article is the most useful type of post to create. High-effort but high-reward!

What If You'd Rather Be Your Own Boss?

As powerful as LinkedIn is for unlocking access to jobs, we totally get it: Not everyone dreams of working for someone else. "I just want to do it myself" is an increasingly common sentiment we hear from job seekers, young and old, especially those of color who question whether they can create change from within the preexisting systems. Young founders litter the landscape of tech and social enterprise start-ups. And in our "Gig Economy," workers of *all* ages express growing frustrations with the traditional job search.

For many professionals (and soon-to-be workers), having meaning and autonomy in a job is more valuable than having security and stability. And in the parlance of our favorite band, the rap pioneers the Beastie Boys, there's "no time like the present to work sh*t out!"

Here's the good news: The same LinkedIn tools that empower you to land your next job also give you a head start when it comes to ditching that job and doing your own thing. Either way, it's all about building your unique personal brand.

Start a Side Hustle

First, let's look at attracting some side work based on your existing skills. For instance, let's say you're a marketing whiz by trade, but you're sick of days full of meetings that never give you a chance to tap your creative side. So you decide to wade into entrepreneurship by first pursuing a little freelance work.

Just like a job seeker, you'll want to start with your LinkedIn profile as your professional brand HQ. But instead of just letting the world know that you're #OpenToWork, you can click "Open to" under your profile heading and then "Providing Services."

Then specify exactly what you can offer:

- Your services

- Your sales pitch

- Your location (including remote work)

- Your availability to LinkedIn members you're not connected to

continued . . .

Now, when LinkedIn users go to the site's ProFinder tool (accessible via the "Services Marketplace" menu under the home screen's "Work" button) and search for your expertise, they'll be able to send you a request for a quote. That means you've got a chance to win a new customer and start to build your business, all on the same site where you've already built up your professional brand.

Hunt for New Leads

If you've gotten a taste of the freelance lifestyle and want more customers and projects—but perhaps faster than ProFinder can provide—you can use LinkedIn to uncover new leads. Search for someone both in a position to buy your services and who'd want to buy them from *you* based on a mutual connection. For example, run an "All Filters" search with "Marketing Executive" in the Title field, then filter for 2nd-degree connections.

Now, just like with job-seeker networking, you can reach out to your mutual contact to broker an introduction and talk directly to a prospective client. You can apply the same search principles to pinpoint potential investors or mentors who can help you along your entrepreneurial journey.

Create Your Own Company Page

Let's say your freelancing goes so well that you decide to take the complete entrepreneurial plunge, quitting your job to go full-time. Now is definitely a good time to create your very own Company Page on LinkedIn so you can start building your firm's online brand, not just your own. A Company Page is a bare minimum for having any kind of professional presence for your business or services, big or small. Specifically, you can start to post company content, build a following, and ultimately develop a sustainable pipeline of future clients to power your business's growth.

All you need to do is:

- Click "Create a Company Page" from the LinkedIn "Work" menu

- Fill out the various fields (name, location, industry)

You're now off and running to post, advertise, build, and grow your biz. No boss required!

Cover Story: A Double-Edged Decision

One of the things that elevates a LinkedIn profile above a resume is that it can provide a deeper sense of the human being behind the accomplishments—your photo, your story (in the About section), and the lives you've touched (via the Recommendations section). So it comes as no surprise that when 1,009 hiring managers were surveyed about their preferences, 76 percent felt that seeing a video of a candidate would be useful.

For your Cover Story video, know what recruiters are looking for and how you can directly respond to that need.

Sure enough, LinkedIn has now enabled its users to do just that. By clicking your profile photo in the LinkedIn app, you can now record a Cover Story—an introductory video that's thirty seconds or shorter. As tempting as it may be to rush right in with a quick video selfie, we strongly recommend thinking it through beforehand. Having worked frequently with professional video producers, we know this is the hardest medium to nail. Unlike a witty tweet or a quick Instagram post, it's not something you can ace off the top of your head. And when a video is bad, it's *really* bad (hello, 95 percent of YouTube!).

So the bottom line is this: If you're not prepared to invest the time to make your Cover Story great, then skip it. It's not yet mandatory (unlike a profile photo) and the consequence of making a poor effort is massive—especially if it ends up ruining an otherwise great profile. But if you do decide to go for it, come back to two themes we've emphasized:

- Know what recruiters are looking for and how you can directly respond to that need. For example, here's a script that's highly on point: "If you're looking for a Customer Success Manager for your start-up, you've come to the right place. As the second

Customer Success hire at Trindle, I helped build our very first CSM dashboard and reduced churn by 27 percent. And now I'd love to bring that relationship-building expertise and passion for working with clients to an organization that's ready to grow quickly." Note how it speaks to the direct function ("Customer Success Manager"), type of organization ("start-up"), and skill set ("CSM dashboard," "reduced churn") that the recruiter is focused on—and it packages it in a friendly, I-can-rock-this-job-tomorrow presentation.

- Don't just assume your video is sending the signal you want. Instead, tap your built network of functional insiders. Send them the video before you publish it to your profile and ask them this question: "What's your gut instinct about this candidate?" That's quite likely how recruiters and hiring managers will process it. So make sure your video is improving that first impression, not hurting it!

Creator Mode: A Turbo Boost for Aspiring Influencers

A massive following on LinkedIn isn't useful for every type of career. (Sadly, we've yet to hear of anyone getting $1,000,000 per sponsored post, like the Kardashians do on Instagram.) But if you've built up a big or valuable audience, it might just get you hired.

For instance, let's say you want to land a sales job in the manufacturing industry; having a large following of prospective clients is like bringing along your own gold mine to the next job interview. Or maybe you're a lawyer with a sizable fan base for your legal blog; which firm wouldn't want to have such a noted influencer on their bench?

If your following can be monetized (or it makes *you* more monetizable to a hirer), consider turning on one of LinkedIn's most intriguing and still new-ish features: Creator Mode.

Unlike a standard profile, which is optimized for recruiters to discover your work experience, Creator Mode rearranges your profile to optimize the visibility of your content. You can just toggle it on and off via your profile's Dashboard. More specifically, here's what else this feature will do:

- Changes your default profile button from "Connect" to "Follow" (and showcases your number of followers)

- Puts your latest content at the very top of your profile

- Adds an extra sentence right beneath your Headline—a high-visibility location—that highlights your primary topics (e.g., "Talks about #manufacturing and #sustainability")

If you truly fall into one of the categories described, this feels like a natural move. In the very likely chance that you don't, however, we recommend that you skip it. If you're being hired for your skills and experience more than your following, continue to focus on the things that matter most: connecting with people in your space and showcasing what you can do!

> **Creator mode: On**
> Get discovered, showcase content on your profile, and get access to creator tools

Anyone can be a thought leader—and build a following—
with LinkedIn's Creator mode.

What If I'm Not Getting Found for the Jobs I *Want*?

This is another common question we get all the time. And while the answer is another "It depends," there are some guardrails and considerations to keep in mind.

The first thing is to circle back to where we started this entire book: thinking critically about what it is that you *really* want in a job. Remember those three circles for what makes a great job: growth, impact, and people. Manifest the opportunities you both want and *can* do into being. That's especially true if they're a bit of a stretch—they should be!

Also, don't judge books by their covers. Sometimes a recruiter inbound message or a request to chat about a specific opportunity might seem random, but you won't really know for sure until you have that conversation. Our advice is to entertain anything that comes your way, even if it appears only tangentially interesting. Once you vet it a bit, you may feel quite differently.

We've also seen many times that a role isn't a dream job, but the company becomes more attractive as you dig in (say there's a great culture, a mission you can get behind, or an opportunity for growth). There's nothing wrong with forsaking the "stretch" goal to get in the door and network your way to a better position once you're in. The savvy job seeker also knows that connection requests can be an opportunity to flip the script and inquire about where that person works, even if there isn't the ideal job available (yet).

Pro Tips for Searching

Consider LinkedIn Premium

This is the most frequently asked question we get from job seekers: "Is LinkedIn Premium worth it?"

Short answer: Nope.

Longer answer: It depends.

While LinkedIn welcomes millions of new members every year who are just entering the working world (making students and new grads its fastest-growing segment), the platform can't sustain the explosive growth rates of its earlier days. So what's a company to do when growth slows? Well, it tries to squeeze current members for more money. (Remember, the site already monetizes member data to sell to recruiters, salespeople, and advertisers—if the service is free, then *you're* the product!) This is the basic idea behind a LinkedIn Premium (aka "Premium Career") membership.

We generally don't think a Premium membership is necessary because so much of the site's functionality—in fact, most everything we've shown you thus far—is available for free. But if you're still early in your Searching and Networking steps, a few Premium benefits might make it worth paying on a month-to-month basis. (You can always start with a free thirty-day trial and extend that a month at a time as needed.) Here are a handful of perks:

- *Search:* If you're in heavy networking mode and doing a lot of advanced People searches (like, hundreds per month), you may eventually hit a paywall asking you to upgrade to Premium. Of course, this requires a *ton* of searches, and there are work-arounds like the Alumni Tool.

- *InMails:* Premium gives you access to InMails (LinkedIn messages that you can send to anyone, even if you're not connected). As you've seen often by now, however, you may be better served by finding a contact's email address on Hunter.io and reaching out directly—especially knowing that most of us still check our work emails many times per day!

- *LinkedIn Learning:* Some courses and modules, including some on the job search itself, are included with Premium (see more on page 275).

- *Company Insights:* This feature gives you access to interesting (if not always essential) trends at the companies you're exploring (see more on page 276).

Okay, so Premium gets you a nice gold-colored badge on your profile, but let's keep it real. Here are some important things that LinkedIn Premium does *not* do:

- Elevate you in either Recruiter or general member search results to help get you found for new opportunities

- Ensure your connection requests (or InMails) cut through the clutter and get read

- Allow highly customized and filterable People searches, like those that are available in LinkedIn Recruiter

- Set up extra job alerts or designate additional job titles or locations you want to get found for

- Flag your candidacy to recruiters or give your applications via "Easy Apply" any special status

Crowdsource Your Search with Polls

One of the most frustrating parts of searching for jobs is that lonesome feeling—that it's just you versus the cold, cruel world of online applications and rejection emails. But we've seen some rather clever job seekers take advantage of LinkedIn's polling feature to tap their network right when they need it most. To do so, just create a post, then click the bar graph icon at the bottom to "Create a poll."

Here's an example: Let's say you're struggling with a resume bullet that just doesn't feel right. You could either waste hours overthinking the question inside your own head (hint: don't!) or you could outsource the decision to the wisdom of your crowd. Try posting a poll like this one:

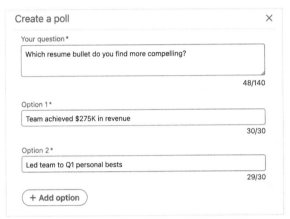

If you're trying to keep your search close to the vest, you can toggle to share with only your connections or a LinkedIn Group you're in (e.g., your alma mater's alumni group). Or, if you'd prefer to tap a large and diverse audience, feel free to share broadly on LinkedIn— or even on other social media like Twitter, if you're truly daring.

And, of course, you can use polls to tap the power of the job-seeking zeitgeist for any number of other scenarios, including:

- The right career path

- The perfect LinkedIn Headline

- The best companies to apply to

- The optimal offer to accept

Hire a Resume Writer

If you find yourself truly stumped as you try to put together a rockstar resume, fear not. The honest truth about hiring, as we've mentioned time and again, is that it's imperfect. One major imperfection is that the skills needed to power your resume or interview (e.g., writing, marketing oneself, and improvisational speaking) aren't necessarily the ones you'll need to be successful on the job.

So if writing isn't your forte, there's no need to force yourself to build that skill—there's a whole galaxy of strong writers who can help develop your resume. And while separating the truly great ones from the hucksters can be hard, LinkedIn's ProFinder tool can help. Here's how:

1. Go to linkedin.com/services or just click "Services Marketplace" from the "Work menu" on the main LinkedIn page.

2. Choose either "Resume Writing" (if you want to build from scratch) or "Resume Review" (if you just need a second pair of expert eyes):

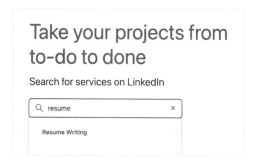

3. Click on "Get proposals" and go through the next steps to specify your needs.

4. Within a few hours, you should have multiple offers to consider. These coaches are vying for your business, so definitely hold out for someone who has:

- Multiple reviews they can share with you (ideally listed as Recommendations on their LinkedIn profile so you can see the real client)

- Sample resumes they can share with you (so you know their style)

- Experience with your desired industry and skill level (since a tech CFO will likely require a much different CV than, say, a junior professor)

Alternatively, if you'd rather tap your own network, LinkedIn also makes that easy:

1. Just start a new post, click the "Ellipses" button, and click "Find an expert."

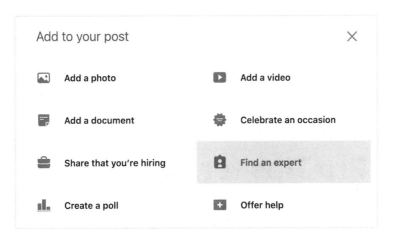

2. Then plug in your desired parameters:

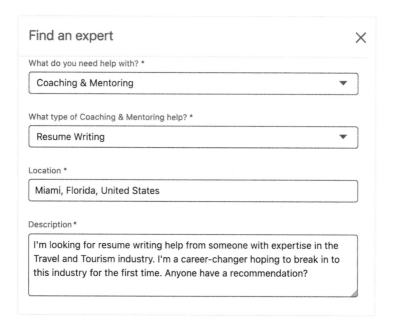

3. And now, instead of seeing only generally qualified options, you'll start to find experts who've been vetted by your own network.

Either way, skip all the hand-wringing over resume-writing and focus on the skills that will matter in the long run—those that will help you rock the job!

Pro Tips for Networking

Connection Best Practices

Here's another one that job seekers ask us all the time: "Should I connect directly with recruiters?"

Answer: "absolutely YES!"

Why? For several reasons. Recruiters are the external face for a company and get candidates into the pipeline—both for a job you really want or for a company you want to work for that doesn't yet have the perfect job open. Besides, what's the worst that can happen? If they ignore or decline your connection request, it's no sweat off your back. There's a minimal chance they'll block you (reduced further if you add a personal note), but even if that happens, it's still no big deal.

Most importantly, recruiters are nodes in the network. They're connected to lots of other people within a company because they either hired them or helped them hire someone. And so when it comes time to find the perfect 2nd-degree contact (e.g., the hiring manager for your dream job), guess what: It's often a recruiter who can broker the warm introduction.

To find the lowest-hanging recruiter fruit, go to "All Filters." In the Keywords section, type in "Recruiter" under Title. Then add filters for 2nd- and 3rd-degree connections (or 1st-degree to remind you whom you already know, and see whom they might know).

Hopefully this has also got you thinking about other "nodes" in the professional world. To build up your network, search for people who have bounced around in different roles or companies (and thus have a large and diverse network). Or look up people in roles like "Career Services" and "Alumni Relations" at your alma mater(s) who are likely connected to both fellow alumni and a range of employers.

Another best practice for connecting is to cultivate a network before you really need it. This isn't just about building your network; it's about making regular and strategic touches. According to LinkedIn research from 2020, you're four times more likely to land your next opportunity when you keep in touch with your network. We recommend getting in the habit of reaching out proactively to specific connections. For example: Did you get a notification about one of your connections' work anniversary, promotion, or new job? Send a congratulatory note.

Especially when economic times are less than stellar or there are weird rumors and vibes from your current employer, these selective touchpoints can yield medium- to long-term benefits. Remember, there's a lot of serendipity in the messy process of hiring. You want to be top of mind at the precise moment your dream job becomes available.

This template to either warm up a cold connection or make a new one has about a two-thirds success rate at eliciting a response or acceptance. The message below follows the template. It is based on shared alma mater, but could just as well be tweaked to focus on a shared connection, cause or volunteer experience, or other shared interest:

COLD-TO-WARM
OUTREACH

Pick the right person and explain why them (and the company), specifically

Clearly state your value and your ask

Play to shared affiliation/ passion (and to their vanity)

Convey you won't waste their time (with message brevity and ask for a short chat)

Hi Craig,

I'm a Darden student (Go Hoos!) hoping to get into fintech after my MBA. I noticed that we have several connections in common, and that you're a marketing leader at Square.

I'd LOVE to learn a bit about your team's priorities and your superimpressive career path.

Any chance you have just ten minutes next week for a fellow Wahoo? I'd greatly appreciate it!

Many thanks,

Jamie

Spin the Wheel with WVMP Roulette

Give credit where credit is due: A savvy MBA student taught us this advanced hack. And it works! We call it "Who Viewed My Profile Roulette," or WVMP Roulette for short.

When you're trying to break into a new space, you are looking for any connective tissue. Profile views are the quickest shortcut to a connection. Why? Because WVMP is the most popular part of LinkedIn—it plays to the two Vs that most compel human behavior: vanity and voyeurism.

> **Don't be afraid to view people's profiles. It's the quickest shortcut to a connection.**

So WVMP Roulette works like this: View the desired connection's profile, multiple times even. Out of some combination of those two Vs and sheer curiosity, chances are strong that they'll view your profile back. That's all you need. Bam! Send them a connection request, InMail, or email starting with, "I noticed we viewed each other's profile," and then pull in the template on the opposite page.

Get Free InMails with LinkedIn Groups

You already know we're not big fans of purchasing LinkedIn Premium just to send InMails—there are plenty other ways to contact industry insiders without spending a cent. And yet, when you're in the midst of networking on the site, it can sometimes feel like a hassle to go off and track down someone's email address. So what if there were a way to send an InMail and not pay LinkedIn for the privilege?

It turns out there is a secret workaround, and it involves LinkedIn Groups. In addition to being a repository of industry wisdom, Groups enable you to communicate directly with other members—even if you're not 1st-degree connections.

Here's how it works:

- Let's say you're trying to find a job or internship in social media and you've come across an insider you just need to get to know.

- Scroll down to the Interests section at the bottom of their profile and see that they belong to a Group called Social Media for Nonprofit Organizations that you've either already joined or decided to join now.

- Now head over to the Group on LinkedIn and click the "See all" link to get a directory of its membership:

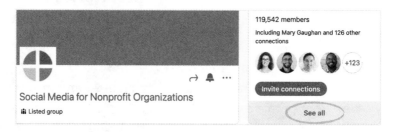

- Finally, search the directory for the right person and then click "Message" right next to their name. Voila—instant outreach to the exact right person:

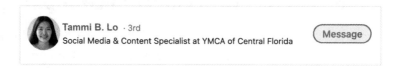

You can now use the money you would have plunked down on that LinkedIn subscription to buy your new contact a coffee when you chat!

Pro Tips for Researching

Try LinkedIn Learning

In 2015, LinkedIn paid a tidy $1.5 billion to acquire online learning company Lynda.com. The child of this union is now called LinkedIn Learning. Similar to course providers like Udacity and Coursera, this platform features a variety of content for upskilling. It can help you develop and show off new credentials you might need to make a pivot. LinkedIn Learning isn't a focus of our trainings, but we include it here because some job seekers we work with have found it really useful.

Two parts of LinkedIn Learning that can be especially helpful:

Aspiring Product Manager

Jatin says:

"LinkedIn Learning helped me a lot in my preparation. I tried to get the best interview preparation courses along with enhancing my fundamental knowledge of Product Management, too."

a) Its courses are highly efficient. Instead of watching an hour-long lecture (like you might on Coursera), you can pick up a new skill at your own pace and convenience with bite-size videos that fit around your workday.

b) It's priced on a monthly subscription model. So while you might pay Udacity hundreds of dollars for a five-month course on Data Analytics, you can get a free trial of LinkedIn Learning for thirty days, pick up a key skill or two you need, and not even pay a cent.

Premium Company Insights

As we detailed previously, Company Pages are crucial sources of information in the pre-interview research phase. We also mentioned earlier in this chapter that Premium members get access to additional data on employers who might have captured your interest.

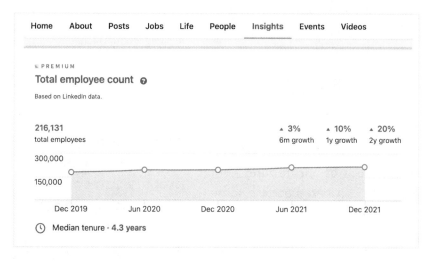

Premium subscribers will see an "Insights" tab on a Company Page.

So just what are these Premium Insights, and how are they useful? It boils down to next-level understanding of a company's hiring patterns and internal hierarchy. You can inspect headcount trends (is the company growing or shrinking?), employee distribution by function (is this a sales- or engineering-dominated firm?), and even which C-level talent is coming and going (did they just bring on a new VP of Marketing or say farewell to their CFO?).

If you're particularly enamored with an employer and crave every available data point, these sorts of insights can be beneficial, but they're a bit hard to act on for interview preparation or outreach. So color us skeptics. But we've found that Company Insights are most helpful during two phases: 1) initial consideration and 2) *post*-interview research and backchanneling.

For example, it's good to get a general sense of whether or not the company is growing and how long employees tend to stay. You definitely want to avoid red flags like a shrinking company, a diminishing desired function at that company, and a heavy attrition rate—all info you can glean on Premium Insights. Of course, you can't exactly use all these charts and granular hiring data for a cover letter or an interview. That said, we have heard about scenarios in which referencing this data during an interview process can indicate your seriousness. You may even pleasantly surprise the interviewers with your knowledge ("I noticed that your sales team is growing at a rate twice that of comparable companies . . . ").

Advanced Research and Interview Hacks Potpourri

Let's close out the chapter with a medley of useful tactics to boost your researching skills:

Search other sites for additional insider information. We mentioned Glassdoor and LinkedIn itself as places to do your due diligence on things like salary, culture, and even interview questions. New(er) related sites pop up from time to time, and they're worth checking out. Two of our favorites are Blind (teamblind.com) and The Org (theorg.com).

Blind is a Glassdoor competitor that collects anonymous user-provided feedback on companies, from salaries to cultural ratings to hiring information. It differs from Glassdoor in its ability to browse by sector and job type, as well as its pure anonymity and therefore candor. (Many companies will try to solicit positive Glassdoor reviews from employees—not a problem on Blind.) Users have described Blind as the new place for "corporate gossip," which is potentially as relevant for job seekers as it is for current employees. Remember, your goal with research is to become an insider!

The Org addresses another frustratingly opaque component of researching companies: the organization chart itself. How do you know where the job or part of the company you're looking at sits within the larger organization? Is it strategically positioned (i.e., reporting to a respected C-level leader)? Is the company itself highly layered and bureaucratic or relatively flat with highly autonomous departments? There are pros and cons to both; layers can mean greater structure, focus, and clarity on expectations, but can also indicate micromanagement and suppression of good ideas. Either way, it's important to know—and gauge your comfort level with—where you'd sit.

Note: Keep in mind that, like any crowdsourced sites, Blind and The Org are only as good as their particular crowds. So be aware that not every firm or industry will be well-represented on these sites. They over-index on tech firms, for instance, and under-index on schools and hospitals.

Follow aggregators. In the Research step, we suggested following companies, thought leaders and influencers, individual members you want to hear more from or can utilize as connective fodder, and specific hashtags. But you can also let content aggregators do the hard sleuthing work for you.

These opinion-shapers and news outlets are increasingly publishing regular newsletters on LinkedIn, which you can follow and get pushed straight to your email inbox. This kind of content is increasingly important to maintain LinkedIn's position as a watering hole for professional expertise, taking on Medium and even more traditional media. Over time, aggregated content will only get more robust and relevant for job seekers and career pivoters.

Start by following popular aggregators like Forbes, Morning Brew, and Business Insider for general workplace insights. Then get more specific to your interests. LinkedIn's "Discover more" hub on the main page will surface even more tailored channels for you as you do so.

Make yourself an insider from the first conversation. Here's one of our favorite lines to use in interviews: "This job description just really jumped off the screen at me." Even if you're not a perfect fit—*no* candidate ever is!—you're basically allaying any concerns from the get-go. It's not only a great starting point to explain why you're a strong candidate, but it also forces you to stay focused on the question the interviewer will care most about: "What is relevant in this person's background that makes them good for *this* particular job?" (Not: "Who is this person generally?")

This opening salvo helps get the interviewer on your side *and* helpfully leads you into answering the "tell me about yourself" question with purpose. And when you've done your research, you can feel confident in doing just that.

The Secret to Building a Bond with Interviewers

There's an old saying: "People will forget what you said, people will forget what you did, but people will never forget how you made them feel." In an interview setting (including informational), ask a question that you know—through your research and intuition—the interviewer will be excited to answer. For most people, this is a question about their successes or pride around overcoming adversity. *Get. Them. Talking. About. Themselves.* The more they do so, the better they will feel about themselves, and they will attribute that good feeling to you! The best interviews are conversations; unless the interviewer seems short on time and by-the-book, you don't have to wait until the end of the interview in the formal Q&A to inquire about them.

CHECKLIST: **Advanced Methods**

Remember that the most successful job seekers (and professionals writ large!) are those with a growth mindset; they're always seeking new strategies to find, and get found for, a better job. It's an iterative process of constant improvement! In that spirit, you can take your job-seeking skills to the next level with these advanced hacks for each of the five key steps in the modern job search.

1. Exploring:

❑ Use Career Explorer to suggest jobs you might be a good fit for, based on your skills and past titles

❑ Try out LinkedIn's Economic Graph reports to get a broad overview of the labor market

❑ Look at LinkedIn's list of in-demand jobs for inspiration

2. Positioning:

❑ Consider the signals you're sending about, and the implications of, how actively (vs. passively) you're job-seeking

❑ Show, don't just tell, by posting original articles and highlighting skills and credentials

❑ Think about adding a Cover Story video to your profile—but only if you have the time and resources to make sure it's great!

3. Searching:

❑ Consider a LinkedIn Premium free trial before jumping into a membership that may or may not be worth it for your particular situation

❑ Try using LinkedIn's polling feature to crowdsource opinions on your job search

❑ Look into hiring a pro if you're stumped while crafting your resume

4. Networking:

- ❏ Connect with nodes in the network

- ❏ Get into the habit of cultivating your network before you need it

- ❏ Play Who Viewed My Profile roulette with coveted connections

- ❏ Message people through LinkedIn Groups to work around the limit on free InMails

5. Researching:

- ❏ Peruse LinkedIn Learning, including free video content related to the job search itself and courses that can help you upskill for your next job

- ❏ If you have (or are trialing) Premium, review Company Page Premium Insights for a deeper dive into hiring trends

- ❏ Round out your research with other job sites like Glassdoor, Blind, and The Org

- ❏ Follow industry newsletters and other pertinent content aggregators

Looking Forward

The journey never ends

> Who looks outside, dreams; who looks inside, awakes.
>
> **—CARL JUNG**

Recapping: The New Game

Here's the reality. No matter how much LinkedIn wants you to treat it like a typical social network ("Post! Share! Like!!!"), the strongest and stickiest motivators for using the platform will always be the need to land a job or the need to fill a job. That's the platform's ultimate purpose, its reason for being. Too many people focus on the 80 percent of LinkedIn that drives no value when it comes to *getting a job*—e.g., not particularly useful things like earning hundreds of Endorsements or liking dozens of posts per day.

But not you. You're now an expert-level Job Search Hacker. So let's recap all you overcame to reach this high level.

The old job search game is one played with undifferentiated resumes, submitted without a referral. Most job seekers are still playing this game. Which makes sense because it's the routine we've been trained to follow since we were students:

1. Go to school: *"My school will help me find and get a job."*

2. Receive directions: *"Include extracurriculars on your resume!"*

3. Follow directions: *"'Member of the Drama League. Check."*

4. Get a reward: *"Good job on your extracurriculars!"*

5. Rinse and repeat: *"I didn't get the job so let me send this same resume out again . . . "*

Admittedly, this is an enticing routine because it removes the scary need to understand how the hiring process really works in the new game. Instead, you can just put your brain on autopilot and follow the conventional wisdom until your submission is finally "correct." And if at first you don't succeed, you don't have to change your approach because you already know that it's "right." You probably just need to apply to more jobs . . . endlessly.

In our experience, contrary to the claims of a "skills gap," there's rarely a shortage of people who could do the job. But there is always, *always* a scarcity of exciting candidates. Why? Precisely because they're playing the wrong game. So many potentially inspiring candidates cloak themselves in a garb of conservative, overly formal language—playing by the resume "rules" to which we've been conditioned—that they make it tough for hiring managers not only to be confident, but to be certain.

Of course, you might get lucky playing by these rules—or perhaps you did in the past, when you had less experience to go on—but these are the exact wrong rules if you want to win the new game consistently.

As we learned time and again throughout this book, the modern job search is about hacking into the hiring process to stand out with both the Human and the Machine: the recruiter and the computer algorithm. The biggest change in today's hiring process is that employers now have access to so much more information:

- 79 percent of US employers check out candidates on search engines *before* making interview decisions.

- 47 percent will immediately discard any candidate, even those who are worthy of serious consideration, if they can't find a strong online presence.

- Usually (and ideally), one's LinkedIn profile is atop those search results, and nine out of ten recruiters—at companies of all sizes—regularly use LinkedIn to find candidates.

But playing the new game doesn't mean discarding all the work you've done on your resume. Couple that resume with the five steps that are the keys to the new job search: **exploring, positioning, searching, networking**, and **researching**. You now have the digital tools at your disposal to do each one well.

Still, we totally understand that, even with a clearer grasp of how the hiring game is best played, it can still feel really intimidating. "Exciting" isn't usually the adjective used by the job seekers with whom we work; "overwhelming" is the more common sentiment. So whenever you're feeling overwhelmed, just return to the principles in this book to help you cut through the clutter and understand what really matters for *finding* and *getting found for* a great new job. And for every step of this often-overwhelming process, LinkedIn is your best friend *and* your Swiss Army knife.

You've got this. We believe in you. Do *you* believe in you?

Where Things Are Headed

Before we close, let's address two closely related questions you may be asking yourself about the future of the modern job search: Are these strategies built for the long-term? And what if LinkedIn is displaced as the world's professional network?

Answers: *Yes*, and *won't happen*. All of these methods—exploring opportunities, positioning your professional brand, searching for specific roles and managers, networking with people who can help, and researching and due diligence—are time-tested and useful for any stage of a career. It's just that they're now done increasingly online. It's way more efficient, and there's no going back. The trend is moving in only one direction: more technology, at more stages of the process. Not less.

Here are the top trends shaping the future of hiring, as of late 2020, per a LinkedIn survey of recruiters:

- 78 percent of recruiters say diversity in hiring is a very or extremely important trend

- 50 percent of recruiters say the same about using data to drive smarter hiring decisions

- 35 percent of recruiters expect AI to be a critical trend in the coming years

As you can see, recruiters will likely have even more weighing on their shoulders in the years to come. Which means you can expect even greater reliance on technology to ease that burden.

As for LinkedIn itself, if you've absorbed the concept of network effect, you can easily intuit why LinkedIn is not going anywhere. It's already brushed aside numerous challenges to its business model. Facebook has tried to both be a job board and enable targeted professional searching and networking; niche "LinkedIn-for-X" platforms have sprung up for specific industries and groups like manufacturing, the social sector, students, teachers, and more; sites used mostly for posting jobs have tried to expand into human networks. They've all failed.

Why? Because they cannot compete with LinkedIn's massive scale—a virtuous circle that simply reinforces itself as it adds more

LinkedIn is not going anywhere. members, hirers, companies, and salespeople (and the valuable data on all these entities). LinkedIn has no credible competitor. Remember, there was a huge bidding war for LinkedIn, and it was Microsoft's largest acquisition by far. And the reason for that massive $26 billion price tag is the same reason that LinkedIn should matter to you—that with such a huge fraction of global hiring happening there, the platform is incredibly valuable for companies and professionals alike.

Part of why we wrote this book is because we've learned in our coaching, training, and having worked inside LinkedIn that there is a lot of confusion about the company. There are two sources of bewilderment: 1) parsing what actually matters on LinkedIn for job seekers and 2) staying on top of updates to the platform. We've tried our darndest to demystify that first problem; as for the second, our general advice is, "Don't worry about it!" LinkedIn makes minor user interface (look-and-feel) changes regularly, but it rarely changes its base functionality: that is, all the key actions we've shown you in these pages.

And if for some strange reason LinkedIn *does* start making more frequent and dramatic changes, these won't take you by surprise, and you'll be able to separate what matters from what doesn't. Why? Because you're going to make LinkedIn a regular habit. As you do, you may even start seeing changes before other members, since that's how LinkedIn rolls out its updates: to its most faithful users first, expanding to everyone else over time.

In fact, LinkedIn is so deeply entrenched that we predict a complete convergence of the resume and the LinkedIn profile in the next decade. Even Microsoft sees the writing on the wall as the lines blur between the offline and online. The tech giant has already integrated its online suite, Office 365, with LinkedIn, as well as making their Dynamics software more potent with LinkedIn's unrivaled data set. And there's even a Resume Assistant—"powered by LinkedIn"—in Microsoft Word, where the world writes resumes.

Resume
Assistant

How about the future of cover letters? Well, they're now required for less than half of job postings. Many recruiters and managers deem the About section of the LinkedIn profile, coupled with writing samples, to be a worthy substitute. We've participated in more and more hiring processes—as hirers, job seekers, and job-seeking counselors—in which both a resume and cover letter are not required. In our view, this new normal is already here, and it's here to stay.

For the shrinking proportion of employers that *do* require and read cover letters, however, it remains an important part of your application. Consider it a chance to purposefully tell your story and explain why you're the right fit. The emphasis here is on *purposeful*; too many generic cover letters miss the mark completely because they're not highly role-specific. So if you're going to write one, don't just send in a form letter; instead, make it a love letter—one that could only be addressed to the specific organization and role you seek. So we're comparatively bullish on cover letters.

And finally, what about the future of skills? Both hard and soft skills will be the new currency of the new economy. Industry experience will become less important than actual expertise. Both Omar and Jeremy were able to break into tech not by being tech veterans—neither of us had any experience in the sector after business school—but rather by making the argument that we had a cross-sector skill (marketing). The industry was an afterthought—or so our argument went.

As the COVID-19 pandemic shifted nearly every company's way of doing business online and made almost every experience a virtual one, we saw this trend take hold across a variety of industries. Savvy job seekers who successfully pivoted away from slowing industries like travel and hospitality downplayed specific industry knowledge. They instead developed and demonstrated transferable skills (both on their profiles and in the examples cited in interviews). Recruiters will continue to search less by industry, and require less industry-specific experience, in favor of what it takes to actually *do* the job. This is a good thing!

LinkedIn tools like Career Explorer (see page 250), for instance, can help you make this skills translation. If you're early in your career or a flexible pivoter, you may get more traction by focusing on growth industries:

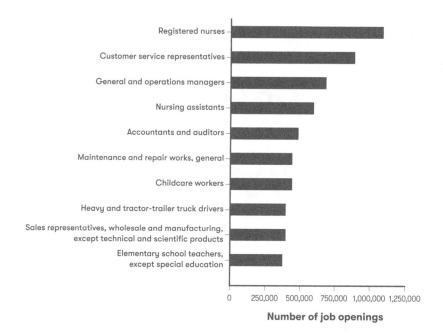

Number of job openings

These are the industries expected to have the most job openings in the United States through 2024.

Look, no one knows exactly what lies ahead. But we're as well-positioned as anyone to stick our fingers to the future-of-work wind. We've trained thousands of job seekers, hired dozens ourselves, and worked in university career services. And we've been inside the belly of the LinkedIn beast as Product Marketers. We have context on both the tools of the new job search and how they're used in practice. At LinkedIn, our job was to bridge the products with the needs of users. A typical Product Manager, by contrast, wants to build cool stuff and is way more technical than we are (to us, Python is a snake and C++ is a grade you might get from a teacher who *really* does not want to give you a friggin' B–).

But here's the most important takeaway when preparing for the future: You don't need us (or anyone else) to be soothsayers. Be your own! How? By keeping tabs on the jobs you want at the places you most want them; positioning yourself well; networking your way in; then repositioning. It's all iterative!

Go Get It!

You've learned the truth of how hiring works. You've taken a peek into the minds of recruiters and managers and seen how they *really* make decisions: consciously, subconsciously, and algorithmically. You've learned their priority order for filling positions, starting with the people they know, the people who make *themselves* known, and right on down to everyone else on merits.

And now you know why it's so hard to get a meaningful look (or even a friggin' response!) from your cold application online. Or why seven in ten people say they want but can't get their dream jobs. Yes, hiring is a messy process, but it's one you can get your arms around and ultimately overcome. You must view the act of applying to a position as a mere step in the job search process—not the whole enchilada. Ideally, you've banged down the door and built relationships so that you're top of mind for when the specific job you really want comes open.

The seeds you're laying may not bear fruit for a while. But they eventually will. This should give you confidence, as should the knowledge that you now know more about the hidden world of hiring than the vast majority of job seekers

Here's some motivation from longtime aspiring Data Scientist Tamunotonye:

"I am still on the journey of getting my dream job. Don't give up, especially when you see so many people sharing good news and you don't yet have yours."

out there. You will become ultrafluent in the strategies in this book by putting them into practice and improving upon them as you get feedback. The truest form of learning is experiential!

You simply never know what might materialize from casting a wide net. You certainly cannot possibly know who knows whom. All you can do is be methodical, put yourself out there, and refuse to give up.

But, of course, as with all social media (LinkedIn included): Take everything you see with a grain of salt. People are not always their true selves online. It's easy to get caught up in what others are ostensibly achieving, but it's much harder to know what's right for *you*.

GNGU: Omar's Story

Omar has a motto in his family: "Garriotts Never Give Up" ("GNGU"). Each year a family member wins the GNGU Award. It's more than a tradition. It's also become a reminder of the hardships we all face—and that we all have a reservoir of inner strength for when we encounter them. Omar is proudly the only five-time winner of the GNGU Award—a credential that's *not* on his LinkedIn profile, however—mostly due to circumstance rather than any kind of superhuman bravery.

When he was diagnosed with liver cancer at age thirty-five and had multiple surgeries—including a live liver-donor transplant—Omar was forced to deprioritize his career to focus on his health. He had to choose survival over raw ambition. And while he sought better work-life balance after the hardest parts were over, he also realized that work is a big part of the meaning he derives from life; it's a primary purpose. So rediscovering his career was an essential part of being able to move from surviving to thriving. Work can motivate us to live fully.

As the poet Adelaide Anne Procter said, "It's never too late to be who you might have been."

Remember that everyone is just trying to figure out adult life—sans any real blueprints. Questions and failures bond us as professionals and humans more than our successes.

At the same time, as much as we've pushed you to dream big, we absolutely get the messy reality of jobs and lives. Just as Omar learned when battling cancer, work can be about survival—physically and financially—more than just dream fulfillment. Do what you have to do.

Dream jobs are much more often the result of baby steps than quantum leaps. Stay patient, but stay hungry. And remember that no job, even your dream job, will ever feel like a 100 percent perfect fit. A crucial part of self-belief is knowing that you're capable of stretching yourself; don't rule yourself out from what might be a fantastic job before you (and the hirer) get a chance to mutually vet.

So keep your chin up, keep your ear to the ground, keep your eyes wide open, and—most importantly—keep yourself in a loving embrace.

And keep pushing yourself forward. Go get it!

Online Resources

Want to take your LinkedIn game to the next level or learn to apply these concepts in a different way? As a purchaser of *Linked*, you get exclusive online access to the following:

- LinkedIn Profile Grader: Get the ten most important parts of your profile evaluated automatically.

- Recruiter Cheatsheet: Get a free guide to the most critical tool in the entire hiring process.

- LinkedIn Masterclass: Get a 90 percent discount on the only LinkedIn course taught by insiders—up-to-date and on-demand.

Use your special code **insider** at **TheJobInsiders.com/book** for this and more exclusive content. You'll also find additional tips and tricks on our blog at TheJobInsiders.com.

Got feedback? Drop us a line at info@thejobinsiders.com.

Other Websites

Throughout this book, we've mentioned a lot of websites to supplement LinkedIn for a variety of purposes. Here they are consolidated in a single place:

AngelList.com posts start-up jobs and facilitates connections between start-up companies, job seekers, and angel investors.

Coursera.com offers digital courses through universities and other content experts, helping professionals and lifelong learners access quality online education.

Glassdoor.com is a platform that allows employees to anonymously upload salary data, company reviews, and information about interview experiences.

Hunter.io collects information from across the internet to help you find the email pattern for any company or even the email of a particular employee.

Idealist.org is a job board that specializes in opportunities in the nonprofit and social-impact sector.

Indeed.com is a general job board that also offers company reviews and salary information.

Jobscan.com compares your LinkedIn profile or resume against a target job description and suggests salient keywords to optimize your application to pass through screening technology.

Jobvite.com provides a market-leading Applicant Tracking System and conducts useful market research for job seekers on trends in the recruiting and hiring process.

TheMuse.com is a job board and career advice site with resources on career exploration, the application process, interview prep, and more.

Salary.com offers compensation data sliced by typical salary bands for a specific industry, function, title, and/or location that interests you.

SlideShare.net (aka "The YouTube for PowerPoints") can help you quickly upskill prior to interviewing with strategic analysis of many companies.

TeamBlind.com seeks to increase transparency in the working world through employee reviews of companies and by allowing users to search by industry and job function. The site prizes total anonymity.

TheOrg.com makes organizational structure charts public, to help both employees of, and applicants to, specific companies understand cultural and operational realities.

Udacity.com is an online educational resource that offers paid and free courses for users to improve their professional skills.

ZipRecruiter.com is another popular general employment marketplace that allows users to browse job postings and salaries.

Further Reading

We're not just standing on the shoulders of career giants—we've been educated by them directly! Here are some of the very best career books from some of the best authors we know:

- *The 2-Hour Job Search, Second Edition: Using Technology to Get the Right Job Faster* by Steve Dalton

- *Recalculating: Navigate Your Career Through the Changing World of Work* by Lindsey Pollak

- *The Peak Performance Formula: Achieving Breakthrough Results in Life and Work* by Bob Lesser

- *The Start-up of You: Adapt to the Future, Invest in Yourself, and Transform Your Career* by Reid Hoffman

- *Designing Your Life: How to Build a Well-Lived, Joyful Life* by Bill Burnett and Dave Evans

And, though not career books, here are two favorite parables for resolute job seekers of any age (with protagonists both named Santiago!):

- *The Alchemist* by Paulo Coelho

- *The Old Man and the Sea* by Ernest Hemingway

May all the universe conspire for you to achieve your goals. With determination amidst difficulty, it surely will.

Acknowledgments

Our LinkedIn journey began thanks to some truly incredible colleagues. As such, we've got to start with a huge shout-out to Gina Pak, Sarah Acton (still the best manager both of us have ever had!), Colleen Jansen, and the incomparable John Hill for hiring and teaming up with us to bring more opportunity to students and alumni around the world.

Then, even after the LinkedIn Student and College team split up, like most great bands, we were able to continue its mission of unlocking opportunity for career starters by partnering with some of the very best folks in Higher Education. Thanks to Jenn Bridge and Kay Dawson at UC Berkeley Haas for challenging us to develop the very first LinkedIn training created by former insiders. To the MBA Career Services & Employer Alliance for enabling us to strut our stuff. To Leslie Lynn at the University of Michigan for giving Jeremy his big break in the career coaching world. To Jenn at Haas and Everette Fortner at the University of Virginia for doing the same for Omar. And to Martina Valkovicova (University of British Columbia); Stella Mantechou (INSEAD); John Bertrand, Onma Lwin, and Mark Brostoff (University of Southern California); and the dozens of other innovative career leaders who believed in us enough to give us our start!

And for helping us take that mission from college campuses onto the pages you're reading right now, our appreciation begins with Alec Shane at Writers House, who took a chance on a book about "the boring social network," and Lisa DiMona, who has believed in our nonfiction vision for many years. And it extends to our diligent and meticulous editor Danny Cooper—and his equally amazing colleagues Rebecca Carlisle, Ilana Gold, Cindy Lee, Chloe Puton, Sarah Smith, Jahanara Alamgir, Kim Daly, Elissa Santos, and the entire Workman team that brought this book to life. As well as to all our incredible colleagues, friends, and leaders who shared their stories in these pages.

We're immensely grateful to all of you who've had a profound professional impact on our lives and on this project.

Finally, on a personal level:

Omar would like to thank Beth and Amaya Garriott for making space for this project amid the demands of adulting. He thanks his dad, Gary, for modeling the truism that if you try to leave the world better than you found it, you imbue your work with purpose. He owes an enormous debt of gratitude to his brother Kristofer for donating his liver to him and to the doctors and nurses who saved his life at multiple turns, affording him the chance to put this book, a true passion pursuit, into the world. He appreciates his mentors— namely, Kinney Zalesne, Mike Lee, Samir Bolar, and Naveen Sikka— from whom he learned (and is still learning) that he can do *anything*, but not *everything*. And a shout-out (bark-out?) to his loving Irish doodle, Sandy, who kept him company during late writing nights at the end of long days in his full-time job.

Jeremy would like to thank his parents, Richard and Iris Schifeling, for letting him take his first job as a paperboy at age ten, thereby cementing the importance of finding a better job forever after. He'd also like to thank his daughters, Ruby and Hannah, for helping him understand that everything—truly, EVERYTHING— is open to negotiation. And he owes so many thanks to his wife, Rachel Burstein, for helping him see that the best career is not nec- essarily the fanciest one, but the one that actually gives you the life you want.

Index

photos
  backgrounds, 119, 121
  profile, 101–102, 115–118, 120
Picasso, Pablo, 58
Piedmont, Shelley, 64
polling feature, 266–267
positioning
  advanced methods for,
    255–264
  checklist for, 138–139
  introduction to, 87–88
  overview of, 55
  recruiters' mindset and,
    88–94
  recruiters' work process and,
    94–102
  steps for optimization, 102–135
positive proactivity, 2
Premium Insights, 276–277
Proctor, Adelaide Anne, 291
profile photos, 101–102, 115–118,
  120
profile views, 190–191
ProFinder tool, 260, 268–269

Q
qualifications, 155
quick wins, 59

R
reactive strategy, 2
reciprocity, 257
Recommendations, 131, 133

Recruiter tool
  About section and, 122–125
  connections and, 109–113
  definition of, 33
  Education section and,
    129–130
  engagement and, 100–101
  Experience section and,
    125–127
  filters used by, 29, 94–101
  following and, 113–115
  importance of, 30
  keywords for, 94–98, 102–104
  location and, 94–96, 98–99,
    104–107
  "Open to work" option and,
    107–109
  photos and, 115–121
  search engine optimization
    and, 128
  Skills & endorsements section
    and, 130–134
recruiters. see also hiring
    managers
  connecting with, 270–272
  definition of, 7
  filters used by, 92, 94–96,
    98–102
  hiring managers versus, 197
  minds of, 88–89, 92, 94, 142
  reasons for rejection from,
    88–89, 90–91
  signaling interest to, 222

About the Authors

Omar Garriott is Global Head of Education for Qualtrics and formerly led education product marketing for Salesforce, LinkedIn, Apple, and Adobe. Despite his corporate bona fides, he is at his core a teacher and mentor—having taught 3rd grade through Teach for America and coached clients ranging from low-income high school students to executives, from undergrads to MBAs, on college and career transitions. He's a proud cancer survivor and an even prouder dad.

Jeremy Schifeling has devoted his career to helping students succeed in theirs. From recruiting top students at Teach For America to leading student marketing for LinkedIn, he's touched the lives of thousands of people just starting their journeys. Along the way, he's served as a career coach for military veterans and business students, built a site to help anyone launch a tech career (www.breakinto.tech), and produced the most-viewed video in LinkedIn's history (tagline: "LinkedIn—it's not just for old people with heavy briefcases").